WATCH LISTEN ASK LEARN

HOW SCHOOL LEADERS CAN *Create an Inclusive Environment* FOR STUDENTS WITH DISABILITIES

BELINDA DUNNICK KARGE

Solution Tree | Press

a division of Solution Tree

555 North Morton Street
Bloomington, IN 47404
800.733.6786 (toll free) / 812.336.7700
FAX: 812.336.7790

email: info@SolutionTree.com
SolutionTree.com

Visit **go.SolutionTree.com/specialneeds** to download the free reproducibles in this book.

Printed in the United States of America

FSC
www.fsc.org
MIX
Paper from responsible sources
FSC® C011935

Library of Congress Cataloging-in-Publication Data

Names: Karge, Belinda Dunnick, author.
Title: Watch, listen, ask, learn : how school leaders can create an inclusive environment for students with disabilities / Belinda Dunnick Karge.
Description: Bloomington, IN : Solution Tree Press, [2022] | Includes bibliographical references and index.
Identifiers: LCCN 2022021625 (print) | LCCN 2022021626 (ebook) | ISBN 9781954631298 (Paperback) | ISBN 9781954631304 (eBook)
Subjects: LCSH: Special education--United States--Administration--Case studies. | Students with disabilities--Education--United States. | Educational equalization--United States. | Special education teachers--Training of--United States.
Classification: LCC LC3981 .K37 2022 (print) | LCC LC3981 (ebook) | DDC 371.9--dc23/eng/20221003
LC record available at https://lccn.loc.gov/2022021625
LC ebook record available at https://lccn.loc.gov/2022021626

Solution Tree
Jeffrey C. Jones, CEO
Edmund M. Ackerman, President

Solution Tree Press
President and Publisher: Douglas M. Rife
Associate Publisher: Sarah Payne-Mills
Managing Production Editor: Kendra Slayton
Editorial Director: Todd Brakke
Art Director: Rian Anderson
Copy Chief: Jessi Finn
Production Editor: Miranda Addonizio
Content Development Specialist: Amy Rubenstein
Acquisitions Editor: Sarah Jubar
Copy Editor: Jessi Finn
Proofreader: Elijah Oates
Text and Cover Designer: Kelsey Hoover
Associate Editor: Sarah Ludwig
Editorial Assistants: Charlotte Jones and Elijah Oates

This book is dedicated to Master Chief Royce Privett.
Through stories of his U.S. Navy career, he taught me that
leadership is about integrity, vision, teamwork, and purpose.

Acknowledgments

I extend my immense gratitude to the doctoral leadership students and graduates of Concordia University Irvine; without our discussions about administrative issues and special education, this book would not exist. You encouraged me to take my knowledge and stories from the field and share the ideas in writing.

I thank all whose stories illuminate the pages of this book, especially Dr. Helene Cunningham, Dr. Greg Hedger, Dr. Barbara Moore, Dr. Angela Taylor, Dr. Scott Turner, and many other administrators who spent precious hours with me brainstorming and building inclusive schools and districts where students with disabilities and their peers are making progress. You allowed me a front seat to the process and gave me free access to view your inclusion data, meet with your staff, and talk to and learn with your students. You consistently reminded me that ultimately all we do is for and about the students and their growth and achievements.

Dr. Bill Scotti, Dr. Larry Hobdell, Dr. Tom Shearer, and other regional educational officers at the U.S. Department of State's Office of Overseas Schools supported my global travel, invited me to conduct special education audits, and asked me to consult with and provide professional learning to many international educators working at schools around the world. From you, I learned the value of collaboration and the importance of consistent messages. Our international community is more inclusive because of people like all of you!

Dr. Soraya Coley, Dr. Dwight Doering, Dr. Reyes Gauna, Dr. Milton Gordon, Dr. David Loy, Dr. Galit C. Reitman, Dr. Matt Rhoads, Dr. Kent Schlichtemeier, Dr. Cyndy Stephens, and Dr. Michael Thomas: I am a stronger educational leader because of your example.

Dr. Richard Eyman, Dr. Ken Kavale, and Dr. Donald L. MacMillan: You introduced me to the love of research and the importance of research-based instructional practices. I tried to tie the lessons you taught me to the tools I have gained from leadership to provide a strong research-based text.

Lynette Ferraro: Your vast special education experience and your words of encouragement spurred me on. You reminded me to keep the text simple and to write from the heart.

Desiree of Irving & Rowe: Thank you for taking the time to photograph me for this book.

I would like to acknowledge the exemplary work of the editorial and production staff at Solution Tree, especially Sarah Jubar, acquisitions editor. From the first phone call to the detailed instructions you provided me about the Solution Tree writing process, you showed me patience and grace. Your close editing and constructive recommendations for revisions made this writing project enjoyable and doable.

I wish to thank the reviewers for their valuable feedback on the content.

Finally, I would not be where I am today without family. Mom, thank you for always being there for me, for being an exemplary educator, listener, leader, professor, counselor, confidant, problem solver, friend, and role model. Desiree, Dustin, Matt, Jackson, and Ryker, you all bring so much joy to my life. And to my best friend and soul mate, my husband, Doug: you center me and bring me daily happiness.

I recall the day I was first given keys to my own classroom. I walked in and kept reciting to myself my confirmation verse, Galatians 5:22: "The fruit of the Spirit is love, joy, peace, patience, kindness, goodness, faithfulness, gentleness . . ." (ESV). I set a personal goal to model the fruit of the Spirit for my students and lead by example. I thank all who have walked alongside me on my educational journey and witnessed my growth and development of knowledge. I believe the fruit of the Spirit are examples of what each of us can do to be inclusive and to help every child learn, grow, and feel like they belong. Thank you for joining me on this journey.

Solution Tree Press would like to thank the following reviewers:

Pamela Bourgeois
Principal, Kleb Intermediate School,
Instructional Officer for Professional Learning (Retired)
Klein Independent School District
Klein, Texas

John D. Ewald
Education Consultant
Frederick, Maryland

Janet Gilbert
Principal
Mountain Shadows Elementary School
Glendale, Arizona

Louis Lim
Vice-Principal
Richmond Green Secondary School
Richmond Hill, Ontario, Canada

Peter Marshall
Elementary School Principal
Halton District School Board
Burlington, Ontario

Blane McCann
Education Consultant
Omaha, Nebraska

Jim Pearce
Principal
Mission School District
Mission, British Columbia, Canada

Faith Short
Principal
East Pointe Elementary
Greenwood, Arkansas

Britney Watson
Principal
Fort Smith Public Schools, Morrison Elementary School
Fort Smith, Arkansas

Dianne Yee
Assistant Professor of Education
Western University
London, Ontario, Canada

Visit **go.SolutionTree.com/specialneeds** to download the free reproducibles in this book.

Table of Contents

Reproducibles are in italics.

TWO

THREE

FOUR

SEVEN

About the Author

Belinda Dunnick Karge, PhD, is a professor in the doctoral studies program at Concordia University Irvine and a professor emeritus at California State University, Fullerton. She taught both general education and special education and served in administrative roles in elementary and high schools prior to teaching in higher education.

Belinda's professional record demonstrates a consistent pattern of research publications; she has produced four textbooks, five curriculum texts, four book chapters, several educational tools, and more than 135 articles. She has made numerous presentations to international, state, and local groups of school district employees and has keynoted several conferences. She serves as a consultant for the U.S. Department of State's Office of Overseas Schools and travels extensively around the world. Research-based instructional strategies, schoolwide change, and inclusive practices are a few areas she consults on.

Belinda received the Council for Exceptional Children's Susan Phillips Gorin Award. She was also honored with the Council for Learning Disabilities' Floyd G. Hudson Outstanding Service Award and the Association for Childhood Education International service award.

Belinda received her PhD in quantitative methods, special education, and educational psychology as well as her master's degree in special education and reading from the University of California, Riverside.

To learn more about Belinda's work, visit www.cui.edu/academicprograms/graduate/edd/leadership/faculty, or follow her on Twitter @dr_karge and on LinkedIn at www.linkedin.com/in/belinda-karge-024b3a30.

To book Belinda Dunnick Karge for professional development, contact pd@SolutionTree.com.

Introduction

A leader takes people where they want to go.
A great leader takes people where they don't necessarily want to go, but ought to be.
—ROSALYNN CARTER

I began my career as a classroom teacher, then a special educator, and then an administrator. I taught in both elementary and high schools in Southern California before moving to the California State University system (California State University, Fullerton; California State University, Northridge; and San Diego State University). There, I instructed students interested in becoming teachers of students with disabilities. I chaired the Department of Special Education at California State University, Fullerton; conducted research with graduate students; and taught classes for both general education and special education teachers and graduate students. My primary focus was supporting general and special education teachers with effective, research-based instructional strategies. I have literally toured the globe as a consultant for the U.S. Office of Overseas Schools, conducting special education audits and assisting schools with providing inclusive services. This experience led me to teach international courses for educational leaders at Johns Hopkins University, the University of Central Florida, and many schools outside the United States.

Surveying and talking to principals about their background in special education have been central to my research. Most educational leaders have no background in special education, or if they are fortunate, they took one course in special education during graduate school (Christensen, Roberston, Williamson, & Hunter, 2013). This is apparent to their teachers, and so is the fact that most principals and administrators don't know how to be strong leaders in this area. When administrators do not know special education laws and policies, it can lead to litigation. And more importantly, when administrators don't know how to include students with disabilities in schoolwide activities, classrooms, and sports, the students fall further behind their peers and do not get the services they deserve.

In 2006, fellow special education professor Beth Lasky and I surveyed principals in California to determine their formal training (Lasky & Karge, 2006). At that time, it was extremely clear that more preservice and in-service professional development were needed. Principals told us they had minimal instruction (one class or even one lecture) on special education in their preservice courses. They reported that they obtained much of the knowledge on the job. As of 2022, we are replicating the study with administrators around the world. The preliminary data confirm that the need identified in 2006 has actually grown and educational leaders need both preservice and on-the-job training in special education.

In 2015, I changed university positions. I moved from working with teachers to working with administrators. My doctoral students at Concordia University Irvine are superintendents, assistant superintendents, district office personnel, principals, assistant principals, and directors of special education. I hear daily tales of their struggles, and I answer many questions related to special education. The primary question I get is, "How can I make my school into an environment where all students with special needs are included and supported?" And that question has served as the motivation to share what I have learned by writing this book.

The goal of this book is to assist current and aspiring leaders to better understand special education services and then lead a school or district to implement inclusionary practices that benefit all students. Of this book's three parts, the first two are devoted to advancing the knowledge that leaders must have in order to be effective. The third part highlights the importance of equity and inclusion and presents eleven steps that leaders, armed with knowledge, can use to implement inclusive practices in their schools. A unique feature of this text is the combined emphasis on the research literature in special education and the research literature in leadership.

The main message I want to convey is that all educational leaders can shift their schools in the direction of inclusive environments. Equity is key to the future of learning. This text is a call to action for those without a special education background. The content provides a resource for closing the gap. It challenges school leaders to watch, listen, ask, and learn about special education. The intended audience for this text includes preK–12 public, private, and charter school leaders at all levels. Table I.1 indicates the various educational roles and a quick overview of how each can use this text.

TABLE I.1: Determining Readers' Roles and How They Can Best Use This Book

ROLE	TEXT USAGE
Principal, assistant principal, head of school, or other key educational leader	This book includes steps for moving a school forward as an inclusive environment for all students, as well as case studies of successful inclusive schools. Key action items for leaders appear throughout, along with ideas for supporting and mentoring special educators.
Dean of students, Advanced Placement coordinator, International Baccalaureate coordinator, or gifted education coordinator	This book contains a wealth of information on equitable access to learning. If we believe that all students can learn at high levels, then ensuring access to learning for all students is essential.
Administrative designee (for example, the education agency representative who is assigned to attend special education planning meetings)	This book offers school leaders responsible for special education action steps for compliance. Key information is also present for the staff who lead the special education process.
Superintendent or assistant superintendent	This book can serve as a quick reference for leaders who are not well versed in legal regulations governing special education. It provides case studies to share and guide as the leaders delegate implementation with support to others.
Human resources director or human resources employee	This book provides essential learning for administrators—something human resources can ask about, require review of, and hold educational leaders accountable to.
Intervention specialist, reading specialist, mathematics specialist, or other support staff member who does not have a special education background	This book provides practitioners a pragmatic guide to inclusive education and key areas to pay attention to related to special education.
General education teacher (teacher leader)	This book includes key terms, case studies, ideas to support all students, and ideas to help people understand why inclusive implementation is so important to school climate and culture.
Special education teacher (teacher leader)	This book provides knowledge of what to expect from educational leaders and how to move schools forward with inclusive practices.
School board member, parent, or guardian	This book provides a simple yet deep understanding of inclusive education and its how and why.
Teacher in training for general education, special education, speech and language, or other area of specialty	This book provides a blend of theory and practice with ample research references.

continued →

ROLE	TEXT USAGE
Member of an administrative certificate or graduate program	This book assists aspiring leaders to better understand special education services and then lead a school or district to implement inclusionary practices that benefit all students.

The book gives school leaders what they need to know about special education. The first part provides the basics of special education. Chapter 1 gives educational leaders strategies to understand special education legislation, litigation, and vocabulary, and the special education field in general. It also explains the six primary principles of the Individuals With Disabilities Education Improvement Act (sometimes known as *IDEIA*, but many educators know it best by the original acronym, *IDEA* [2004], so that is what I use throughout this book). The chapter defines and describes both the individualized education program (IEP) and the 504 plan, and it provides suggestions for how to coordinate team activities, meetings, and systems to fully support students with disabilities.

Chapter 2 explains various service-delivery models and how leaders can ensure students with disabilities receive their education in the least restrictive environment as required by federal law, with the goal of inclusive education. I encourage the formation of a learning services team to coordinate the multitiered system of support (MTSS) and share the responsibilities of referring students to special education and seeing that their IEP goals are met. The chapter also shares and explains examples of different places in which educators can provide services (such as the segregated classroom or the general education classroom).

Anyone who has been in education for a while is aware that personnel make a huge difference in supporting all students, especially students with disabilities. In part 2, I focus on the personnel who provide this support. General and special education teachers (chapter 3), paraeducators (chapter 4), and related services personnel (chapter 5) hold things together within a school; how effective leaders support them, work with them, and strengthen their skills are key to hiring and retaining them. It is vital that leaders know who their personnel are and how their training will support various students. Building relationships and communicating meaningful administrative support lead to retention of special education teachers. Teachers want to remain at schools where the leadership honors their skills, works collaboratively with them to solve problems, and helps all students at the school be included and successful. Ensuring personnel are using research-based instructional strategies and up-to-date techniques builds the strength of the learning services team.

Finally, an understanding of the whole system and how its parts work is necessary to ensure equity for all and then establish and maintain an inclusive school, which is the focus of part 3. Chapter 6 highlights inclusion and equity and the many considerations that leaders must keep in mind as they center inclusion in the school climate. Inclusion has been around since the 1980s, and the chapter highlights ample evidence that students with disabilities do better in inclusive settings, yet we still have schools that don't know how to include.

Chapter 7 gives specific steps for establishing an inclusive school.

1. Review current practices.
2. Involve the leadership team.
3. Do some action planning.
4. Conduct professional learning.
5. Read the research.
6. Encourage family engagement.
7. Design and implement an inclusion plan.
8. Implement data-collection measures.
9. Monitor implementation.
10. Revise and adjust.
11. Celebrate and share successes.

Throughout the book, there are inserts providing actions administrators can immediately take to improve inclusion practices and support students with special needs. Also, the book features case studies that offer concrete examples of inclusion in action. All the case studies are true and come from my years consulting with schools throughout the United States and around the globe. I have changed the school and student names; however, each case study is from my personal experience. Several reproducibles are provided as examples of tools for successful inclusive implementation. Educational leaders should have a schoolwide initiative to support *all* student needs. There is no one model. Every school needs to design its own process. However, understanding that special education is a service, not a place, and that this service should be conducted in the general education classroom whenever possible is the key to inclusive schools (IDEA, 2004). This book gives leaders the tools to establish an inclusive environment where all students learn and where special education needs are met.

Part 1

WHAT EVERY LEADER SHOULD KNOW ABOUT SPECIAL EDUCATION

ONE

LEARNING THE LEGAL BASICS OF SPECIAL EDUCATION

All you need is the plan,
the road map, and the courage
to press on to your destination.
—EARL NIGHTINGALE

The administrator's call came at 10:30 on a Friday morning: "I know you are a special education expert; I am panicking because I just received a court subpoena on a case for a student at my school. I don't know the student or the parents, and I did not attend the IEP meetings. How is it that the court is expecting me to testify?" The appearance date was a week away.

Sadly, in that short week, the administrator (whose name I have not mentioned to preserve his privacy) was not able to fully comprehend the legal aspects of special education. Nor did he comprehend the importance of knowing all students at a school site (and their parents or guardians) regardless of attending IEP meetings or not. When asked basic questions about special education during the court testimony, he was not able to respond. When queried about the specific student, he could not explain any of the supports, the accommodations, or the continuum of least restrictive placements at his own school site. When the judge requested he comment on his prior conversations with the parents, he drew a blank. The district lost the case.

An educational leader attends to many roles on a daily, weekly, and monthly basis. High on the list is being informed and educated. Ultimately, the preceding school district lost the case because the school leader did not know the legal expectations of the Individuals With Disabilities Education Act (IDEA, 2004). He did not realize the courts would expect him to be knowledgeable about the law, to connect with the student and parents, and to articulate the special education services provided at his school. Sadly, this scenario is common. Campus administrators may not lead the special education meetings; however, they are responsible for collaborating with their administrative designee at the meetings and understanding the student and parent situation. The more involved leaders are, the less likely it is that costly legal issues will arise. Also, this involvement means we can spend more intentional time supporting all students on the campus. Educational leaders cannot come to the job with the mindset that simply providing special education services satisfies the appropriate actions. This chapter clearly defines what *appropriate* actually entails and how noncompliance with these requirements is a violation of the U.S. legislation tied to free appropriate public education (IDEA, 2004).

Special education is a relatively new field. The Education for All Handicapped Children Act was first introduced in the United States in 1975. The premise was that all students with disabilities should be educated in public schools with their peers at no cost to the parents. The requirements of the law were based on many lawsuits leading up to the congressional decision to regulate support for students with disabilities. Most previous laws came to fruition due to parents of students with disabilities who advocated for the rights of their children (Bartz, 2017; Karge, Ringlaben, & Schwartz, 1996; Rothstein & Johnson, 2021).

The Education for All Handicapped Children Act makes it so states and local education districts receive federal funds to help support the costs of special education (Cortiella & Horowitz, 2014). Despite the existence of this law, legitimate concern related to compliance and best education practices exists (Maggin, Hughes, Passmore, Kumm, & Scaletta, 2020). Part of this is simply the fact that many educational leaders do not know the law and do not realize the critical importance it should have for their school, district, or other educational setting.

Soon after the United States implemented the 1975 legislation, other countries followed. For example, the People's Republic of China passed legislation in 1982 (Kritzer, 2012), Canada enacted the Canadian Human Rights Act in 1985, and the Australian Human Rights Commission issued the Disability Discrimination Act of 1992. In my global travels, which include accreditation and special education audit visits, I have found that the United States is still an international leader in special education legislation.

In *How Successful People Think: Change Your Thinking, Change Your Life*, John C. Maxwell (2009) writes, "Focused thinking harnesses energy toward a desired goal" (p. 11). Superintendents, principals, and other key educational leaders must be change agents who drive their schools toward goals (Kouzes & Posner, 2017; Lasky & Karge, 2006; Tracy-Bronson, 2020). If the goal is to harness energy to support every student in the school, then this means intentionally studying and focusing on all that is necessary to ensure every student's needs. It means understanding litigation as well as supporting general and special education teachers and other service providers to offer the best quality instruction possible in the general education environments so that all students have equitable opportunities to learn and succeed in society. *All students can learn* should be the underlying belief that educational leaders cultivate (Huberman, Navo, & Parrish, 2012).

Action for Administrators

Unless otherwise noted, the laws described in these pages are federal litigation that took place in the United States. Individual states, provinces, and countries may have different legal policies or mandates to follow. Check with your local education agency to confirm the specific procedures you are required to follow.

This chapter focuses on IDEA (2004) and its legal requirements, including IEPs, specially designed instruction, and additional considerations. I also discuss Section 504 of the Rehabilitation Act of 1973.

Individuals With Disabilities Education Act

Congress sought to end the long history of segregation and exclusion of students with disabilities from the American public school system with the implementation of Public Law 94-142, the Education for All Handicapped Children Act of 1975, later renamed the Individuals With Disabilities Education Act, or IDEA (1990), and reauthorized in 1997 and 2004. This law defines thirteen categories of disability for students who are eligible for special education services: (1) autism, (2) deaf-blindness, (3) deafness, (4) hearing impairment, (5) intellectual disability, (6) multiple disabilities, (7) orthopedic impairment, (8) other health impairment, (9) serious emotional disturbance, (10) specific learning disability, (11) speech or language impairment,

(12) traumatic brain injury, and (13) visual impairment, including blindness. These categories are defined in IDEA section 300.8 (see https://sites.ed.gov/idea/regs/b/a/300.8). IDEA (2004) makes explicit the expectation that students with disabilities are entitled to the same education and opportunities as everyone else:

> Disability is a natural part of the human experience and in no way diminishes the right of individuals to participate in or contribute to society. Improving educational results for children with disabilities is an essential element of our national policy of ensuring equality of opportunity, full participation, independent living, and economic self-efficiency for individuals with disabilities.

IDEA is the primary legal reference for supporting the funding of free appropriate public education of students with disabilities. Since its passing, this landmark legislation has yielded great progress in securing the rights of more than seven million students with disabilities (U.S. Department of Education, 2020). IDEA (2004) requires public schools to provide special education (specially designed instruction) and related services for students. Students are entitled to supplemental and related services in the general education classroom with their peers (Walker, Johnson, & Randolph, 2021). Identification and evaluation of students must be delivered at no cost to the parents. These ideas comprise the six primary principles of IDEA.

1. Zero reject
2. Free appropriate public education
3. Least restrictive environment
4. Due process
5. Parent participation
6. Nondiscriminatory evaluation

See the appendix (page 178) for a reproducible at-a-glance summary of the six IDEA principles. The following sections discuss each principle in more detail, along with the reauthorization of IDEA (2004).

Zero Reject

The *zero reject* principle, which holds that no child can be denied an education, is a direct result of several key court cases, including *Brown v. Board of Education of Topeka* (1954). In the United States, every public school must provide an education to every child; a school cannot reject a student based on disability. Parents or guardians who reside in the United States can go to their local public school and request services. This requirement also includes Department of Defense schools in various locations around the globe, as they are considered U.S. public schools. Private schools located in the United States are able to set admissions criteria and can deny services. American international schools located overseas can also set admissions criteria and deny services, as these schools are not considered U.S. public schools.

Zero reject means a district cannot exclude a child from being a student. The district cannot say that students are "too disabled" to learn or that a significant behavior issue impacting their learning might exclude them. If a school believes a student has a contagious disease, it still must provide learning opportunities through methods such as home schooling or online learning. In sum, every student enrolled in public education in the United States must have the opportunity to participate in learning.

Free Appropriate Public Education

Just as the Supreme Court ruled in *Brown v. Board of Education of Topeka* (1954), the Fourteenth Amendment gives specific rights to an appropriate public education at no cost to students or their families. *Brown v. Board of Education* established the precedent of zero reject that later cases applied to students with disabilities to ensure they receive free appropriate public education. Progress monitoring, transition services, and thoughtful planning and services are all guaranteed in a free appropriate public education (Walker et al., 2021). Under a consent decree, in *Pennsylvania Association for Retarded Children (PARC) v. Commonwealth of Pennsylvania* (1971), the state of Pennsylvania agreed to provide full access to a free public education to students with intellectual disabilities. *Mills v. Board of Education of District of Columbia* (1972) was a similar scenario; the U.S. District Court for the District of Columbia ruled that school districts were constitutionally prohibited from deciding they had inadequate resources. In both cases, groups of parents who said their children could learn and should receive an education allowed the cases to gain prominence. Parents' voices matter.

The U.S. Supreme Court has referred to IEPs as the centerpiece for ensuring the free appropriate public education provision (Weatherly, 2021). The most common way we note free appropriate public education is progress on IEP objectives. IDEA (2004) and case law define *appropriate* as "meaningful gain" and "some educational benefit." This means that a student's programming (IEP objectives and instructional strategies) must show gain (progress) and receive benefit from education. The most commonly litigated issue in due process cases across the United States is failure to provide a free appropriate public education (Rothstein & Johnson, 2021). The bottom line is that without an *appropriate* education, a school is violating students' free appropriate public education as guaranteed in federal law.

Least Restrictive Environment

All students with disabilities have the right to a free education that is specifically designed to meet their unique needs. Furthermore, all students with disabilities deserve to be educated in an environment with their peers without disabilities. Increasingly, advocacy groups comprising parents, community members, and policymakers have encouraged this integration (Rodriguez & Murawski, 2022). This principle, the *least restrictive environment*, says that to the maximum extent appropriate, students with disabilities—from birth to their twenty-second birthday—must be educated with students without disabilities. This means all students should receive instruction in a general education (regular) classroom with their nondisabled peers, unless they prove that they are unable to learn in that setting. According to IDEA (2004), if a student cannot make gains or receive educational benefit in the general education classroom, that setting may actually be a more restrictive setting for that student. If the least restrictive cannot confer a free appropriate public education, then the continuum of services must be available.

The continuum of services states that students who cannot be educated without help in the general education classroom should receive some type of specifically designed instructional support that allows them to remain in the classroom, fully included with the other students, 100 percent of the time. Sometimes this means the students will need the support of a paraprofessional, or it might look like the general education and special education teachers co-teaching. If this is not possible, the students may need time in a smaller pull-out classroom and time to mainstream back into the general education classroom, or they may need specialized support in a separate environment for one period a day and then spend the remainder of the day in general education.

Placement decisions are made by the IEP team consisting of the student's parents or guardians, an administrator, the student's teachers, other professionals, and the student, when appropriate (Smith & Tyler, 2014). The team considers various parts of the continuum of services (see figure 1.1).

Only after experimenting with the full range of services should the team agree to place a student in a self-contained classroom for specialized support with other students with disabilities. Students in this scenario would spend most of their day with other students with disabilities, excluded from general education students except when mainstreamed back into a general education classroom. After all other options have been tried and found unsuccessful, then the more restrictive placements may

Least Restrictive Environment Continuum of Services	Extent of removal from interaction with peers
☐ General education classroom	Least Restrictive
☐ General education classroom with consult and paraeducator	
☐ General education classroom with specialized academic instruction or related service member (co-teaching)	
☐ Resource for specialized support (separate environment by period)	
☐ Behavior intervention classes (separate environment by period)	
☐ Self-contained classroom offering specialized support and general education classroom for part of the day	
☐ Self-contained classroom offering specialized support with opportunities to participate with noneligible students in nonacademics and extracurriculars	
☐ Self-contained classroom full-time	
☐ Self-contained classroom at another school or nonpublic school	
☐ Residential treatment center or homebound instruction	Most Restrictive

Source: Karge, 2021.

FIGURE 1.1: The continuum of services for students with disabilities.

be appropriate. For example, a high school student with severe dyslexia and significant behavior challenges may need a more restrictive placement for specific instructional and behavior-monitoring purposes. The special education services would then be the least restrictive placement, as they offer the only way for the student to make academic, social, and emotional progress. The placement depends on the team's decision, and the team must always realize that special education is a service, not a place, and when possible, that service should be in the general education classroom with general education peers (Lipsky & Gartner, 2012).

Special education is a service, not a place, and when possible, that service should be in the general education classroom with general education peers.

When determining placement for schooling, every team member must consider where students will be when they graduate from school. Society doesn't have banks for persons with disabilities, nor are there stores just for persons with disabilities; so why are there such classrooms and schools (Karge & Lasky, 2007)? When students are educated with their peers, they are more successful in society (Cole, Murphy, Frisby, Grossi, & Bolte, 2019). I cannot say it enough: special education is a service, not a place.

Action for Administrators

Assess the least restrictive environment continuum of placement at your school site. Make certain it is a true continuum and not just a jump from general education to a segregated special education classroom.

Due Process

Students with disabilities and their families are provided specific due process with regard to special education. U.S. citizens have procedural due process to allow them to challenge the government's intrusion on their liberties. Students placed in a special education program have the same right of due process to ensure that at the time of placement, and at least annually thereafter, this environment is and continues to be the least restrictive and offers an appropriate education.

Due process is considered the ultimate procedural safeguard for parents of students with disabilities. The idea is that an impartial hearing officer hears both sides of a dispute (parent versus district) and renders a decision. Under certain circumstances, parents who prevail in special education proceedings are entitled to reimbursement of legal and other costs. All students are entitled to due process before suspension or expulsion from school. Under due process, no changes can be made to a student's placement or program without prior notification of the parents. Parents have the right to question and challenge special education services. Students have a right to be represented by an attorney or advocate in school-related disciplinary matters.

The first case of special education due process decided by the Supreme Court occurred in 1982. A student with moderate hearing impairment, Amy Rowley, was participating in a general education classroom based on her IEP. She received one hour of tutoring daily, as well as speech and language therapy. Amy's parents asked for a sign language interpreter to be present in the classroom every day. The district refused, interpreting the free appropriate public education requirements to mean that a sign language interpreter was not necessary. The parents believed a sign language interpreter was a necessary related service under these requirements. Ultimately, the Supreme Court ruled that Amy *did* receive educational benefits under a free appropriate public education, as she had been promoted from grade to grade and had experienced an appropriate education without a sign language interpreter, and thus, she was not entitled to an interpreter. In *Board of Education of the Hendrick Hudson School District v. Rowley* (1982), the court clearly noted an appropriate education does not mean "the best education."

Parent Participation

The fifth principle of IDEA is *parent participation*, meaning that parents have the right to participate in every decision related to the identification, evaluation, and placement of their child suspected of having or already identified as having a disability (Sears, Peters, Beidler, & Murawski, 2021). The parent rights, called *procedural safeguards*, help ensure the relationship between parents and schools is more than just an event (the parent-teacher conference, back-to-school night, or open house); it is a relationship that grows and is nourished over time.

Family engagement is also the sixth step to implementing inclusive practices (see chapter 7, page 145). Most parents spend more time with their children than educators do. Parents are the experts on their own children and should be consulted and considered members of the education team. If a parent is not involved, the school must find out if another family member (for example, a grandparent or aunt or uncle) or legal guardian is serving in this advocacy role (Rodriguez & Murawski, 2022).

Action for Administrators

Build relationships with parents. Let them know that you know the legislation related to IDEA and you are there as a change agent to support the educators working with their child. Let them know you care and want to support their child in any way you can.

Nondiscriminatory Evaluation

When conducting assessments to identify students who need special education services, the assessor or assessors must use two or more assessment instruments, and those instruments must be administered in the student's native language. This is the sixth principle of IDEA, and it is termed *nondiscriminatory evaluation*. In 1979, parents filed the *Larry P. v. Riles* case against the state of California, claiming that the state's method of classifying students with disabilities was culturally biased against students of color. The students were placed in special education based on one assessment: an IQ test. The court ruled there should be a battery of assessments to support placement in special education. Similarly, in 1969, leading up to the *Diana v. State Board of Education* case, nine students were discriminated against because their assessment was administered in English while their native language was Spanish. The students were moved to special education based on an assessment by a monolingual psychologist, who later was deemed an unqualified assessor. The 1969 case was settled out of court in 1970. Since then, schools have qualified assessors give tests in each student's native language.

The *Diana v. State Board of Education* (1970) and *Larry P. v. Riles* (1979) cases led to the landmark decisions that all students must be tested in their native language or mode of communication and more than one assessment must be used for identification purposes. Furthermore, parents must give permission for every phase of special education, from referral to program placement, and the proposed plan must include goals and objectives.

Reauthorization of IDEA (2004)

The six principles of IDEA form the baseline of special education law and regulations. This IDEA regulation has been reauthorized several times. In 1986, Public Law 99-457 added infants and toddlers and provided individual family service plans. Then a landmark decision in 1990, Public Law 101-476, changed the name to IDEA, added transition plans, and added individuals with autism and traumatic brain injury. And in 1997, Public Law 105-17 added attention deficit hyperactivity disorder to the "other health impairment" category, added functional behavioral assessments, and changed transition plans to become a component of the IEP. Then, in 2004, Public Law 108-446 required special education teachers to be highly qualified, and it mandated testing, eliminated IEP short-term objectives and benchmarks, changed learning disability identification procedures, and allowed alternative educational settings in situations when drug or weapon use is involved.

Unfortunately, the field of special education is complicated by many acronyms and initialisms. If school leaders know these terms, they can assist parents learning to navigate their children's educational system. Figure 1.2 offers a partial list as a reference guide. Please help staff understand that these abbreviations can be very intimidating and should not be used when communicating with parents or guardians unless the staff provide full explanations.

ABA	Applied behavior analysis
ADD	Attention deficit disorder
ADHD	Attention deficit hyperactivity disorder
APE	Adapted physical education
APH	Aphasia
AT	Assistive technology
AUT	Autism
BL	Blind
CAC	Community advisory committee for special education
CATS	Career and transition services
CBI	Community-based instruction
DBL	Deaf or blind or both
DEA	Deaf
DD	Developmentally delayed
DHH	Deaf or hard of hearing
DI	Differentiated instruction
DIS	Designated instructional services (sometimes called *related services*—that is, language and speech, adapted physical education, occupational therapy, social work, and so on)
ESY	Extended school year
FAPE	Free appropriate public education
FBA	Functional behavioral assessment
FFH	Family foster home
Hughes Bill	California legislation regarding management of serious behavior problems of students with disabilities
IDEA	Individuals With Disabilities Education Act
IEP	Individualized education program
ITP	Individualized transition plan
LAS	Language and speech
LCI	Licensed children's institution
LD	Learning disabilities
LEP	Limited English proficiency
LID	Low-incidence disability (meaning a severe disabling condition with hearing, vision, or orthopedic impairments, or a combination)
LRE	Least restrictive environment
MH	Multiple handicap
MTSS	Multitiered system of support
OT	Occupational therapy
PT	Physical therapy
RTI	Response to intervention
UDL	Universal Design for Learning

FIGURE 1.2: Guide to special education abbreviations.

Visit ***go.SolutionTree.com/specialneeds*** *for a free reproducible version of this figure.*

Individualized Education Program

Under the IDEA federal legislation, the document that U.S. educators use to determine specific special education services for an individual student is the *individualized education program* (*IEP*). Many international schools across the globe use the term *individual learning plan*. However, schools in the United States do not accept individual learning plan documents. An IEP is a written plan that outlines a student's unique needs and the special education and related services needed for the student with a disability (Rothstein & Johnson, 2021). In many education circles, it is referred to as a *contract*. However, keep in mind that an IEP is not a legally binding contract. It does not guarantee that all IEP goals and objectives will be met by the end of the school year. A school district cannot be held liable if it does not meet the goals and objectives that an IEP lays out. The IEP is a legal commitment for the school district to provide the special education and related services listed therein and, most importantly, to make a good-faith attempt to assist the student in meeting those goals and objectives. Educators use the IEP as a management tool to ensure a strong match of individual needs to services. The IEP assessment cycle begins with parents' consent for evaluation and ends with parents' consent for student placement and for the entire written document. Parental involvement is key and affirmed by legal precedent. The *Endrew F. v. Douglas County School District* (2017) case ruled parents are required to have "meaningful opportunities to participate in the education of their children."

A lot of time and effort goes into the creation of students' individual IEPs. By following a set process, schools can ensure that all students who need them will receive IEPs that guarantee necessary services. A dedicated IEP scheduler can help ensure that the process goes smoothly. This in turn ensures that students receive specially designed instruction to meet their IEP goals.

IEP Process

The sequence for IEP events is detailed in figure 1.3.

Initially, when a student is identified as possibly having difficulty learning, basic screening and identification begin. The parent is contacted for input, and the teacher tries numerous strategies and interventions and collects data on the student's progress. This is the prereferral intervention phase. Every school has a team to implement this process, the most common being the student study team or child guidance intervention team. In chapter 2 (page 31), I introduce the learning services team (LST), which fulfills this role; this all-purpose team designs the multitiered system of support and includes the prereferral intervention within a three-tier system.

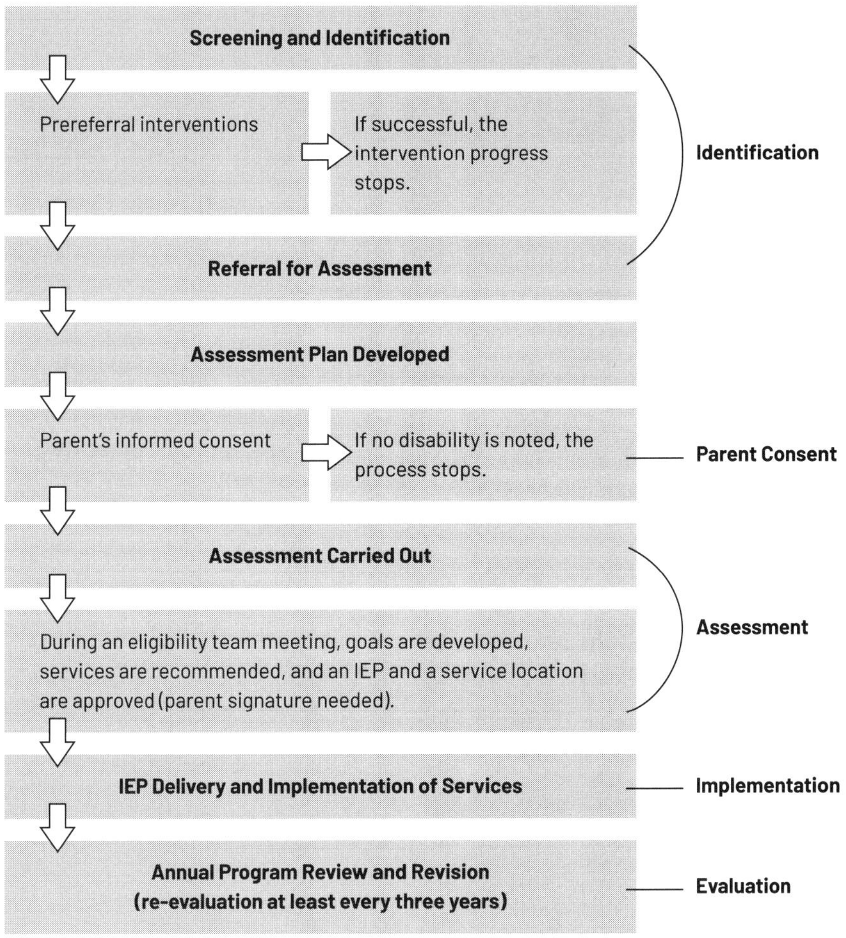

FIGURE 1.3: The sequence of IEP events.

Visit ***go.SolutionTree.com/specialneeds*** *for a free reproducible version of this figure.*

Regardless of the name used, the team comprises professionals who offer suggestions for intervention and keep the parent informed. If this intervention is successful, the process stops. However, if the student continues to have challenges, a referral for assessment takes place.

The IEP team develops the assessment plan by carefully determining what types of assessment are necessary. Formal and informal assessment data should come from a variety of sources. These may include standardized assessments (given by a licensed professional assessor, such as a psychologist, medical doctor, speech and language pathologist, or someone in a similar role), curriculum-based assessments and observations conducted by personnel at the school (administered by the general education or special education teacher), or both. The parent must provide informed consent.

Once all assessments and observations are gathered, an IEP meeting takes place. The IEP team determines eligibility for special education. Eligibility is based on the thirteen categories of disability under IDEA (2004).

Participants in an IEP meeting include an administrator or designee who is representing the education agency (that is, the school or school district), special education teachers, general education teachers, one or more parents or guardians, the person conducting the assessment, the student (when appropriate), advocates, and others as appropriate. The education agency representative is a person who is qualified to provide or supervise special education services and is able to speak to the availability of resources in the school or district. Typically, this is the educational leader (administrator) at the school. However, in high-profile cases where the district expects challenges or litigation, someone from the district office, with the proper background, attends the meeting.

The administrator (or the designated representative from the education agency) sets the stage for the meeting by assuring the parents (or guardians) they are members of the IEP team and their voices matter. When introductions take place at the meeting's start, introduce the parents first. Fully explain the parents' rights at the beginning of the meeting, provide the parents with a copy of a document listing these rights, and ask them if they have any questions about their rights. Let parents know that their procedural due process is important and that all members of the team take it seriously. These simple statements can defuse future legal actions.

If a parent is unable to attend or chooses not to attend the IEP meeting in person, try an alternative means of participation (for example, a telephone call or video conference). Document all attempts to gain parent participation (note the date and time of telephone calls, save copies of correspondence, and so on).

The actual writing of the IEP is a collaborative team effort during the meeting. To save time, it is acceptable to write a draft of goals and objectives ahead of the IEP meeting; however, all persons involved, including the parents, must receive this draft prior to the meeting. I strongly recommend that the goals and objectives be those the student can achieve within a year according to the student's ability level. Long lists of goals are frustrating. Keep the list concise and in direct support of the student's academic, social, emotional, and physical growth.

At the meeting, psychologists or those who conducted the assessment must describe the instruments used and the assessment results in easy-to-understand language. The team then uses this information to create the goals and objectives. If a draft was shared ahead of time, make sure the assessment results align with the goals and objectives. Parents should be considered full partners in the decision making and goal setting. Be sure to allocate time for parent input and questions.

The components of the written IEP include the following.

- Statement of performance, including academic, behavior, and mental health needs
- Disability category for receiving services
- Annual goals stating how the student will receive general education curriculum
- Related services, supplementary aids, or both
- Extent of participation in regular education
- Dates and duration of services
- Statement of individual appropriate accommodations
- Evaluation or progress-monitoring procedures
- Transition plan (created by the time students turn sixteen years old)
- Age of maturity (for students eighteen or older)
- Signatures of all participants

Attorney Julie J. Weatherly (2021) recommends, "IEP teams should use the *stranger test* when developing IEP content." This means anyone reading the student's IEP should have a very strong conceptual knowledge of the student's educational strengths, challenges, and current levels of academic and functional performance. After reading the IEP content, people should feel like they personally know the student.

The actual IEP form varies from school district to school district and from state to state. If you conduct an internet search for *image of IEP*, you will see the wide variety of forms educators use to meet the IDEA requirements. I especially recommend the following.

- https://iep-template.com
- https://handypdf.com/pdf/iep-template-01
- www.jotform.com/pdf-templates/iep-plan-template

The IEP section on the present level of academic achievement and functional performance describes the student's strengths, challenges, skills, and abilities at the time the IEP is written. Grade-level standards are the norm for reporting academic achievement.

Functional performance refers to daily life competencies that go beyond academics, such as behavior, communication, social skills, and mobility.

In consideration of the least restrictive environment, the IEP team must determine the student's ability or inability to participate and receive services in general education classrooms (*Thornock v. Boise Independent School District No. 1*, 1988). The team must make every effort to keep the student with a disability in the general education setting for specially designed services.

IEP meetings can range from as short as thirty minutes to as long as three hours or more, especially if the student receives a lot of related services. Schedule the meeting with a beginning time and an end time. If the end time arrives and the meeting is not over, honor everyone's time, and schedule an additional meeting for another time. At all meetings, everyone present should sign an attendance sheet and then sign if they agree or disagree with the IEP's content once the team has reached consensus. This two-signature process is legally important, especially if the meeting takes place over multiple days or if an individual member does not agree with the rest of the team on the decision made at the meeting.

Action for Administrators

Take the lead. Make it a priority to be at IEP meetings. Know what placements and services are available in your school and district. Lead the meetings by maintaining the agenda, time lines, and speaker list. Be respectful to all attendees, making sure all voices are heard, especially the parent voices.

Once the IEP team develops the goals and provides a service recommendation, and parents approve and sign the IEP, the program services begin. During the implementation phase, there should be frequent contact among parents and all related services providers (explained in depth in chapter 5, page 101). The IEP team monitors the student's progress consistently and reviews the IEP annually. As required by IDEA, every three years, the process begins again with a complete re-evaluation.

Action for Administrators

To determine the appropriateness of the IEP, ask these questions.

"Were objectives derived from appropriate assessments for the student's age and functioning level?"

"Was the IEP (objectives and accommodations or modifications) developed based on present levels of performance?"

"Are there IEP objectives in all necessary domains (areas of need), and can progress be documented?"

IEP Scheduler

A key component of procedural safeguards under IDEA is appropriate notice of meetings. This notice must be in written form and in conversational terminology familiar to the general public. It is critical to appoint someone in the school as the IEP master scheduler, who provides appropriate notice of meetings to all attendees. Sometimes this scheduler might be the psychologist or a lead special educator. Other times it might be an administrative assistant. Whoever is appointed creates and monitors a master schedule to ensure parents are invited in a timely manner, general education teachers and other team members know ahead of time so they can provide input, and certain things ultimately run smoothly.

Mills v. Board of Education of District of Columbia (1972) stipulates the constitutional due process principle (Rothstein & Johnson, 2021), which, as stated earlier, means that students are entitled to annual checks to ensure their placement in the least restrictive environment. Approximately 10 percent of a school's population may be students with IEPs. If, for example, you are the principal of a large comprehensive high school with two thousand students, this could mean two hundred students in your school will require special education services. Adhering to the legal time lines of annual and triannual IEP meetings is important to effective leadership for special education. Figure 1.4 (page 26) provides a sample from a schoolwide IEP schedule; schools commonly create schedules like this within Microsoft Excel or a Google spreadsheet (https://google.com/sheets).

Month	Student	IEP Review Date	Type of IEP Meeting	Date to Send Invitations (Notice of Meeting)
September	J. K.	9/4	Initial	8/4
	G. Z.	9/12	Annual	8/12
October	A. S.	10/4	Triannual	9/4
November	D. Q.	11/13	Annual	10/13
December	S. R.	12/3	Annual	11/3

FIGURE 1.4: Sample of a schoolwide IEP schedule.

Specially Designed Instruction

Regardless of their placement, all students with disabilities must receive specially designed instruction. IDEA (2004) defines *specially designed instruction* as instruction that is clearly linked to students' academic and functional needs documented in their IEPs. Teachers deliver this instruction to help students learn and to assist them in reaching their IEP goals. This means that teachers must ensure they design this instruction to be accessible to students. Sometimes it means helping the student understand a required standard by changing the content in such a way that the student may more thoroughly grasp the content. For example, a teacher may add pictures to an electronically designed worksheet so the student has a visual aid to better understand the content. Other times it means using a different methodology to align with a particular disability or otherwise changing the delivery of instruction. For example, if a general education teacher lectures on a topic for twenty minutes during class, the special education teacher may reteach the content to the student with a disability, highlighting the lecture's main ideas to ensure depth of knowledge.

A properly trained special education teacher knows how to implement specially designed instruction effectively. Although teachers may use accommodations or differentiation to support specially designed instruction, these two terms are not synonymous. *Accommodations* means providing access, including use of calculators, highlighters, and sentence starters, or using strategies like breaking information into smaller parts. Accommodation adjusts how to help students meet the goal. *Differentiation* is the *philosophy* and understanding that all students are different and their needs vary according to their background, culture, disability, and so on (see pages 158–159 for more details on these terms). This is a given in classrooms around the globe. Differentiation is for all students, not just students with disabilities, but when educators use differentiation with students with disabilities, significant growth is evident (Tomlinson, 2014; Wu, 2013).

Action for Administrators

The special education teacher can provide specially designed instruction in any setting, including in general education classrooms using a co-teaching model (see chapter 2, page 51). Sometimes educational leaders mistakenly think specially designed instruction can be accomplished only in segregated environments.

The terms *special day class* and *resource specialist person* have been eliminated in many areas of the United States because they refer to placements. These terms are no longer used because those settings no longer exist, as all students with disabilities are educated in the inclusive environment. Instead, special education teachers are referred to as *specially designed instructors* because that is their area of expertise in the general education classroom as they co-teach, collaborate, and consult with general education peers. Internationally, the term *learning support specialist* or *inclusion specialist* is frequently used. Sometimes the terminology is contractual. For the purposes of this book, I use the term *special education teacher*. The special education teacher referred to is assumed to have ample training at the university level (often a master's degree) and is state or country certified to teach students with disabilities.

Additional Considerations

Even as leaders work to implement inclusive practices and provide for the requirements of IDEA, they have a number of additional considerations to keep in mind. These include standardized assessments and budgeting.

Standardized Assessments

The federal mandate under IDEA is that all students with disabilities be included in standardized assessments. This creates challenges, as general education teachers sometimes think having students with disabilities enrolled in their classes will lower standardized assessment scores, which could reflect on their teaching. This is a good place for the leadership and the special education teachers to advocate for students with disabilities. For example, many students with autism and learning disabilities do very well on high-stakes standardized assessments. These scores can even assist with raising the class mean (Wu, 2013). Even if test scores drop through no fault of the teacher, that is no reason to deny students access to high-quality tiered instruction.

Researchers Adai A. Tefera, David Hernández-Saca, and Ashlee M. Lester (2019) conducted interviews of minority high school students with disabilities. These students discuss the need to display tremendous grit when teachers make them feel less than adequate for receiving low test scores. Grit, which many educators would consider a positive attribute for students to develop, can have problematic overtones when it comes to students from marginalized communities because of the potential for victim blaming; that is, teachers blame low achievement on a lack of grit rather than a disadvantaged background (Tefera et al., 2019). Leaders need to advocate for students' rights and observe and understand students' perspectives (for example, those related to high-stakes testing). However, leaders must also assure teachers that if their overall test scores fall, leaders will recognize that this is due to a combination of things, which may include having a student with a disability in their class. This in no way means the leader will abandon them. Leaders must support their teachers and assist them with ways to provide intervention and support. Inclusion facilitators (that is, special education teachers) can offer unique skills and training to aid general education teachers with interventions, strategies, and accommodations for students with disabilities who have lower assessment scores. These facilitators can help all the teachers move from the mindset of "*my* students" to one of "*our* students" (Kurth & Gross, 2015).

Budgeting

Take the time to get to know your special education director and district fiscal officer and to determine what you can and cannot accomplish with different funding sources. For example, under IDEA (2004), funds may go toward supplementary aids and services such as the following.

- A classroom paraeducator
- A personal paraeducator
- Assistive technology devices, services, or both
- Behavior management
- Teacher training
- Social inclusion, social-emotional supports, or both
- Itinerant instruction

This means schools can use IDEA (2004) funds to support these areas. Special education has several sources of funding. For example, in California, 46 percent of special education funding comes from local funds, 45 percent comes from state funds, and only 9 percent comes from federal funds (R. Cochlin, personal communication,

June 28, 2022). Although as a leader, you are used to wrestling with budgeting issues, special education funding can be tricky. While the services provided on the IEPs and under IDEA are free to students and families, they are not free to the schools! "Free appropriate public education means . . . provided at public expense, under public supervision and direction, and without charge" (Rothstein & Johnson, 2021, p. 137). Talk to your fiscal experts to determine how funds are distributed. States that comply with the IDEA mandates are eligible for funds from the federal government. These funds are distributed based on a funding formula that takes into account how many students with disabilities there are and how severe the disabilities are (Rothstein & Johnson, 2021). However, schools extensively use local and state funds to cover costs. These local and state funds come from various sources depending on where the school is located, how many students with disabilities are present, and what types of government and private moneys are available.

Section 504 of the Rehabilitation Act of 1973

Every student eligible for special education services under IDEA is also eligible under Section 504 of the Rehabilitation Act of 1973; however, the reverse is not true. The 504 plan is like an IEP and may be used as a process to support students with disabilities who need reasonable accommodations but do not need more comprehensive special education support. For example, a student with attention deficit disorder or attention deficit hyperactivity disorder (ADHD) who could function in school and whose disability did not interfere with school activities would be covered by Section 504 but not by IDEA. Meanwhile, a different student with the same condition would have coverage under IDEA if that condition did in fact interfere with school activities. A reasonable accommodation for this student might be time to go to the health office or the nurse for medication. Section 504 prohibits discrimination under federal law; it is a civil rights law to support students. It states:

> No otherwise qualified individual with a disability in the United States, as defined in section 705(20) of this title, shall, solely by reason of her or his disability, be excluded from the participation in, be denied the benefits of, or be subjected to discrimination under any program or activity receiving federal financial assistance.

Examples of students eligible for Section 504 who typically aren't considered to have a disability are students suffering from a broken bone, students who are pregnant, or students diagnosed with cancer.

Table 1.1 (page 30) is a simple breakdown to help educators understand the difference between IDEA and Section 504.

TABLE 1.1: Understanding the Difference Between IDEA and Section 504

IDEA	SECTION 504
Funding statute	Not a funding statute
Thirteen discrete categories of disabilities	Broadly defined areas of special needs
Procedural due process	Procedural due process
Section 504 students not covered under IDEA	All IDEA students covered by Section 504
IEP created and implemented to convey educational benefit	504 plan created to document accommodations
Consent for placement needed	No consent for placement
Annual review	No annual review

Every school in the United States has a format for IEPs. Check with your district's special education director or your local planning area's special education director for the IEP forms you are required to use. Not every system, however, has an established protocol for Section 504. Reach out to your district's special education director or your local planning area's special education director to request a checklist for 504 eligibility review and to discuss Section 504 parent procedural safeguards.

Conclusion

This chapter's content just scratches the surface of special education legal requirements. My intent is to provide educational leaders with must-know information about the six principles of IDEA, the IEP process, and Section 504. Special education is a complicated field. Surround yourself with people who can inform and support you. Your local education agency representative or district director of special education can give you many details that will enhance your leadership abilities to support parents, educators, and ultimately the students with disabilities whom you serve. Avoid unnecessary litigation by knowing the legal mandates and understanding how to apply them to the students you serve.

Chapter 2 will detail service-delivery models and how you can support all students in your school by establishing a multitiered system of support that identifies response to intervention and students' academic, social, behavioral, and emotional needs. This may or may not include a schoolwide positive behavior support system. However, I recommend both to ensure high-quality supports. The chapter will also cover inclusion, co-teaching, learning centers, and self-contained (segregated) classrooms. These are the basics of what every leader should know about special education.

TWO

STRIVING TO MEET THE LEAST RESTRICTIVE ENVIRONMENT: SERVICE-DELIVERY MODELS

Here is a powerful yet simple rule:
always give people more than they expect to get.
—NELSON BOSWELL

It is essential that schools deliver services to students who need them in an efficient and organized way. The congressionally mandated report *The Condition of Education 2020* indicates 7.1 million or 14 percent of public school students receive special education services (Hussar et al., 2020). To serve these students, schools require a reliable way to identify who needs support, what support they need, and the best way to provide that support.

Personnel and service-delivery models differ greatly across the United States and around the world. For example, in a large comprehensive high school in Mexico, there is a counselor for every grade level and only one special education teacher. Yet a small private high school in Africa has a learning support person (special education teacher) for every grade level and only one counselor. In some schools, the services are all provided in the general education classroom, and other schools use a more segregated class approach. However, one common goal runs through all programs: meeting the individual needs of each student in the least restrictive environment.

This sounds great, but in practice, it is not always so easy. As discussed in chapter 1 (page 14), the least restrictive environment has many levels. As an educational leader, you must plan the service-delivery model at your school site based on the needs of your student population and the staffing available. Make this a top priority.

In chapter 7 (page 145), I provide eleven steps for establishing an inclusive school. The first step is to *review current practices*. As you read through this chapter, think about how you are striving to meet the least restrictive environment on your campus. Take time to really review your current practices, including what teams you have established to support inclusive practices and what service-delivery model or models you implement. As you do this, I strongly encourage you to *involve the leadership team* (step 2 of the eleven steps) in these discussions and decisions related to practice. Begin thinking now about how you might *do some action planning* (step 3) to proactively move your school toward inclusive practices by designing a learning services team that can brainstorm and plan for implementation of an effective schoolwide multitiered system of support.

The U.S. Department of Education's (2020) *41st Annual Report to Congress on the Implementation of the Individuals With Disabilities Education Act, 2019* chronicles that 64 percent of all students with disabilities spend at least 80 percent of their day in general education classes. When possible, students should be educated in the general education classroom with their general education peers. The best way to do this is to establish a multitiered system of support at your school. The MTSS should demonstrate an integrated, comprehensive, schoolwide approach to instruction, differentiated learning, student-centered learning, individualized student needs, and the alignment of systems necessary for *all* students' academic, behavioral, emotional, and social success.

This chapter focuses on the successful implementation and running of an MTSS. First, I discuss the formation of a learning services team, then I get into some details of the MTSS itself and how to use it to ensure all students get support, and finally, I discuss special education service-delivery models.

Learning Services Team

Schools should put together a learning services team (LST) to oversee the implementation of the MTSS and to coordinate referrals. In my travels globally, I have heard *student study team* and *child guidance intervention team* used as the names of this team. I prefer *learning services team*, as the team's primary goal is to coordinate the learning services for Tier 1 and Tier 2 intervention and to serve as an avenue for students prior to special education referral. The LST is a schoolwide team. Once special education referrals occur, an IEP team forms to support the individual student according to needs; this team is different for every student. That is, the teachers and learning services personnel who support the specific student are members of that student's IEP team (see chapter 1, page 9). The LST members can collaborate to provide for greater cohesiveness, coordination, and instructional continuity and complement existing curriculum and instructional programs. The team should consist of some combination of administrators, general education teachers, special education teachers, counselors, psychologist, speech and language pathologist, intervention coach, nurse, reading teacher, language teacher, and other specialists at the school. Staff who support every tier within the school system should be represented on the team.

Every school is different, and each will need to decide which LST members can efficiently collaborate to support the MTSS. School A may have a small team of three general education teachers, two special education teachers, and the administrator. School B may have a much larger team consisting of a representative of every grade level or content area in the school as well as a psychologist, a counselor, a speech and language therapist, special education teachers, language support teachers, and administrators.

The team meets regularly to reconfigure resources and coordinate service delivery. This team may bring services to the classroom or remove students for brief periods of time to support them and administer services. *Special education is a service, not a place* (IDEA, 2004). I cannot repeat this enough; it's that important. The service can be provided in general education classrooms or other locations on campus. The value added is the *service*. The goal is continuous and coherent support. The LST should include not only collaboration between school psychologists and administrators to promote systems-level change (Eagle, Dowd-Eagle, Snyder, & Holtzman, 2015) but also collaboration among all specialists and support staff available at the school site. This allows a broad focus on academics, behavior, and mental health (including social skills, social-emotional wellness, physical well-being, nutrition, and overall health).

Encourage team members to share responsibilities during meetings. Figure 2.1 (page 34) provides a suggested template for LST duties.

The LST builds capacity by collaboratively making data-based decisions for the school's MTSS. This team must base the MTSS's design and increased intervention intensity on the needs of individual students and the availability of staff to support them. The LST should review both quantitative data (that is, standardized and

Duty	Requirements	Who Performs the Duty
Recording	Document the meeting in the LST log sheet (see page 185). Record notes during the meeting. Make three copies of the meeting notes (for the parent, the cumulative file, and the student's teacher). Put the original meeting notes in the team book or online file. Put a copy of the meeting notes in the student's cumulative file. Deliver or electronically send the meeting notes to the student's teacher. Deliver or electronically send the parent a copy of the meeting notes with a thank-you note.	
Scheduling	To schedule meetings, put a calendar in the office, or use an electronic calendar and give all educators access to it. Send a letter or email home to inform parents of the team meeting one week in advance. Call parents to remind them of the meeting two days prior to the meeting. Maintain the team time line checklist.	
Preplanning	Send a reminder to the student's teachers with a list of things they need to bring to the meeting. Ask the teachers if they need help gathering information, and assist them. Meet with the teachers to review the interventions implemented with the student and have samples ready for the meeting.	
Follow-up	Fill out the summary form (page 186) during the meeting. Make sure all interventions are tried before a second team meeting is scheduled. After the second team meeting, if testing is not recommended, work with the classroom teachers to implement follow-up strategies. Compile a list of parents who are willing to talk to other parents about special education, retention, and so on.	
Other	If the student is transitioning from another school, collect data from the previous school. If the student works with a private tutor, submit a parent request to speak to the tutor.	

FIGURE 2.1: Template for LST duties.

Visit ***go.SolutionTree.com/specialneeds*** *for a free reproducible version of this figure.*

formative assessments) and qualitative data (for example, teacher and parent perceptions and teacher comments on report cards) at the school.

The work of this team needs to be visible to faculty and staff at the school. Decide how this might be implemented. Take time at faculty meetings to cover what the team is doing, or send out this information via an electronic newsletter. Share case studies and successes so all can take pride in progress. The key is to foster a team effort. Your special education teachers and your other specialists are part of the team; include their voices at the meetings.

Action for Administrators

Form an LST, be present at the meetings, brainstorm with the team, and design a cohesive schoolwide system whereby students receive MTSS services. Make certain all special education teachers and specialists are members of the team. The expectation should be that updated data are evaluated at each team meeting.

Multitiered System of Support

Once the LST has participated in some action planning (step 3 of the eleven steps to an inclusive school), it is time to design an MTSS model specifically for the school. Don't rush through this process! *Conduct professional learning* (step 4) and *read the research* (step 5). Authors Matt Navo and Amy Williams (2022) give leadership teams the tools to create a school or district MTSS framework; their book *Demystifying MTSS* is an excellent source for professional learning. Authors Jessica Djabrayan Hannigan and John E. Hannigan (2021) have also written an excellent MTSS start-up guide that can assist with both professional learning and the research to gain knowledge before implementation. As team members write the school's MTSS handbook, which serves as a central school resource, consider all stakeholders. *Encourage family engagement* (step 6), as families are key members of the stakeholder group. Families need to understand the systems in place at their children's schools and how to request access to the various tiers if needed.

Although implementations can vary, at its core, MTSS is based on a three-tier system of instruction and intervention. The notion of MTSS is that all students receive universal best instruction in the general education classroom (Tier 1). Teachers use research-based instructional strategies for core curriculum instruction. This means differentiated learning, as well as student accommodations, universal design, and maybe even some co-teaching. However, we know from the research that this does not work for all students, and some students need more targeted support (Tier 2) or intensive support (Tier 3; Blackburn & Witzel, 2018; Mitchell, Bruhn, & Lewis, 2016). As you will see in this section, special needs services are a step beyond the three tiers. Note that students receiving Tier 2 support maintain access to Tier 1 instruction. Similarly, students in Tier 3 often receive support at Tier 2 and retain access to Tier 1 instruction.

Tier 2 is designed for targeted support. In addition to the support and Tier 1 instruction they receive in the core classroom, some students get more support from the LST in deficit areas. The LST provides this support for six to eight weeks and then re-evaluates to see whether the student is ready to go back full-time to the general education classroom (Tier 1). For example, say a fourth-grade student is reading at the third-grade level. The student has strong phonemic awareness, phonics, and comprehension; however, her fluency is very poor. Through schoolwide data progress monitoring, the LST is aware of the situation and administers a fluency pretest to the student, which reveals she reads fluently with 68 percent accuracy. During Tier 2 intervention, the student is placed in a small group with the reading teacher, who uses the Wilson Fluency/Basic program (www.wilsonlanguage.com/programs/fluency-basic) for twenty minutes daily for six weeks. At the end of the six weeks, the student is reassessed, and her score improves to 83 percent accuracy. The student is able to go back into the general education classroom and becomes a more capable reader just from the intervention. She did not need to be referred to special education services.

Tier 3 is intended for the very few students who need intensive support—typically students who are missing foundational skills for the grade or course or who need a learning or language plan to support their personal learning goals and objectives. These students receive the core instruction and support from Tier 1 as well as support of increased intensity and time through Tier 2 and Tier 3 (Blackburn & Witzel, 2018). For example, imagine a fifth-grade student who has just enrolled in an American international school in Eastern Europe. The student is reading in his first language (Russian) at the fifth-grade level; however, he is reading in English at the second-grade level. This student participates in eight weeks of Tier 2 intervention with a small group of classmates. During the thirty-minute intervention time, the English language teacher facilitates choral and oral reading. Additionally, the student receives one-on-one Tier 3 support from an instructional assistant (paraprofessional) three times a week for thirty minutes. During this time, the student participates in a six-week online program from the Institute of Reading Development (https://readingprograms.org/Programs/5th-grade). This online program reinforces fluency and comprehension. The English language teacher also meets with the student for thirty minutes two times a week to provide explicit instruction in comprehension. This process is repeated for two cycles of eight weeks each. After these sixteen weeks, the student is on grade level and does not need referral to special education.

Figure 2.2 provides a basic MTSS diagram.

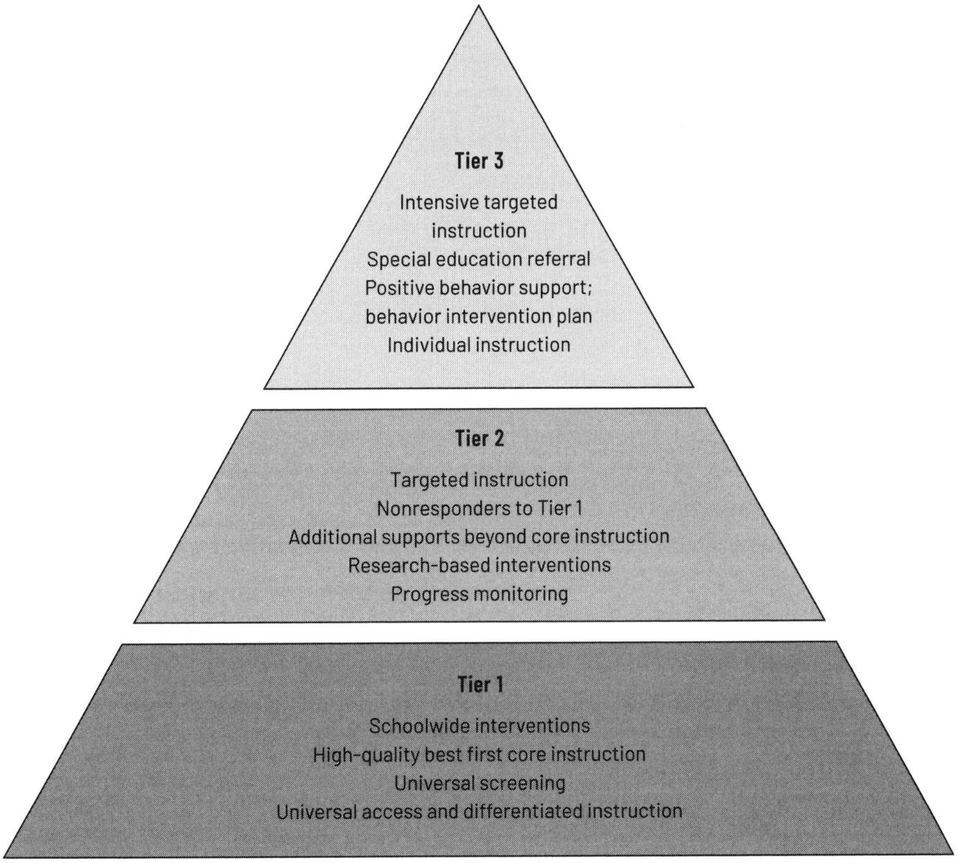

Source: Karge & Lasky, 2012. Used with permission.

FIGURE 2.2: Multitiered system of support.

What we have learned from using MTSS in the United States is that students sometimes need to be pulled out for six to eight weeks to receive intensive intervention at Tier 3 and then go back into the general education classroom for Tier 1 and Tier 2 instruction. This is not required, nor should it be the norm for every student. The goal should be to set students up for success by teaching them basics they will need in the inclusive classroom. For some, this means what to do if they don't understand directions. Others spend the time in a supplemental program—for example, a program on basic mathematics facts, a fill-in-the-gap area, or whatever students lack that is keeping them from succeeding in the general education classroom. Students maintain their seats in the general education classroom and only leave for approximately thirty minutes for this intensive instruction.

There is little agreement in the literature about when a student should officially be considered a special education student on the MTSS continuum. In fact, it makes sense, as identification and assessment should be independent and individual for each student. What is more critical is that the MTSS is developed as a systematic response to ensure all students are successful (Berkeley, Scanlon, Bailey, Sutton, & Sacco, 2020; Hannigan & Hannigan, 2021). Austin Buffum, Mike Mattos, and Janet Malone (2018) define this systematic response as a five-step process.

1. Identify the individual students who need assistance.
2. Connect the student's learning needs with the necessary intervention.
3. Implement a monitoring process (to make certain the intervention is working).
4. Revise the intervention as needed.
5. Extend or end the intervention based on mastery of essential curriculum.

Students who are unsuccessful during the tiered approach may need to be referred for special education services. For long-term Tier 3 students who have been receiving Tier 3 support for six months or more, the LST must initiate a referral for special education assessment. The LST should carefully use fidelity assessments to identify students who need assistance by discussing student assets and areas of challenge, continually evaluating the effectiveness of the school's programs, and considering the adoption of interventions validated in the literature (Lee & Gage, 2020; McIntosh & Goodman, 2016). Furthermore, the team should carefully review student progress and the time the progression has taken to determine continued need. MTSS is meant to be a schoolwide system for intervention, serving any student in the school who needs support. If the intervention is ineffective or is taking longer than expected, it is time that the LST refer the student for special education assessment. In checking for a specific learning disability, a local education agency may use a process that determines whether the student responds to scientific, research-based intervention as part of the evaluation procedures (IDEA, 2004).

In checking for a specific learning disability, a local education agency may use a process that determines whether the student responds to scientific, research-based intervention as part of the evaluation procedures (IDEA, 2004).

Where Did the Concept of MTSS Come From?

In 2001, President George W. Bush formed a special commission to study how special education services might be improved and to give input to the reauthorization of IDEA. The President's Commission on Excellence in Special Education consisted of many researchers in special education. After days of discussion, commission members went to the congressional education committee and shared that an issue in the field was students were receiving learning disability labels when, in fact, they did not have a disability. The commission determined that these students had just not received or been exposed to solid research-based instructional practices. The work that followed in U.S. education was based on the commission's report (U.S. Department of Education, 2002).

The term *response to intervention* (*RTI*) was used to describe a three-tier system of support where students received research-based instructional strategies. The concepts behind intervention have strong historical roots in reading research as early as the 1960s; however, this commission brought forth the benefit to the special education community. The historical roots are summarized in literacy learning researcher Elfrieda H. Hiebert's (2015) journal article "Changing Readers, Changing Texts: Beginning Reading Texts From 1960 to 2010" as well as in researchers John J. Hoover, Leonard Baca, Emily Wexler-Love, and Lauren Saenz's (2008) research summary of the national implementation of RTI. Some students had a strong response to the intervention, and they did not need to be referred or tested for special education services. The assumption was that when students experiencing learning difficulty received more effective instruction sooner, it would prevent a learning disability diagnosis.

Prior to RTI, schools commonly used what was known as the *wait to fail* approach (Blackburn & Witzel, 2018) along with the intelligence quotient (IQ) discrepancy model. Students were assessed for IQ and then compared to achievement measures. When students were ineligible for services under this model, services were denied. And the following year, when they were tested again, they were further behind. For example, the young student who does not have phonemic awareness skills later has challenges with word attack skills, leading to challenges with reading comprehension.

With the passage of the reauthorization of IDEA (2004), Congress granted state and local schools special authority to use RTI as part of the identification process for learning disabilities. Specifically, does the student respond to scientific, research-based intervention as part of the evaluation procedures? Much evidence exists to advocate for using RTI as a progress-monitoring tool for students with or without disabilities (Callender, 2014; VanDerHeyden, 2011). A comprehensive review of the literature demonstrates that RTI impacted the academic achievement of the students involved and their performance on standardized assessments (Ridgeway, Price, Simpson, & Rose, 2012). RTI evolved into MTSS as a variety of systems were incorporated, including but not limited to academics, behavior, and mental health.

Implementing a successful MTSS involves a lot of moving parts. An MTSS includes more than just academic supports. As part of the MTSS, school leaders need to consider the integration of a schoolwide positive behavior support system and student mental health support. Each MTSS model is designed specifically by and for the school; thus, each school should write a schoolwide MTSS handbook to document and convey to the education community the specifics of the individual MTSS program.

Schoolwide Positive Behavior Support System

Hill M. Walker and colleagues (1996) originally introduced the tier system to advocate support for behaviors and social-emotional needs. Their seminal work suggests interventions as a multilevel approach, including primary behavior support for all students (Tier 1), secondary behavior support for targeted groups who are at risk of behavior challenges (Tier 2), and tertiary behavior support for the small percentage of students who have severe problematic behaviors (Tier 3). When schools implement MTSS with a focus on addressing learning challenges after such challenges become evident, these behavior support tiers establish generic systems of support and positive behavioral interventions and supports (PBIS) designed to *prevent* learning and behavior problems (Lane, Menzies, Oakes, & Kalberg, 2019; McIntosh & Goodman, 2016). Federal special education legislation (IDEA, 2004) references PBIS.

The systemic approach of schoolwide positive behavior support allows for proactively planning solutions for discipline, including reduced student suspensions, fewer office discipline referrals, lower expulsion rates, and higher teacher satisfaction with student behavior (Grasley-Boy, Gage, & Lombardo, 2019; Lee & Gage, 2020; Wienen et al., 2019). A meta-analysis of 8,781 schools conducted by Ahhyun Lee and Nicholas A. Gage (2020) reports statistically significant increases in academic achievement and reductions in discipline referrals when the three-tier schoolwide positive behavior support system is implemented.

Suspensions and expulsions are more common for students with disabilities than for their general education peers (Anderson, 2020; Steinberg & Lacoe, 2017). In an examination of the relationships among absenteeism, disciplinary outcomes, and educational setting, Kaitlin P. Anderson (2020) finds that across five years of data, students in inclusive settings have fewer disciplinary incidents and better attendance. Students in inclusive settings receive significantly fewer suspensions. See https://pbis.org for details on the over twenty-five thousand students in schools worldwide that use a schoolwide positive behavior support system to meet individual student needs.

It has become clear that MTSS integration includes the basic principles of response to intervention and schoolwide positive behavior support systems (McIntosh & Goodman, 2016). Additionally, MTSS is a comprehensive schoolwide system designed by and implemented at the school to provide systematic supports for all students (Hannigan & Hannigan, 2021). These supports may be academic, behavioral, social, emotional, physical, or a combination. This positive, success-oriented system uses specific assessment and intervention techniques to help remove educational, behavioral, or affective stumbling blocks for all students in the general education classroom.

MTSS and Mental Health

The MTSS tier structure should be designed to include academic, behavior, and mental health support. *Mental health* is a state of well-being exemplified when students realize their own abilities, productively manage life stresses and personal emotions, and contribute to the world by participating in community events, activities, or service projects (World Health Organization, 2005). Academic success alone does not determine a well-rounded individual. Social relationships, feelings of belonging, and mindfulness of one's own abilities have determined success in many students' lives (Hande & Karge, 2021). Thus, establishing tiers to support levels of social, emotional, and physical health in combination with emphases on academics and behavior can lead to strong MTSS implementation.

Figure 2.3 (page 42) illustrates a system where the tier structure is designed to include academic, behavior, and mental health tiers. Including mental health in MTSS is a 2020s concept, yet preventive frameworks originated in the mental health domain in the early 1960s (von der Embse, Rutherford, Mankin, & Jenkins, 2019). Figure 2.3 also includes an expandable table where the team can list what the school is doing at each tier level to enhance the school's multitiered system of support.

MTSS Handbook

The school should have an MTSS handbook that provides all the procedures and shared forms used to enhance services. This handbook supports differentiation and ultimately explains the plan for inclusive services at the school. Putting everything in one place and outwardly displaying the plan for providing services to all students will encourage all stakeholders to rise to the task of efficiently supporting students. The MTSS handbook can be posted on the school's website for all to access, including both internal stakeholders (employees at the school) and external stakeholders (community partners and families).

Structure for the School's MTSS Tier Development

Suggested Tier Structure

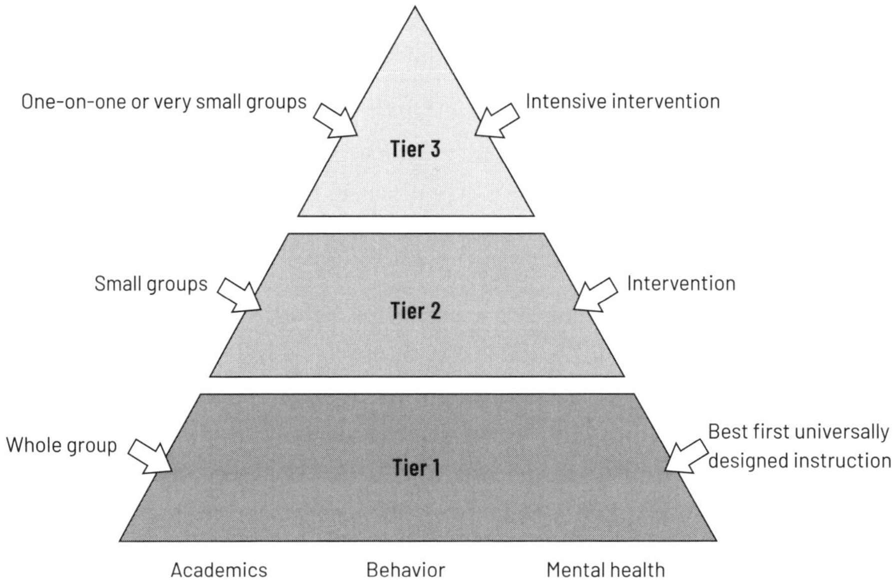

	Academic Supports	Behavior Supports	Mental Health Supports
Tier 1 (General education)			
Tier 2 (Interventions)			
Tier 3 (Intensive interventions)			

FIGURE 2.3: Worksheet for MTSS tier development.
Visit ***go.SolutionTree.com/specialneeds*** *for a free reproducible version of this figure.*

Consider the following for the MTSS handbook.

- **School inclusion plan:** Once you have read this book, you will have access to the eleven steps for establishing an inclusive school. Step 7 is to *design and implement an inclusion plan*. I strongly suggest that the MTSS handbook begin with the inclusion plan. This sets the stage for the reader.

- **Design of MTSS (graphic visual):** This image clearly shows schoolwide Tier 1 interventions as general education classroom interventions and the ways students receive Tiers 2 and 3 support services.
- **Intervention processes flowchart:** This is a way to visualize where the LST provides interventions used at each tier to support academics, behavior, and mental health. This depends on your school resources.
- **Sample weekly schedules:** These would include schedules for special education teachers, speech specialists, counselors, nurses, and all team members. Many general education teachers do not understand the roles of special education teachers and other support specialists at the school. Sharing the daily schedule of each gives general education teachers a look at the depth of detail to scheduling and the rationale behind why the special education teacher or specialist cannot be in their classroom full-time.
- **Forms:** Include copies of tools that will see frequent use. The appendix of this book contains reproducible templates for these: "Sample Learning Services Team Referral Form" (page 179), "Sample Parent Notice of a Learning Services Team Meeting" (page 183), "Student Response Form for the Learning Services Team" (page 184), "Learning Services Team Log Sheet" (page 185), "Learning Services Team Summary Form" (page 186), "Sample Special Education Referral Form" (page 188), and "General Education Student Information Form" (page 189).
- **Examples of roles and duties:** Have all team members write a description of their responsibilities, with a special emphasis on what special education and intervention staff roles are.
- **Suggestions for what educators should bring to meetings:** These might include report cards, observation notes, samples of student classwork, formative assessments, behavior or attendance records, and so on.
- **Definition of differentiation:** Share the research here. Many stakeholders may not know what differentiation is. A good definition of *differentiation* to use here is tailoring instruction to meet individual needs (Tomlinson, 2014).
- **List of accommodations:** Provide a list from which teachers might draw as they differentiate.
- **Resources:** Share with stakeholders resources available at your school, in the community, or online that might be beneficial for MTSS implementation.

Action for Administrators

Did you know that sometimes special education teachers feel disconnected and lonely, especially at schools where they are the only specialist? You can create a supportive environment where they feel part of the team and demonstrate leadership at the school just by having them participate in MTSS and allowing their voices to be heard.

The MTSS in Action

With an effective MTSS up and running, school leaders can implement a process for moving students through the system to ensure everyone receives the appropriate level of support. This should start with a thorough data review, then continue with referral to the LST as necessary.

DATA DAYS

Consider hosting data days three times a year as opportunities for the LST to review data for the whole school. I encourage schools I work with to come up with more creative names for these days, and I often suggest the name *We Care Days*. The LST should ensure that state or provincial, district, school, and classroom curriculum-based data are available and transparent. Step 8 of the eleven steps for establishing an inclusive school is *implement data-collection measures*; this step is absolutely essential. An effective leader should take steps to make sure the school environment is such that everyone feels safe sharing and discussing data. This begins with building trust within the LST and then establishing continued trust as teachers, parents, and others collaborate with the LST to measure and review collected data and determine next steps for supporting all students. The team also considers staff, student, and parent input as well as attendance, discipline, and social-emotional learning data. The administrators (principal and assistant or vice principal) should be present for data days, along with all other members of the LST. Leaders can ensure success by providing substitutes and bringing additional teachers into the discussion when they have information about specific students.

On data days, the team evaluates data for every student in the school. In a healthy school environment, the majority of students remain in Tier 1. Based on the data, the team may form intervention groups (Tier 2) or plan one-on-one intensive interventions for individual students (Tier 3). For example, in an elementary school, the

LST may determine that a group of students lacks the ability to do fractions and equations. Upon closer examination, it may become clear that the group is struggling with number sense. Thus, the team would flag this group as in need of intervention. At the secondary level, a group of students may have substantially lower writing scores than their peers do, so the team would form one group to work on writing strategies and another for writing process support.

LST REFERRAL PROCESS

When the LST flags students during data days, or when school staff or parents otherwise have reason to believe students are not succeeding in Tier 1, the LST further considers the students. The LST uses a strengths-based problem-solving process that includes school staff, students, and parents. And the LST makes educational decisions based on student data (hard evidence from the common assessments, standardized assessments, social-emotional learning assessments, curriculum-based assessments, behavior and social-emotional learning data, and any other individual student data). The referral process gives the LST an organized way to address the strengths and intervention needs of individual students, and it represents a key piece of the larger multitiered system of support.

Action for Administrators

Establish a meeting protocol, such as the following example, and use it regularly.

1. Introduce participants.
2. Explain the purpose of the meeting.
3. Have the summary form available as a handout or on a screen for the group to reference.
4. Provide a time limit for the meeting (approximately thirty to forty minutes).
5. Appoint a timekeeper.
6. Proceed through the meeting in the same order as the agenda outlines.
7. Set up a follow-up date prior to the end of the meeting.
8. Provide copies of the plan to all relevant parties. Log the date.

There are a number of forms the LST can use to keep the referral process organized and documented.

- The appendix provides a sample LST referral form (page 179). Teachers most commonly use this form to bring to the LST's attention a student who is having challenges and might need tiered support and perhaps, ultimately, a referral to special education. This same form could be used during LST data days to flag a particular student.
- A sample parent notice of an LST meeting appears in the appendix (page 183). When the LST receives a referral form from a teacher or another school employee, or when a student is flagged at a data day meeting, the team sets up an LST meeting to discuss the individual student. At this time, the teacher must call the parents or caregivers to let them know that a meeting will take place. Typically, the teacher is the parents' primary contact person at the school; having their child's regular teacher make the initial contact is less threatening to the parent than having another member of the LST do so. During these phone calls, the teacher makes the parents aware of the meeting and gives them appropriate notice. The notice form reaches the parents via email, the postal service, or both, depending on school policy. The form invites the parents to the meeting and informs them that areas of student strength and weakness in academic skills, classroom behavior, social interactions, and attendance will be discussed, including any specific concerns that are the reasons for the referral. The form also lets parents know that, during the meeting, a precise plan to assist the student in finding success at school will be developed. Parents are not required to attend the LST meeting; however, they are strongly encouraged to be there, as they are a key component of their child's education success. If the student is later referred for special education services, an IEP team meeting will be scheduled, and IDEA requires parents to be informed and to provide input for the IEP meeting. The parent notice form for the meeting asks parents to please think about the listed topics and be ready to discuss them at the meeting.
- As individuals are referred to the LST, student input is also important. When appropriate, have the student complete a questionnaire to share information of value to the team. A sample reproducible student response form for the LST is in the appendix (page 184).

- I strongly encourage maintaining a simple LST log sheet to document all student referrals. A sample log sheet is in the appendix (page 185). This log will be especially useful to determine what interventions have been tried and what previous supports the student received before the IEP referral.
- After the LST meeting, keep track of meeting notes, conversations, and actions on the LST summary form located in the appendix (page 186).

The LST meets and reviews the student's situation and makes recommendations. Typically, these recommendations are for Tier 2 or Tier 3 supports under the school MTSS plan. The agenda for the meeting includes reviewing the student's strengths, historical information, and academics. The team looks at mobility between schools over the course of the student's education, including preschool and summer school. If the student was retained, the team notes this. Student attendance is reviewed, including any truancy concerns. The team reviews all available data, discusses what interventions have been implemented, clarifies current concerns, and then makes recommendations. Figure 2.4 (page 48) offers an example meeting agenda.

Again, the LST applies a strengths-based problem-solving process to address the intervention needs of students who are exhibiting significant difficulties in academics, behavior, social-emotional learning, mental health, or attendance. This collaborative approach provides for cohesiveness, coordination, and instructional continuity as it complements existing curricula and instructional programs. After a specified intervention period, the team reconvenes to review student outcomes based on data gathered as part of the agreed-on interventions. At the follow-up meeting, the team again makes all decisions based on data. If the student is not making progress, the team may recommend a special education referral.

Example decisions a team may make include the following.

- Close the case (the student has successfully met the goal).
- Adjust the LST plan to address current or new student concerns.
- Consider a referral to alternative programs or services.
- Consider a possible referral for special education services.

The team should consider a special education referral only if it suspects a disability and it has exhausted all resources in general education. In that case, the team documents the student response to interventions and helps ensure an appropriate referral to special education. Students must be eligible under one of thirteen handicapping conditions identified by IDEA (2004). The LST compares ability to achievement to

1. Purpose of meeting, procedures, and introductions
2. Student strengths (at home and at school)
3. Student history
    a. Health
    b. Birth history (Was the student born prematurely, or were there any complications at birth? As an infant, did the student spend time in the NICU?)
    c. Early milestones (At what age did the student first crawl? Walk? Talk?)
    d. Surgeries, accidents, ear infections, and allergies
    e. Vision and hearing
    f. Family history of learning disabilities
    g. Home living status (primary language spoken at home)
4. Academic history (prior LST referrals and outcomes)
5. Mobility (review of all schools attended)
6. Retention
7. Attendance
8. Data
    a. Most recent state or provincial and teacher-made assessments, as well as student work samples
    b. Standardized test scores
    c. Curriculum-based assessment scores
    d. Grades
    e. Behavioral data and discipline issues
    f. Social-emotional data
9. Current interventions and outcomes
    a. Academic interventions and student response
    b. Behavior interventions and student response
    c. Accommodations
10. Concerns
    a. Academic (teacher, parent, and student)
    b. Behavioral (teacher, parent, and student)
11. Actions

FIGURE 2.4: Example LST meeting agenda.

*Visit **go.SolutionTree.com/specialneeds** for a free reproducible version of this figure.*

look for a significant discrepancy that adversely affects education performance. Also, the LST determines which member of the team will complete an official special education referral form. Completion of this form begins a sixty-day assessment period, as specified by IDEA. This means that the student must have a complete evaluation within sixty days of the referral. A sample special education referral form is in the appendix (page 188).

Action for Administrators

Be cautious about prelabeling a student with a disability. This is a heavy label. Make sure your LST has exhausted all research-based interventions before moving ahead with the referral documentation for special education services.

Once the student has been referred for special education placement, then the legal process governed by IDEA begins (described in chapter 1, figure 1.3, page 21). At the point where the IEP team is developing the student goals, the team comes up with a recommendation for where those goals should be met. In other words, it answers these questions: What will the service location be? Will the student receive all services in the general education classroom, or will some of those services take place in different special education service-delivery models?

Special Education Service-Delivery Models

The IEP team has a number of options to consider for delivering special education services. Most importantly, it must consider the least restrictive environment for the individual student. As I noted in chapter 1, the IEP team should analyze the continuum of services (figure 1.1, page 15). And the team should only recommend that services take place in a more restrictive setting if it determines the student cannot receive services in the general education classroom. In the sections that follow, I explore some service-delivery models that take place in the general education classroom, and then I discuss co-teaching. After that, I briefly explain the more restrictive settings, which might include a resource room or learning center, a behavior intervention class, a self-contained class, a residential treatment center, or homebound instruction.

General Education Classroom

Ultimately, every student should be educated in the general education classroom. However, students sometimes need additional supports in order to be successful in this setting. At the beginning of the school year, the LST should inform the general education teacher of how many students with IEPs are enrolled in the class and what types of services and accommodations each student will need. For reference, see the sample "General Education Student Information Form" reproducible in the appendix (page 189).

In some cases, a student may have a peer support system already established. For example, the student with an IEP may have a designated peer who takes notes and shares them with the student. A specific colleague may be assigned to consult or co-teach with the general education teacher (see the Co-Teaching section on page 51 for more about this service-delivery model). The IEP team should communicate this information at the beginning of the school year. Another possibility is to provide specialized academic instruction within the general education setting.

GENERAL EDUCATION CLASSROOM WITH A CONSULT AND A PARAEDUCATOR

If the IEP team determines that the least restrictive environment for an assigned student is the general education classroom with a consulting special education teacher and a paraeducator, the special education teacher who is assigned to consult will need some planning time with the general education teacher. In this case, I use the term *consult* to mean that the special education teacher will share ideas and collaborate with the general education teacher outside the classroom. The special education teacher may need some scheduled time to observe the student with the IEP in the environment and give suggestions for how the paraeducator can work with the student and support the teacher (chapter 4, page 83, includes more details on working with paraeducators). In this model, special education teachers act as an ear to listen and a colleague to provide suggestions; however, they themselves are not working inside the general education classroom. Instead, an assigned paraeducator would implement the special education support services under the supervision of the special education teacher.

GENERAL EDUCATION CLASSROOM WITH SPECIALIZED ACADEMIC INSTRUCTION OR A RELATED SERVICE MEMBER

A common practice is for the general education teacher to have a special education teacher or related service member come into the classroom and provide specialized academic instruction or related services directly to the student with the IEP (chapter 5, page 101, features more details on related services). In these cases, personnel may give one-on-one instruction, or they may give instruction to a small group of students (featuring just students who have IEPs or both the students with IEPs and general education students). Special education teachers or related services personnel fulfilling this role usually have a caseload of several students, so they must juggle their schedules and move from general education classroom to general education classroom to provide services.

Co-Teaching

Within the MTSS structure, the service-delivery option of co-teaching has a place in both Tier 1 and Tier 2. Co-teaching is often used to maximize quality research-based teaching. For special education or other specialized services (for example, for English learners), co-teaching gives teachers a way to provide instruction in the general education classroom instead of sending students to segregated settings (Friend, 2019). For secondary schools, where content is heavy and students should not miss content explanations and instruction, research supports the effectiveness of co-teaching when implemented with fidelity (Hamdan, Anuar, & Khan, 2016; King-Sears, Stefanidis, Berkeley, & Strogilos, 2021).

Co-teaching is defined as two teachers working together in a classroom with groups of students, sharing the planning, organization, delivery, and assessment of instruction as well as the physical space (Friend & Barron, 2016). Both teachers are actively involved in all aspects of instruction. When special education teachers co-teach and work alongside general education teachers, they not only see and learn the curriculum but also view students in their primary environment and can provide immediate recommendations (Karge, 2015; Karten & Murawski, 2020). Special education students have firsthand access to the general education curriculum (from the general education expert), and they receive the necessary and legally required specially designed instruction (from the special education expert; Theoharis & Causton, 2014). Tier 1 and Tier 2 students receive best first instruction in the general education classroom with two certified teachers (Murawski & Scott, 2017). *Best first instruction* means giving every student the best instruction possible in the general education classroom (Plotinsky, 2020). This best first instruction meets standards-based content-area or grade-level requirements and is culturally responsive and relevant. It is a proactive attempt to make sure instruction is strong before intervention takes place.

The Swedish government cites co-teaching as a way to promote sustainable, evidence-based, inclusive practices in education (von Ahlefeld Nisser, 2017). Inclusivity becomes a way of thinking—the norm—driven by values such as participatory democracy, team building, and collaborative decision making. Co-teaching is seen as a school system strategy for continuous improvement (Walsh, 2012).

As schools plan and roll out the inclusive co-teaching model, it is crucial that everyone clearly understands, discusses, and accepts the concept and procedures of the special education teachers working in classrooms alongside or as consultants to general education teachers (Friend & Barron, 2016; Karge, 2015; Karten & Murawski, 2020). Leaders must allocate planning time. There should be time at the beginning of the year during orientation and then, once the school year has begun, a few collaboration days with substitute teachers available so that co-teachers can meet and engage in deep preplanning. This time will yield growth in student achievement because when all adults working in a room know what the expectations are, they can cover more content, and higher-order thinking and inquiry can take place (Karge, 2015; Murawski & Scott, 2017).

Often when teachers co-teach, they tend to cluster students with disabilities in the co-taught class. Ideally, try to keep the percentage of students with IEPs at 20 percent if possible—at most 30 percent—with the remaining 70 to 80 percent comprising general education students without IEPs. You want the population to reflect the general population and contain natural proportions. You don't want the class to feel like a "special education" class.

The research on co-teaching demonstrates that it is popular among students themselves (Murawski & Scott, 2017; Strogilos & King-Sears, 2019). I believe that students of any age, from first grade to high school, like to have additional help and support in the classroom. As one student puts it, "I like having two teachers because they are nice. I also like it because the other teachers help the other kids. We have two helpers. It is fun to have two teachers" (M. Catrell, personal communication, June 1, 2015).

Co-teaching opens the door for standards-based instruction in tandem with instructional strategies designed to make the material accessible for all learners in the general education classroom (Bottge, Cohen, & Choi, 2017). Improved student outcomes and achievement gains are apparent when co-teaching is implemented with fidelity (Huberman et al., 2012; Tremblay, 2013). Remember, having the special education teacher in the classroom, modeling and working alongside the general education teachers, is typically better than relying on a pull-out environment. General education teachers will greatly benefit from seeing specially designed instruction as well as effective and efficient modeling of accommodations and differentiation from special education.

Eleven Co-Teaching Strategies

I have expanded on common forms of co-teaching originally introduced by educators and researchers Lynne Cook and Marilyn Friend (1995) and created three ways to think about moving through the co-teaching sequence: (1) supportive co-teaching, (2) team co-teaching, and (3) advanced co-teaching. I go into much greater detail in *Engage Co-Teach* (Karge, 2015), but the following list provides a brief overview of eleven strategies and how they fit into these three categories.

Supportive Co-Teaching

1. **One teach, one assist:** One adult (typically the general education teacher) plans and teaches, and the other circulates and assists as needed. Researchers Thomas E. Scruggs, Margo A. Mastropieri, and Kimberly A. McDuffie (2007) state that although this first strategy is not recommended in the literature, it is the dominant co-teaching strategy. I believe this is primarily because teachers have not received proper professional learning opportunities covering the other forms of co-teaching.
2. **One teach, one observe:** One adult plans and teaches, and the other systematically collects data through observation. This second teacher may observe a predetermined targeted student, students, or a groups of students.
3. **One teach, one support:** One adult plans and teaches, and the other "does something to enhance and support the instruction" (Karge, 2015, p. 6). The supporting teacher might, for example, take notes on the board, create a graphic, paraphrase the other teacher's statements, or summarize the lecture content for the students.

Team Co-Teaching

4. **Graze-and-tag teaching:** One adult plans and teaches, and the other adult "grazes"; then the roles shift. This allows both teachers to share their expertise and approach the material in different ways. The idea comes from the sport of wrestling, in which wrestlers take turns leading in different forms and positions, allowing for engaged viewing.
5. **Parallel teaching:** Two teachers collaboratively plan and use the same lesson plan. However, the whole group is divided into two separate, diverse groups of students. Both adults instruct only their own group. Often the smaller group size leads to more content coverage (Karge, 2015).
6. **Station teaching:** Two teachers collaboratively plan the overall lesson, and both teachers plan their own content for the individual station they will teach. Students are divided into groups: one teacher works with one group, the other teacher works with another group, and additional groups of students work independently.
7. **Alternative teaching:** Teachers collaboratively plan for instruction where they will divide students into two groups. One adult teaches enrichment while the other adult provides specialized instruction for reteaching.

Advanced Co-Teaching

8. **Conversation teaching:** Teachers collaboratively plan for a talk show–style educational conversation, in which the two adults will speak to each other in front of the students to teach a concept or go over a historical event. When using this strategy, teachers refrain from asking students questions—the students are listeners absorbing the content.
9. **Role-play teaching:** Teachers collaboratively plan a role-play and present it to the entire group of students. The role-play may involve performing a skit, engaging in a debate, presenting a think-aloud, or doing a characterization. The show the teachers put on captures students' attention. The students recall this unusual performance and "generalize the knowledge obtained from viewing" (Karge, 2015, p. 19).
10. **Interactive teaching:** Teachers collaboratively plan and use a variety of the co-teaching approaches to interact during the teaching process. Both take the lead in active instructional responsibilities during one period or portion of the day.
11. **Shared teaching:** Teachers collaboratively plan, fully sharing responsibility, classroom resources, student assessment data, reflective evaluation of classroom practices, and student work. Typically, for shared teaching, co-teachers work together all day or for multiple periods in the same classroom.

Action for Administrators

When observing co-teachers, check that the educators are using one or more of the eleven strategies for co-teaching. Encourage strategies 4–11 for more veteran co-teachers; these strategies encourage equity of instructional responsibilities.

When co-teaching is taking place, leaders should see something beyond what they would see if only one teacher were in the classroom. Co-teaching partners might be teaching collaboratively, debating, or role-playing and in some way demonstrating and instructing in a different way than if either teacher were alone. The value of the collaboration and depth of knowledge two teachers can bring to learning for all students is second to none.

Resource Room or Learning Center

While some Tier 2 interventions and special education services can take place within the general education classroom, Tier 3 instruction, some Tier 2 instruction, and some special education services typically do occur in a different location. Historically, special education services that are located outside the general education classroom have been referenced as *pull-out services*, meaning the student is taken out of the classroom. Students receive these services in a different environment, often a resource room or learning center. Students maintain their enrollment in the general education classroom and only leave for specific instructional activities. Then they return to their general education classroom for the remainder of the day. If special education students receive instruction in a resource room or learning center alongside general education students who are getting Tier 2 or Tier 3 instruction, they are still getting some of the advantages of an inclusive setting.

Students often consider the resource room or learning center to be the special education teacher's classroom. Sometimes the staff member assigned to work in the area is known as the resource specialist person. Students go to the resource room for thirty minutes to half a day to receive one-on-one or small-group instruction. Some schools have moved away from the resource room in favor of a learning center model. The learning center, while still a physical location and still considered a pull-out environment, is staffed by special education teachers, paraeducators, speech and language specialists, occupational therapists, intervention teachers, reading specialists, and other specialists.

Substantial progress and growth can certainly take place in these pull-out environments; however, growth often flatlines because students struggle to generalize what they have learned when they return to the general education classroom (Burt & Whitney, 2018).

Behavior Intervention Class

In some cases, the behavior intervention class is the least restrictive environment for students with severe emotional disturbance, ADHD, autism, or significant behaviors that may impact students in the general education classroom. Students receive their instruction in the behavior intervention class while learning appropriate behavior skills with the goal of moving back into the general education classroom once the behaviors are under control. Small behaviors can be quickly addressed before they become debilitating to the student. Students learn to self-monitor and to advocate for themselves when they become frustrated or need individual time to cool off. They also learn simple mnemonics such as ASC ("always stay calm") to help prepare them for reentry into the general education classroom.

Self-Contained Class

The *self-contained class*, which has also been known as the *special day class*, is a place where a teacher provides specialized, self-contained services and supports in one classroom (or a series of classrooms for secondary subjects) all day. Sometimes the teacher assigned to work in the special day class is referred to as the special day class teacher. This teacher is usually a certified special education teacher. An IEP team places its student in the special day class because it determines this is the least restrictive environment for the student's learning needs. Often, IEP teams determine that students require specialized instruction beyond what they can receive in the general education classroom.

A concern when placing a student with a disability in a segregated environment is that a self-fulfilling prophecy may occur (Rothstein & Johnson, 2021). For example, the special education teacher may structure the day to teach only the IEP goals, and though the student may meet these goals, without access to the general education curriculum, overall expectations drop. Additionally, the student cannot benefit from typically developing peers who model expectations or set the bar at a higher-order learning level.

The research literature indicates many behavior and social-emotional issues arise in the special day class setting, as students with disabilities have no general education role models and often mimic each other's behaviors (Parekh & Brown, 2019). Schools can prevent this by assigning students with disabilities enrolled in special day class a general education classroom at their grade level (in elementary) or in a content-area strength (in secondary). Students can then spend a few minutes a day in this environment and gradually work up to more time in the general education setting. This always keeps the door open for the least restrictive environment.

Action for Administrators

Make certain all students with disabilities in your school are assigned to an age-appropriate general education classroom. If they are enrolled in special day class, select a general education class that they can work toward participating in and feeling a part of. Work with your superintendent and school board to include these students on the general education roster.

Residential Treatment Center or Homebound Instruction

The most restrictive placements on the least restrictive environment continuum are the residential treatment center and homebound instruction. These placements are typically referenced as out-of-district placements, as the student receives services outside the public school system. Anytime an IEP team recommends an out-of-district placement, it costs a significant amount of money. These services are expensive! As mentioned, we always strive for the least restrictive environment. But when it comes to this end of the continuum, "in spite of its restrictive nature, the placement will be considered appropriate if it is necessary for the students to benefit from education" (Rothstein & Johnson, 2021, p. 219). Note that these services are not considered inclusive and should be recommended only for extreme cases and situations where more inclusive settings were tried first.

Conclusion

Collaboration among educators is a foundation for effective contemporary schooling (DuFour, DuFour, Eaker, Mattos, & Muhammad, 2021). An attainable way to ensure effective collaboration is to establish an LST. This team will work with colleagues to design, implement, and evaluate a schoolwide MTSS, where general education teachers, special education teachers, and other professionals collaboratively strive to attain the least restrictive environment for all students. When students are not making progress in the general education classroom (and all other possibilities have been exhausted), the IEP team may recommend a more restrictive placement, such as a segregated learning environment. However, the goal must always be to move the student back into the mainstream as quickly as possible. The IEP team should evaluate student placement at every IEP meeting and, when possible, the general education classroom should be the first choice.

Schools can support success for all students by including students with disabilities in a co-taught general education classroom for part of the day. Co-teaching gives students access to the general education curriculum while they receive specialized instruction with the accommodations and supports they need to be successful in school and society.

In the Wallace Foundation's report *How Principals Affect Students and Schools: A Systematic Synthesis of Two Decades of Research*, the authors outline effective principal practices; the strategic management of personnel and resources is a top practice (Grissom, Egalite, & Lindsay, 2021). Strategically establish a schoolwide MTSS that provides effective intervention in academic, behavior, and mental health areas and uses the unique talents of your learning services team and other school personnel to enhance the model. Chapter 3 provides specific ideas for supporting and mentoring the special education personnel at your school.

Part 2

HOW EFFECTIVE LEADERS SUPPORT SPECIAL EDUCATION PERSONNEL

THREE

SUPPORTING AND MENTORING SPECIAL EDUCATION PERSONNEL

The young do not know enough to be prudent,
and therefore they attempt the impossible—
and achieve it, generation after generation.
—PEARL S. BUCK

Teaching is hard work. Teachers certified in special education are required to teach all the same grade-level standards and core curriculum as their general education colleagues, in addition to knowing how to implement specially designed instruction as required by each student's IEP. Additionally, special education teachers must write all IEPs and attend all IEP meetings for every student on their caseload. Connection with parents is ongoing, not just relegated to parent-teacher conferences and back-to-school nights. These teachers are expected to co-teach, collaborate, or both with general education colleagues and provide authentic opportunities for students to engage with typical peers. Minimizing behavioral outbursts and social-emotional and self-regulation disputes alongside increasing achievement growth adds to their multifaceted set of challenges. Typically, schools contract this undertaking on the same pay scale as general education.

There is a global teacher shortage (Carver-Thomas, Burns, Leung-Gagné, & Ondrasek, 2022; Love & Love, 2022). Forty-six percent of U.S. teachers quit before their fifth year (Carver-Thomas & Darling-Hammond, 2017; Eggers & Calegari, 2011). The severe shortage of special education teachers is well documented (Billingsley & Bettini, 2019; Paris, 2013; Tyler & Brunner, 2014). The average special education teacher remains in the classroom for only five years (Ondrasek, Carver-Thomas, Scott, & Darling-Hammond, 2020). With this high rate of attrition, schools face great challenges ensuring that a qualified specialist with disability expertise will be available when needed. Graduates of elementary teaching programs may find job opportunities scarce, yet ample special education positions are available (Reitman, 2018). Special education teachers are more prone to exit teaching than general education teachers are (Carver-Thomas & Darling-Hammond, 2017).

Schools have a retention rate of over 95 percent for ten years and beyond when special education teachers receive support in the areas of individual relationships, pedagogical knowledge, self-perception of competence, mentorship, and professional learning and reflection (Reitman & Karge, 2019).

In their journal article "Special Education Teacher Attrition and Retention: A Review of the Literature," Bonnie Billingsley and Elizabeth Bettini (2019) synthesize thirty studies highlighting the importance of quality teacher preparation, working conditions, school characteristics, and nonwork factors. Schools achieve a retention rate of over 95 percent for ten years and beyond when special education teachers receive support in the areas of individual relationships, pedagogical knowledge, self-perception of competence, mentorship, and professional learning and reflection (Reitman & Karge, 2019). Another study finds there is a 96 percent retention rate for ten-year veteran special educators; these educators report that extensive mentoring and pedagogical training, among other supports, contributed to their willingness to remain in teaching (Karge & McCabe, 2014). With the chronic shortage of special education teachers, it is *critical* that educational leaders support the teachers in the classroom to ensure their retention.

And support doesn't just mean showing up. Your support needs to be well tempered with knowledge. Building a skill set in special education takes time and is developmental in nature. The following experience captures the danger of not developing this skill set as a leader:

> Here we go again; in my nineteen years teaching, this is the seventh principal I must train. Today, the administrator was in the classroom just as a

> student with autism was having a meltdown, and a student with ADHD was greatly bothered and was running in circles. The general education students were ignoring both and doing their work. Do you think the administrator could ignore? Heck no, they had to go up to the student with autism and make matters worse. I am sure I will hear about this after school. (B. Backster, personal communication, September 28, 2021)

The preceding comment comes from a veteran special education teacher who has demonstrated exemplary success with co-teaching. However, she is frustrated. She feels the administrator does not trust or value her work. When the administrator stepped in, the teacher saw it as a disruption, not an attempt to provide assistance. How can you, as a leader, avoid missteps like this and truly support your teachers?

In this chapter, you will learn how to become a respected, trusted, and knowledgeable leader by supporting the special education staff as you build relationships and provide opportunities for increasing pedagogical knowledge. This leadership includes, most importantly, helping teachers understand and use research-based instructional strategies, allocating time for proper mentorship, and advocating for professional learning. You can also have awareness of your teachers' learning continua and encourage and support the teachers as they progress.

Action for Administrators

If you are new to a school or have a new special education teacher, observe and listen first. Build a relationship with the teacher, seek to understand the students with disabilities, and find out what is necessary before stepping in.

Relationship Building

You can collaborate and build trusting relationships with your teachers by utilizing the *build* rapport, *inspire* feedback, *celebrate* success, and *exceed* results (*BICE*) leadership program (Nolan, 2017). Figure 3.1 (page 64) illustrates this very useful two-week, step-by-step framework.

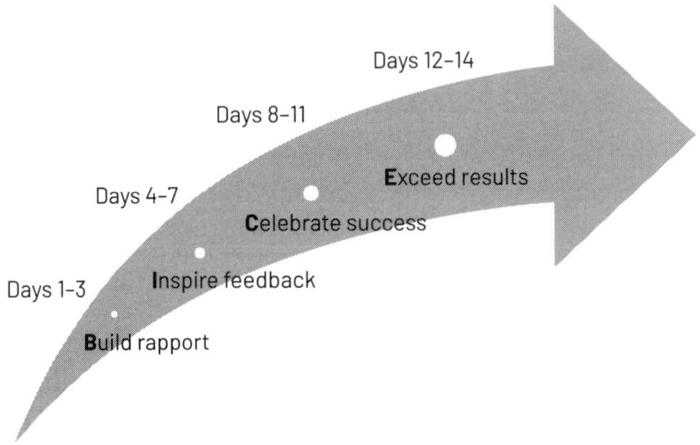

Source: Nolan, 2017. Used with permission.

FIGURE 3.1: The four-level BICE leadership program.

During the first one to three days, build rapport by emphasizing open lines of communication with the special education teacher. Leave a positive note on the teacher's desk or send an email about something unrelated to teaching. The primary goal is to make a connection. Engaging in a basic conversation unrelated to work (perhaps by commenting on a photo on the teacher's desk) will help create a personal connection (Nolan, 2017).

At some point between days 4 and 7, visit the classroom when students are present and watch—without taking notes—for no longer than five minutes. Sit down and absorb what is taking place. Immediately after the observation, send the teacher an inspiring note of feedback based on something positive you saw the teacher doing in the classroom. Comment on the use of instructional grouping; share a note of praise on a component of the instructional delivery (for example, an explicit instruction technique, a hands-on experience, or an effective learning center), use of technology, or a depth-of-knowledge area. The short observation will inspire feedback.

The beginning of the second week is a time to celebrate success. Take time to go into the classroom again. This time, look for three strength areas and one growth area. Send an email or write a note to the teacher describing in detail the areas of strength and giving specific suggestions for the growth area.

Toward the end of this second week, implement the last level: exceed results. Send a short email to all the staff related to the area of focus. If a special education teacher were working with or co-teaching in the English department, you might send something similar to the following examples.

- "The English department had 70 percent of objectives written on the board for students to see. Let's go for 90 percent!"

- "The English department effectively used small-group instruction for essay writing. Let's try pairs!"

This is a goal-setting opportunity for the entire staff, not just special education personnel. Knowing that one teacher needed growth means others may as well. Instead of calling out the special education teacher, setting a school goal can help build teamwork and positive relationships.

The BICE leadership program takes only two weeks to implement. Data have shown significant administrator-teacher relationships can be built in this short amount of time, and the classroom observations can be used to enhance the entire school or academic department. The program's benefits also include increased teacher job satisfaction (Nolan, 2017).

Administrators can use figure 3.2 (page 66) to track their progress and action steps as they apply the BICE program to build relationships with special education teachers.

Taking these two weeks to implement BICE will enable leaders to develop much-needed relationships between themselves and special education teachers and also increase trust. Schools where the administrator is present in classrooms and works side by side with teachers exhibit the highest level of trust among their staff (Travis, 2021). Once school leaders have established trust, they can triangulate data from various sources to evaluate the special education teacher and the progress students with disabilities are making at the school. Leaders should use the following evidence points to make evaluative conclusions about teacher performance (Travis, 2021).

- **Observational evidence:** This might include notes and impressions from classroom walkthroughs or visits.
- **Evidence of student growth:** This evidence should be related to IEP goals and student formative and summative data that are documented and assessed frequently and at least yearly according to IDEA.
- **Evidence of collaboration:** This should comprise indicators of working with general education teachers. These indicators include but are not limited to co-teaching lesson plans, notes to general education teachers about various student accommodations or modifications, and observations of general education and special education teacher interactions inside and outside the classroom.
- **Evidence of professional learning:** This might include working toward advanced-degree certifications, attending district-sponsored professional development sessions, and pursuing online course participant badges or certificates.

Special education teacher's name:			
Days 1–3 Dates: ______-______ Build rapport.	Days 4–7 Dates: ______-______ Inspire feedback.	Days 8–11 Dates: ______-______ Celebrate success.	Days 12–14 Dates: ______-______ Exceed results.
Create an open line of communication and make a connection with the teacher. Choose at least one of the following activities. ☐ Leave a positive note on the teacher's desk. ☐ Send an email about something unrelated to teaching. ☐ Engage in a basic conversation unrelated to work. ☐ Write your own idea: __________ __________	Visit the classroom when students are present and watch—without taking notes—for no longer than five minutes. Immediately after the observation, do the following. ☐ Record something positive you saw the teacher do in the classroom: __________ __________ ☐ Your short observation will inspire feedback. ☐ Send the teacher an inspiring note of feedback based on the positive thing you recorded.	Go into the classroom again. Look for three strength areas and one growth area. ☐ Record the strength areas and growth area. First strength: __________ __________ Second strength: __________ __________ Third strength: __________ __________ One growth area: __________ __________ Specific suggestions: __________ __________ ☐ Send an email or write a note to the teacher describing in detail the areas of strength and giving specific suggestions for the growth area.	☐ Send a short email to all the staff related to the area of focus.

Source: Adapted from Nolan, 2017.

FIGURE 3.2: BICE program progress form.

*Visit **go.SolutionTree.com/specialneeds** for a free reproducible version of this figure.*

- **Evidence of differentiation:** Look for indicators of differentiated instruction in observed lessons, in suggested accommodations to general education teachers, and in lesson plans.
- **Evidence of parent communication:** Keeping open lines of family engagement (step 6 of the eleven steps to establish inclusive schools) is critical to student success. This means maintaining the required IEP

paperwork and also the informal calls home to let parents know when their children received an A on their mathematics test or worked well with peers during a small-group history lesson.

Review each of these types of evidence at least annually with the new special education teacher or a veteran teacher new to special education. In some states, such as California, this induction period lasts two years (Sierra & Karge, 2020). This type of evaluation and support should become an annual routine for all leaders, as it demonstrates a sincere interest in teaching excellence. School-improvement researcher Toby A. Travis (2021) recommends that when leaders review each element, they should discuss both celebrations (affirmations) and future goals (areas in need of improvement).

Pedagogical Knowledge

Exemplary special education teachers have a refined collection of strong pedagogical practices in their instruction toolboxes. Whether you observe a segregated special education classroom or a co-taught general education classroom, students should be working on grade-level standards via Tier 1 strategies with specially designed instruction. This can be challenging for all involved. The well-meaning special education teacher may focus only on the IEP goals; meanwhile, the students fall further and further behind in the grade-level or content-area standards, as they are not receiving the same instruction as their typical peers. As detailed in chapter 2's exploration of MTSS (page 35), the teacher must provide a balance so students are exposed to all curricula.

Every special education teacher needs opportunities to increase pedagogical knowledge. A simple way to incorporate such opportunities is to include the special education staff in grade-level or content-area team meetings and curriculum conversations. Make sure the special education teacher has copies of all necessary teacher guides for the grade levels or content areas of all students on their caseload. This is critical professional learning, which is step 4 of the inclusion implementation process described in chapter 7 (page 145).

At a new special education teacher induction meeting I attended, the facilitator asked how the district teacher meetings went the day prior. I listened as one teacher responded, "I was not invited, so I just worked on my own lesson plans." Another stated, "I did not know which grade-level team discussion to join, so I did not attend any." Yet another shared he attended the English department meeting, and the other teachers asked him why he was there. He had to explain that he co-teaches English in one period and teaches an English class for students with disabilities during another period.

Special education teachers commonly comment on being excluded from various school meetings. As the administrator, take the lead, include your specialists in the appropriate grade-level or content-area meetings, and list them by name with the other teachers so all involved are aware of who is to attend. Just as students with disabilities benefit from inclusive general education experiences, so do your special education teachers. As you *design and implement an inclusion plan* (step 7 of the eleven steps for establishing an inclusive school), make sure all teachers (and all related services personnel—more on this in chapter 5, page 101) feel connected to the school community. The educational leader is the community organizer, the person who brings the school together (Nordick, Putney, & Jones, 2019). Including the special education teacher in all school faculty meetings, events, and collaborative experiences provides a primary means of connection to ensure a thriving school community. We educational leaders have many other ways to support teachers' pedagogical knowledge, such as highlighting research-based instructional practices, mentorship, and professional learning.

Research-Based Instructional Practices

As an educational leader, you can increase pedagogical knowledge by guiding special education teachers to research-based practices and resources that have shown strong evidence of positive outcomes for students with disabilities (Karge & Reitman, 2016).

All teachers face challenges. However, special education teachers have the task of educating students with some of the most multifaceted behavior and learning needs (McLeskey, Waldron, Spooner, & Algozzine, 2014). Every minute of instruction counts. Remember, special education is a service, not a place. Regardless of where the instruction is occurring (in the general education classroom or in a segregated environment), take the steps to ensure your teachers are using high-leverage instructional practices to design individual instruction for students with disabilities. These research-based practices can leverage student learning. This may seem obvious, yet education researchers Bryan G. Cook and Samuel L. Odom (2013) report many effective teaching strategies that could substantially improve student achievement are not habitually used. The research is clear: improving instruction leads to academic improvement (Master, Loeb, & Wyckoff, 2014).

The Council for Exceptional Children and the Collaboration for Effective Educator Development, Accountability, and Reform (CEEDAR) Center co-created a list of twenty-two high-leverage practices in special education (McLeskey et al., 2014). These fall under four subheadings: (1) assessment, (2) collaboration, (3) social and emotional behavior, and (4) instruction. Figure 3.3 lists the practices for assessment, collaboration, and social and emotional behavior. Figure 3.4 does the same for instructional practices.

Assessment	Collaboration	Social and Emotional Behavior
Use multiple sources to understand students' strengths.	Increase student success; collaborate with professionals.	Establish a consistent, organized, respectful learning environment.
Design and implement an education program with stakeholders who interpret assessments together.	Organize and facilitate effective meetings with parents and professionals.	Provide positive and constructive feedback to guide student learning and behavior.
Improve student outcomes by using student assessment data, analyzing instructional practices, and making adjustments.	Make families a major part of the collaboration, and give them a voice in all the team does to support learning and secure needed services.	Teach social behaviors. Conduct functional behavioral assessments for behavior plan development.

Source: McLeskey et al., 2014.

FIGURE 3.3: High-leverage practices—Assessment, collaboration, and social and emotional behavior.

Instruction
Identify and prioritize long- and short-term learning goals.
Systematically design instruction toward specific learning goals.
Adapt curriculum tasks and materials for specific learning goals.
Teach cognitive and metacognitive strategies to support learning and independence.
Provide scaffolded supports.
Use explicit instruction.
Use flexible grouping.
Use strategies to promote active student engagement.
Use assistive and instructional technologies.
Provide intensive instruction.
Teach students to maintain and generalize new learning across time and settings.
Provide positive and constructive feedback to guide students' learning and behavior.

Source: McLeskey et al., 2014.

FIGURE 3.4: High-leverage practices—Instruction.

Educational leaders need to be aware of research-based teaching strategies and how effectively these strategies can support *all* students, but particularly students with disabilities. Research can be confusing and complicated, but it does not have to be. *Research based* means a strategy has been tested over time, in a variety of settings, with different students, and the same result has occurred. For example, we would deem a strategy research based if it has worked over a fifteen-week period in California, Tennessee, and New York with students of different ages and abilities and it resulted in the same data outcome growth. Guiding teachers toward this research is important to step 4 (*conduct professional learning*) and step 5 (*read the research*) as you establish an inclusive school. The inclusive school thrives when teachers use research-based best practices and document students' achievement.

Action for Administrators

Share these links to resources for research-based instructional practices.

The What Works Clearinghouse (https://ies.ed.gov/ncee/wwc) provides educators with the information they need to make evidence-based decisions. It focuses on the results of high-quality research to answer the question, "What works in education?"

The IRIS Center (https://iris.peabody.vanderbilt.edu) is dedicated to improving education outcomes for all students, especially students with disabilities from birth to age twenty-one, through the use of effective evidence-based practices and interventions. The IRIS Center website shares research-based modules; see https://bit.ly/3NOWvbB for a specific explanation of evidence-based practices.

TeachingWorks (https://teachingworks.org/work-of-teaching/high-leverage-practices) lists high-level instructional practices researched and confirmed for fidelity by the University of Michigan.

The National Center on Intensive Intervention (https://intensiveintervention.org) is a strong resource for teachers of students with severe and persistent learning and behavior needs.

The Council for Exceptional Children's twenty-two high-leverage practices for persons with disabilities (https://highleveragepractices.org/about-hlps) are supported by the research of the Council for Exceptional Children and published in collaboration with the CEEDAR Center.

The University of Kansas has excellent resources all based on the top research in the field. See https://specialconnections.ku.edu for assessment, curriculum, and teaching strategies.

Help your teaching staff understand that when they take pieces of different strategies or approaches they have seen and put them together, it may not work because this loses the fidelity of the practice. The term *fidelity* in this context means implementing the strategy or technique in the way the researcher or developer intended. Exemplary studies have demonstrated positive student outcomes when teachers use research-based instructional strategies with fidelity (Champion, 2015; Reitman, 2018; Scheetz, Waters, Smeaton, & Lare, 2005).

Leaders must understand and ask questions about teaching practices instead of making assumptions. The research on special education and on instruction in general changes regularly, and it is difficult for any leader to keep up with all research-based techniques. An upper-grade inclusion specialist (the assigned title at her school in South Dakota) shared with me the following:

> In working with a student who is dyslexic and confuses *b* and *d*, I was using a research-based practice introduced by Marilyn Sprick [2021] as lead author in the Third Quest's *Parallel Universe* where students are to put a dot under the *d* every time they write. My principal walked in and told the student to erase the dots! (R. Daniels, personal communication, January 10, 2022)

Leaders need to do the difficult work of watching, listening, and asking questions. Instead of jumping in and telling the student to erase the dots, this leader should have waited until *after* the lesson and asked the teacher to explain the teaching technique. The strategy this teacher was using is a simple accommodation technique for the individual student's specially designed instruction.

As leaders, we tend to rely extensively on our own experiences. However, most educational leaders do not have training in special education (Lasky & Karge, 2006; Przekwas, 2021). We have to trust and learn from our special education teachers. Teacher self-efficacy is linked to student achievement (Thornton, Zunino, & Beattie, 2020). When teachers know and believe in their research-based instructional practices, we must walk alongside them and build their confidence. This is why it is critical that we watch, listen, ask, and learn to create an inclusive environment for all students.

Mentorship

I am a realist, and I know that not every special education teacher is exceptional. For this reason, assigning the new or struggling special education teacher to a mentor who has expertise in research-based practices is crucial for teacher success. Some schools systematically assign mentors to new teachers. Mentors can help veteran teachers who are moving from general education to special education or from elementary to secondary, as well as teachers who are new to the school.

To *mentor* means to walk alongside. Meaningful content for specific mentorship is crucial (Anderson & Karge, 2020). The key is to make certain the assigned mentor has strong special education content and instruction knowledge (Cornelius, Rosenberg, & Sandmel, 2020). The mentor needs to have experience delivering specially designed instruction to the same grade level or content area as the mentee teaches. Educators should see mentorship as a supportive and educational process of growth (Abu Zaineh & Karge, 2019).

Allocate time for proper mentorship. This may mean bringing in a substitute for one or both teachers so the mentor can observe the mentee in the classroom or so the mentor and mentee can have dedicated collaboration time. If evidence-based strategies and high-level practices are a focus, the mentor and mentee will need time to review the various practices and discuss how to implement them into teaching practice.

Mentoring time should be scheduled in addition to just-in-time support. The schedule guarantees timely check-ins and discussion about critical areas of teaching. Scheduling allows for school-based coaching to take place, while school-based coaching allows for prompting and feedback to occur in the natural environment of the classroom (Bradshaw et al., 2018). When mentors are available for just-in-time support (that is, immediate support), the mentees feel valued and supported (Sierra & Karge, 2020).

Educational leaders should create a culture of collective responsibility among the leader, the mentor, and the special education teacher (Cornelius et al., 2020). When teachers receive appropriate support, they become self-confident and remain in the teaching profession longer (Przekwas, 2021).

WATCH LISTEN ASK LEARN

Action for Administrators

School leaders maximize the professional learning of special education teachers by demonstrating an awareness of the contextual challenges of the special education environment and allowing innovation in professional learning design.

Professional Learning

As mentioned, *conducting professional learning* (step 4 of the eleven steps to establishing an inclusive school) is vitally important to implementing inclusive practices. Do your professional development sessions provide professional learning for *all* teachers? So many times, administrators say they hold weekly or monthly professional development sessions, but they do not see improvements in the outcomes of students with disabilities. Upon investigating further, these administrators may find the training sessions were in areas irrelevant to or not frequently used by the special education teacher. Sadly, the general education professional learning did not highlight inclusion of students with disabilities, nor did the training specifically connect to the everyday challenges that special education teachers (and related services personnel) face. Special educators need to receive professional learning designed to deeply enrich their practice as teachers of students with disabilities. Researchers Jessica L. Hagaman and Kathryn J. Casey (2018) report a primary reason special education teachers leave the field is inadequate access to professional learning.

Educator practice can benefit greatly from well-designed professional learning (Cordingley et al., 2015; García & Weiss, 2019). Too often, professional learning means "listening to stale talks accompanied by endless slides" (Cordingley et al., 2015, p. 3). I believe high-quality professional learning is achieved, in contrast, when the learning is continuous and engaging and it takes place over time. When a school or district contracts a speaker, it often establishes discussion groups and learning communities to allow time for engagement and processing of the content (Stewart, 2014). In these situations, even if the content is unrelated (or perceived to be unrelated) to inclusion, discussion can create a bridge toward a learning opportunity and open doors to mindfully processing the content and how it connects to the specific teaching environment the teacher is in. Learning Forward, in collaboration with forty organizations, designed specific standards for high-quality professional learning for educators (https://learningforward.org/standards). The organization purposefully moved away from the term *professional development* and uses the term *professional learning* instead to demonstrate the importance of educators taking an active role in their own learning. This means allowing innovation in professional learning design. When teachers have a voice in their professional learning, their development as professionals is more evident (Farris-Berg & Dirkswager, 2013). Consider alternate forms of professional learning, such as explicit discussions, learning walks, book clubs, movie club, research club, authentic literacy, or strategy of the week. The following sections go into further detail on each.

EXPLICIT DISCUSSIONS

Relevant content, subject knowledge, and pedagogy are all critical to student outcomes, yet how often do educators discuss them after graduate school? Provide a safe space for teachers to share how they accommodate and differentiate to support individual learning; these explicit discussions can raise the bar for all involved. Schedule time for explicit discussions on how to translate what the teachers learn to classroom practice.

For example, Karen Rogers (2020) suggests categories that a group of educators can use in an explicit discussion on grouping strategies for high-ability and gifted learners.

- **Flexible grouping:** Students are differentiated either across grade-level classes, between grade levels, or within a single classroom in high-achievement areas.
- **Self-contained homogeneous classrooms:** The top students in a grade level are placed in a single classroom for all advanced learning.
- **Within-class grouping:** Students within a single classroom are grouped by performance level for specific differentiation in content areas.
- **Cooperative grouping by ability or performance level:** High-ability students are placed with other high-ability students (groups of three or four or dyads) to work on differentiated tasks or assignments collaboratively.
- **Cluster grouping:** High-ability or high-performing students are placed together in one mixed-ability classroom. The sizes of clusters range from three to ten.

Each of these categories is supported by as few as seven to as many as twenty-three studies (Rogers, 2020). The explicit discussion about this topic could begin with an overview of the studies in this area and then move into an opportunity for educators to share what each grouping might look like with various content at the school. You could easily replicate this discussion at your school site. After the discussion, ask the teachers what topic they would like to explicitly discuss in the next professional learning session.

Discussions such as this can build effective communities of practice where educators engage in a collaborative inquiry cycle to strengthen their instruction and classroom culture (Feller, Myers, & Smith, 2022). PLC at Work architects Richard DuFour, Rebecca DuFour, and Robert Eaker, whose work focuses on school improvement, cite collaborative inquiry cycles in their definition of a professional learning community, which relies on continuous, job-embedded learning by educators as the key to improving student learning. This cycle consists of data analysis, goal setting, collective inquiry, and action research (DuFour et al., 2021).

LEARNING WALKS

A *learning walk* is a simple, intentional, and nonevaluative professional learning opportunity in which educators visit classrooms to observe (Fisher & Frey, 2014). The concept is a small team of educators enters the classroom. The teacher and students know there will be visitors; however, the visitors do not engage in any way with the teacher and students. The visiting educator's role is to watch and learn.

I suggest that each educator consider the following questions.

- "How is the environment in this classroom enhancing instruction? What could I do in my own practice based on this learning?"
- "What types of relationships have developed in this classroom? What could I do to enhance my relationships with students, parents, and staff I work with?"
- "What type of instruction is occurring? Am I observing strategies that I could implement in my own teaching?"
- "As I move around the classroom, do I see evidence of differentiation and specially designed instruction? Are these practices I can implement in my classroom?"
- "Are schoolwide systems of behavior in place? What is the teacher doing to implement these systems? What are the students doing to maintain appropriate behaviors in the classroom? Is there anything here that I can use in my practice?"
- "Inclusion means *all*. As I observe, do I see *every* student engaged and learning? What techniques does the teacher use to engage *all* students? Is there a technique I can use in my own classroom?"
- "What other observations am I documenting that I might use to improve my own practice?"

Using the think-write-pair-share strategy (Karge, 2014), the small team of educators comes together either shortly after the observation, after school, or the next morning (you don't want a lot of time to pass). Each educator *thinks* and *writes* down the answers to the preceding questions prior to the debrief meeting or at the beginning of the debrief meeting. Educators are paired to *share* responses to all questions with a colleague. The professional learning ends with an open sharing time in which all educators share at least one thing they learned that they will take back to their own classroom and implement. This share is attended by the educators who were teaching, assisting, or providing a service while the small group visited their classrooms. This in turn gives the observed educators a chance to do some observing of their own as they see the think-write-pair-share strategy modeled for them.

BOOK CLUBS

A common complaint of special education teachers occurs when a professional learning event or session does not apply to them. Consider offering monthly professional learning book clubs for small groups of educators. Every teacher is required to participate; however, each small group can choose a relevant book that empowers contributions from special education teachers. Suggestions for special educators might include the following.

- *Explicit Instruction: Effective and Efficient Teaching* (Archer & Hughes, 2010)
- *What Really Works With Exceptional Learners* (Murawski & Scott, 2017)
- *Doable Differentiation: Twelve Strategies to Meet the Needs of All Learners* (Kise, 2021)

All attendees should read the assigned pages ahead of the meeting and, if possible, implement one or more of the strategies and discuss the strategies during the book club meeting. I recommend each person read one chapter a month. Another option would be to use a jigsaw strategy: divide the chapters, and come back together after a month so all attendees can share the key concepts they learned from their assigned chapter of the book.

MOVIE CLUB

Many fabulous movies show the public the abilities of persons with disabilities. Documentary filmmaker Dan Habib (2007, 2012) has many good documentaries on inclusive education. Two of my favorites are *Including Samuel* (Habib, 2007) and *Who Cares About Kelsey?* (Habib, 2012). Teachers and school staff can join for a movie afternoon and view and discuss various disability-related films, documentaries, or both. *Forrest Gump* (Zemeckis, 1994), *My Left Foot* (Sheridan, 1989), *Children of a Lesser God* (Haines, 1986), *Mask* (Bogdanovich, 1985), *Front of the Class* (Werner, 2008), *Rain Man* (Levinson, 1988), *Mr. Holland's Opus* (Herek, 1995), and *Stand and Deliver* (Menéndez, 1988) all open the door for rich conversations and opportunities to relate to either a teacher or a person with a disability. These films can inspire people and can provide an open forum for discussion and learning to take place.

RESEARCH CLUB

There are many obstacles that can prevent successful inclusion. When leaders share extensive research about the benefits of inclusion, they may quell any reservations expressed by the staff and parents. I work with several school leaders who electronically send out research tips of the month to the faculty, the staff, and sometimes the larger school community. They share article syntheses with one another and then pass them on to the various schools they represent.

Research helps drive implementation of high-level programs and provides ideas of individualized school models to create. A school in Japan with a large population of students with learning disabilities and ADHD exemplifies successful implementation of a research club. Any educator at the school is welcome to join colleagues in the research club for an hour-long discussion twice a month. At each club meeting, a different teacher or school leader shares an article. The stipulation is if teachers or leaders share articles, they must tell their colleagues how the articles influenced their practice, providing fertile ground for successful ideas to spread.

At a school in Italy, the headmaster (equivalent to the superintendent) sent out various journal articles related to inclusive education and instruction. After reading the research, the teachers decided to replicate some of the studies at their own school. They shared the research results with other employees on a teacher-led research day. Seeing these results coming from their own students, the teachers were highly motivated to improve their practice, and the changes they made led to better results for their students.

Another example of successful implementation of a teacher research club occurred at a school in North Carolina that has a large population of students with autism. All the middle school teachers and school leaders read Donald Oswald's (2005) article "An Encyclopedia of Autism Interventions." After that, they used the following five key components of the autism spectrum disorder inclusion collaboration model to influence a schoolwide change process: (1) environmental and curricular modifications, (2) attitudinal and social support, (3) coordinated team commitment, (4) recurrent evaluation of inclusion procedures, and (5) school-home collaboration. The research club explored articles in the five areas and used the process to gain momentum and implement extensive supports for including students with autism at the school.

A common theme throughout all these examples is that educators remain up to date as new research becomes available in the field.

AUTHENTIC LITERACY

At the core of every discipline should be authentic literacy. *Authentic literacy* is the ability to enjoy literacy in a meaningful way that connects to community and personal values (Eastman & Rasmussen, 2021). Continual discussions among educators and students about the ability to read, write, and speak can lead to improved student outcomes. Travis (2021) purports that everything else falls into place when schools intentionally focus on authentic literacy. However, many students move on from their education without strong authentic literacy skills; a significant portion of the workforce has very limited authentic literacy skills (Vignoles, 2016).

Teaching literacy is beneficial for both students and teachers. The research in special education has long supported that teacher growth in the teaching of literacy improves practice (Murawski & Scott, 2017). A principal of a large comprehensive high school in Dallas, Texas, has shared with me that his tip for successful inclusive education is to help all teachers in the school see themselves as literacy teachers (J. Dowling, personal communication, December 5, 2011). He explains that when content-area teachers share their favorite books and authentic reading materials connected to their content, students usually open up to discovery and conversation. In his school, every student is included. There are not separate classes for general education and students with disabilities. He encourages teachers to share real-world examples with all students to help them understand how the content area (science, mathematics, history, physical education, music, and so on) requires reading in its various jobs and career opportunities. This centering of authentic literacy provides intrinsic motivation for students to learn and understand more. The principal also encourages his teachers to use picture books to demonstrate topic connections and asks them to, when possible, provide visuals that align with the content they are teaching. These simple practices have allowed students with executive function challenges, learning disabilities, and autism to learn to fully participate. The serendipity, as he explains it, is that other students in the school also benefit from these simple teaching strategies (J. Dowling, personal communication, December 5, 2011). Teachers improve their practice, and all students improve their outcomes.

STRATEGY OF THE WEEK

In the faculty newsletter or at a faculty meeting, introduce a new instructional strategy. The strategy may come from Robert J. Marzano's (2017) *The New Art and Science of Teaching*, Karge's (2014) engagement strategies, or another resource. Ask several teachers to use the strategy and share the outcome the following week. Or challenge the teaching staff to use it and report back on the implementation the following week.

An international school in Asia that I worked with set a schoolwide goal to integrate engagement strategies. The leadership purchased *Engage 11: Strategies to Promote Student Engagement* for every teacher (Karge, 2014); this teaching tool contains eleven strategies.

1. Tell-help-check
2. Give one, get one
3. Magic wand
4. Think-write-pair-share
5. Talking chips
6. Ambassadors
7. Idea wave
8. Scaffolding
9. Three-step interview
10. Team-pair-solo
11. Questioning the author

For example, the first strategy, tell-help-check, is a cooperative learning strategy. The idea is for students to work with a peer. One student *tells* the other student something content related, and the second student *helps* by adding comments; then they *check* their work together. An algebra teacher at the school in Asia used the strategy to review for an upcoming exam. The teacher reported during the share-out that students indicated they remembered what their partner had shared during the tell-help-check, and they believed this helped them do better on the exam. The science teacher used the strategy during a lab experiment. The students were to tell their assigned peers how to do the experiment (walk them through the steps) and then check the results posted by the teacher. The teacher reported the perceived value of the strategy was the depth of knowledge demonstrated by the various peers. And a co-teaching team of language arts and special education teachers reported using the strategy for a book-review activity. Their example demonstrated the value of thoughtful peer groupings on projected outcomes. They reported that by carefully pairing their students, they were able to have every student participate in a discussion of a recently read book; this was unlike the class discussion they had conducted the week before, in which only a few students spoke. The teachers also talked about the formative assessment they were able to use during the strategy. These three examples motivated others on the teaching team to use future strategies and share their outcomes.

The following week, the give one, get one strategy was introduced. The music theory teacher used the strategy and a reproducible form (figure 3.5) to review for an exam. She asked the students to record in each of the top six boxes an idea that they wanted to recall for the exam. She had them work independently on this part. Then they were to move around the classroom, looking at what others wrote, giving some ideas to others, and adding some ideas for themselves on the bottom four lines of the form. The activity was so successful that she allowed all students to use this one form during the assessment; everyone passed with a B or better. More importantly, she felt the students really understood the music theory concepts.

Record the things you would like to remember from this presentation in the boxes.

Give some of your ideas to others. *Get* some of their ideas for yourself.

1. ______________________________
2. ______________________________
3. ______________________________
4. ______________________________

FIGURE 3.5: Give one, get one form.

Visit ***go.SolutionTree.com/specialneeds*** *for a free reproducible version of this figure.*

The co-taught history class (general education and special education teachers) used the form to reinforce the learning after viewing a historical documentary. The students were able to write or draw pictures of six things (one in each box) that they learned from the film. When they met with other students to fill in the bottom portion, many had to use the back of the form because they were getting so many ideas. The special education teacher commented that she had not previously seen students with disabilities integrated in this way. She said she did not even know who was who as everyone participated and enjoyed the learning opportunity. When the students returned to their seats, they did a share-out of some of the top ideas. The general education teacher felt their responses were stronger than his Advanced Placement history class's.

It is plain to see that teachers who learn new strategies can potentially revitalize their own practice while kick-starting the engagement and motivation of all their students; for students with disabilities, this can be especially meaningful.

The Learning Continuum

Just as there is a learning continuum for K–12 students, there is a continuum for new teachers and for educators who are new to special education. Teachers go through stages in their growth progression as they develop skills to teach. A new special education teacher or a veteran teacher new to special education will go through what educational psychologist Frances F. Fuller (1969) calls the *stages of development*: (1) self, (2) task, and (3) impact. Teachers in the *self* stage are primarily concerned with getting through the day; they spend a good deal of time focusing on their own day-to-day survival. Eventually, their focus moves to taking care of daily teaching, writing lesson plans and IEPs, and beginning to feel successful with the *task* of teaching. Finally, teachers reflect on the *impact* they are making, looking at student outcome data and evaluating lessons.

For some, these stages occur very quickly (over a month), and for others, progressing through the stages takes many years. When teachers move from school to school or do not receive the supports they need, they tend to remain in the self and task stages and never reach impact (Hall & Hord, 2015). As the administrator, you can help by understanding the various developmental stages and encouraging teacher growth and assessment as well as personal insight and reflection on one's own stages of development. Researchers who have studied these stages believe it takes approximately five years for an educator to attain the impact level (Fuller, 1969; Hall & Hord, 2015; Reitman, 2018).

Two ways that you can encourage teachers in their progress through the learning continuum are by providing IEP follow-up and welcoming innovation.

IEP Follow-Up

Leaders inspire, empower, and model effective practices. You can inspire special education teachers by touching base with them monthly and asking if students are meeting their IEP goals. This keeps you informed as to what kind of progress students are making, and it makes teachers feel they are not alone and someone is there to follow up on IEP implementation. It empowers teachers to be able to have a casual conversation about student progress monitoring. As you learn of students who are making progress, send notes home or email parents (and copy the teacher on the message) to share the good news. This gives parents the feeling that you are looking after their children and following their progress. Taking the time to communicate growth establishes a positive relationship that will be invaluable should you have to contact the parents for absenteeism or a behavior challenge. When the leader models effective communication with parents, especially around the IEP, it builds confidence and moral support for the special education teacher.

Importance of Welcoming Innovation

Novice special education teachers often bring innovation and new ideas. Leaders should welcome and embrace this enthusiasm. Sometimes veteran teachers are inspired by the joy and excitement the new special educator brings to the school. New teachers may have received training on new technologies or programs; make every effort to get these teachers the tools they need to succeed and teach to their potential.

Share your personal passion with your new teachers. Let them know you were in their shoes, had a strong mentor (if you did), and want to provide them with the same. Reflect *with* instead of *at* the new educators, and listen. Let them know you will support their innovation and assist in any way you can to support their chosen career.

Conclusion

This chapter began with data on special education teacher retention and attrition. If special education teachers are going to remain in the field five years and beyond, they need support. Mentoring is a necessary practice, and evidence from around the globe shows that leadership support can inspire high student achievement in novice teachers' classrooms (Darling-Hammond, 2017). A respected, trusted, and knowledgeable leader can support special education staff by building relationships and providing opportunities for pedagogical knowledge to increase. This support includes encouraging the use of research-based instructional strategies, allocating time for proper mentorship, and providing innovation in the required professional learning. Leaders can also be aware of each teacher's learning continuum and strive to offer assistance through the stages of growth. These leadership strategies are also productive in maintaining all teachers.

Leaders can also support special educators by ensuring that these teachers have appropriate assistance in the classroom and that general education teachers have appropriate assistance when the special educator is not in the general education classroom. Chapter 4 details how to work with the paraeducators (assistants) who walk alongside the general and special education teachers on a daily basis.

FOUR

SUPPORTING PARAEDUCATOR PERSONNEL

It is always the simple
that produces the marvelous.
—AMELIA BARR

As a leader, you may think building capacity and trust in relationships sounds simple, yet it's critical. These relationships go beyond the teachers in the school. The definition of *teaching* has shifted away from the past perception of providing general education with one group of students and expanded to incorporate many other roles, including working collaboratively with assistants. It is important to connect with, support, and mentor those who work day to day and side by side with teachers providing services for students with disabilities.

Adults who assist in schools go by many different titles (instructional assistant, teacher's aide, therapy assistant, job coach, paraprofessional, inclusion assistant, educational aide, and teaching assistant, to name a few). For the purposes of this book, I prefer and use the term *paraeducator*. The prefix *para-* means to walk alongside, as does the term *mentor*. Though they have different roles, just as mentors do, paraeducators walk alongside teachers to support their work. The paraeducator typically provides assistance to the students; the mentor coaches and provides assistance to the teacher.

The prefix para- *means to walk alongside, as does the term* mentor. *Though they have different roles, just as mentors do, paraeducators walk alongside teachers to support their work. The paraeducator typically provides assistance to the students; the mentor coaches and provides assistance to the teacher.*

Likewise, the teacher must walk alongside and support the paraeducator. This role can be challenging, as most teachers did not learn in their teacher education program how to supervise adults. A special education teacher may be assigned several paraeducators to supervise and provide directions for the time the paraeducator supports students in general education classrooms. Or the special education teacher may be the assigned supervisor for paraeducators working alongside them in a segregated classroom. Sometimes a new teacher is assigned a paraeducator with many years of experience.

In this chapter, I discuss the many facets of the paraeducator's role as well as how leaders can ensure paraeducators are valued and valuable members of the school team. Professional learning for paraeducators should be included in step 4 of the eleven steps for ensuring an inclusive school (chapter 7, page 145), as it is an essential consideration throughout this work.

The Paraeducator Role

Think about how inclusive practices will work at your school if you currently have only segregated special education programs. Consider the value high-quality paraeducators bring to facilitating an inclusive setting. For example, consider a segregated primary special education classroom with three first graders, four second graders, and three third graders. If this classroom has one special education teacher and three paraeducators, you can coordinate schedules as you move into an inclusive setting; you can make it so the four adults rotate into grade-level general education classes for teaching small groups, preteaching, and reteaching skills or concepts. The students benefit because they are with their grade-level peers and hear the grade-level content from the general education teacher, and the teachers benefit because they can collaborate, consult, and co-teach as needed. Inclusion changes the view of the physical setting where students receive their services and gives students access to general education.

As the school moves forward with implementation of inclusive practices, it may need additional paraeducators to support the accommodations and appropriate educational environment of students with disabilities. The following case study shares an administrative experience at a small school with only one special education teacher and a need for more adult support.

> *At Para School, a rural school in Iowa, I worked with an innovative leader who facilitated the design of a viable inclusive program. The school had only one special education teacher. As educators met to creatively construct learning environments for thirty-six students with disabilities at the school site, it became clear the budget would not allow for another full-time special education teacher. The team convened and analyzed every IEP to think critically about how to design appropriate inclusive learning supports for each student. The team realized that hiring several part-time paraeducators, each with expertise in different areas, who could support students under the special education teacher's supervision was a sustainable option.*
>
> *Communication between the teachers and the paraeducators should be ongoing. Because of this, the interview process made it clear up front that the paraeducators must attend a weekly meeting with the special education teacher. At this meeting, the special education teacher (direct supervisor of paraeducators) went over the weekly schedule, shared lesson plans for situations in which the paraeducators were to lead a small group, taught the paraeducators how to teach accommodations to their assigned students, and discussed daily journal entries. Each paraeducator was required to document daily interactions with students. A sample of such documentation appears in figure 4.1 (page 86). This simple quick write gives the special education teacher evidence of how paraeducators used their time and which students received support.*
>
> *The paraeducators were hired knowing they would work in general education classrooms. Para School hired one specific paraeducator as a one-on-one paraeducator for a student with impaired vision. This person received some very basic training related to the student's disability; duties included always remaining aware of the student's safety without being overprotective, offering verbal cues, and introducing the student to equipment and space through verbalization as well as through touch. Finally, the special education teacher explained the critical importance of peers and the use of the buddy system and consistently discussed these topics during weekly meetings.*

Time	Group or Individual	Support Provided
8:30–9:00 a.m.	Fluency group of grade 3 and 4 students	Altered reading chorally and individually; last five minutes, used cloze reading procedure (as was instructed at weekly meeting)
9:10–9:40 a.m.	Vocabulary group of grade 1 to 3 students	Played vocabulary game, then pretaught spelling words using strategy learned at weekly meeting
9:49–10:00 a.m.	Recess for lower grades	Supervised—encouraged Silvia to join jump rope game
10:00–10:30 a.m.	Grade 2 general education classroom	Listened to instruction, then had Luis write out the steps the teacher had provided for the mathematics problem; walked around and assisted students who needed support
10:30–10:50 a.m.	Break	Break
10:50–11:20 a.m.	Grade 4 general education classroom	Supervised computer station—checked Joan's, Charlie's, and Karen's work; all on target today
11:20–11:50 a.m.	Grade 3 general education classroom	Did fun role-play with Mrs. K that she scripted; I was Ms. Noun, and she was Mr. Verb. All our special education students were on task and engaged.
11:50 a.m.-12:30 p.m.	Grade 6 general education classroom	Helped a student, John, having a difficult time with the assignment; I read aloud the directions to him and had him repeat. He was frustrated. We took a short walk. When we returned to class, and he read aloud directions again, this time, he was able to get to work.

FIGURE 4.1: Sample paraeducator daily documentation.

At the school described in the preceding case study, weekly sessions with the special education teacher proved to be valuable professional learning opportunities for both the paraeducators and the special education teacher. At times, the principal joined the weekly meetings to observe the standard of practice that the educators established. The principal noticed that the meetings were all one sided at the beginning, with the special education teacher sharing what the paraeducators would do during the week. As the paraeducators became more comfortable in their roles, they also provided suggestions and insights to the teacher. After the highly successful inclusive program was shared at a districtwide meeting, other schools in the area adopted the weekly meetings and documentation strategy. Similarly, a small high school in the community hired itinerant paraeducators to administer and score tests and quizzes. The school conducted professional learning for the paraeducators to provide the dos and don'ts of assessment. For example, paraeducators received specific testing instructions related to individual student IEPs.

- Allow students to make audio recordings of their answers (then transcribe them for the teacher).
- Provide students with the opportunity to have tests read orally.
- Allow students to use charts, calculators, or manipulatives on the tests.
- Provide partial credit for various correct steps in a problem-solving process.
- Read test instructions aloud to students who request it based on the IEP details provided by the teacher.

Probably the most challenging situation a paraeducator is tasked with relates to managing student behavior. Professional learning in this area is essential. When school behavioral support coaches provide paraeducators with ongoing professional learning, student behavior improves (Bradshaw et al., 2018). Like other educators at the school, paraeducators need to understand the *ABCs of behavior* (antecedent, behavior, and consequence) and how to handle various situations that may occur when they are providing instructional support to students either in general education classrooms or in smaller groups. The ABCs of behavior model comes from the work of psychologist B. F. Skinner in 1945. He reasoned that every complex issue in science has its own functional analysis. Skinner's analysis of behavior is such that problems must be defined by controlling variables. Over time, professionals in the education field have learned to appreciate this scientific approach to how antecedents and consequences directly impact behavior (Skinner, Wellborn, & Connell, 1990), as this is the background to applied behavior analysis.

The reauthorization of IDEA in 2004 outlines:

> A state may allow paraprofessionals who are appropriately trained and supervised under state standards to assist in the provision of special education and related services. The training can be provided directly from the supervisor (often a teacher), or it can be a group professional learning session at the school or district.

Most of the time, teachers do not receive training in how to work with paraeducators in their university certification programs (Douglas, Uitto, Reinfelds, & D'Agostino, 2019; Karge, Pierson, & Robinson, 2011). There are some very effective and compelling training videos available. For example, the ParaSharp program has job-specific tools available online (see www.321insight.com); this program's discussion guides align with four- to thirteen-minute videos on addressing issues related to professional roles and responsibilities, avoiding power struggles, and understanding basic special education. The primary duty of a paraeducator is to work with students; thus, professional learning needs to include instructional supervision.

The importance of professional learning is a thread that runs through every facet of the paraeducator's role. Leaders can ensure that paraeducators receive the support they need to succeed in their role by being aware of these facets, including the duties of paraeducators, the tasks paraeducators perform, the importance of confidentiality, the challenges of providing one-on-one support, the possibilities related to Tier 2 interventions and learning centers, and the role of bilingual paraeducators.

Duties of a Paraeducator

Paraeducators' duties are based on the specific contracts under which they are employed. These duties often include working with small groups or individual students and implementing curriculum adaptations, specific behavior strategies, instructional strategies, or social-learning strategies. A paraeducator may monitor and assist students as they participate in independent learning activities. Sometimes school leaders call on paraeducators to assist students with personal hygiene needs as stated in the students' IEPs. Paraeducators may also prepare learning materials. When expectations from the supervising teacher (the special education teacher) are clear and specific, paraeducators can effectively implement the student routines and perform better, ultimately leading them to support students with disabilities.

Kent Gerlach (2017), leading expert in research on paraeducators, writes that it is important to look at paraeducators' skills and experience in maintaining safe learning environments, communicating students' progress, and implementing effective lessons initiated by related services personnel or the teacher. Teachers have many key topics to discuss with the paraeducator at the beginning of the year or when the paraeducator is first assigned to them. According to Gerlach (2015), questions on these topics include the following.

- What are the short- and long-term goals for the specific students the paraeducator is to work with?
- What will the paraeducator's role be in the classroom?
- What routines and instructional procedures will the paraeducator use?
- How should the paraeducator communicate with the teacher?

For paraeducators to become true members of the team, they need to know the school philosophy and procedures, the mission and values, the policies and procedures that are standard to every employee, and the leadership personnel. If the school has an MTSS handbook (see chapter 2, page 41), the paraeducator should have access to it and have time to read and discuss it with the immediate supervisor (special education teacher). Schools must share regulations regarding bullying, teasing, and harassment. They need to clearly outline child abuse and neglect procedures as well as school safety and emergency procedures for earthquakes, tornadoes, fires, weapons on campus, and so on. Understanding the distinction between teacher and paraeducator roles and knowing the principal is the building leader are key elements to ensuring success.

Tasks Paraeducators Can Perform

Paraeducators can be trained to do many tasks to support the unique learning needs of students with disabilities. Ultimately, the person employed in this role must be supervised. Use the task checklist in figure 4.2 for contract development. The supervising teacher can also use the checklist to coach the paraeducator.

- ☐ Reinforcing skills using materials and activities as directed by the teacher
- ☐ Explaining and reteaching a lesson (after watching the teacher provide the instruction)
- ☐ Coaching students through a sequence of tasks
- ☐ Checking homework or work completion
- ☐ Monitoring students during seatwork or group activities
- ☐ Providing daily assignment support
- ☐ Reading a book to a student or listening to a student read a book
- ☐ Checking backpacks or assisting with the organization of backpacks or desks
- ☐ Lifting, rotating, or supporting students with physical needs
- ☐ Taking data for monitoring or charting behavior
- ☐ Conducting a small-group lesson using the lesson plan provided by the certified teacher
- ☐ Accompanying students to a therapy session, a classroom, the bus, lunch, the bathroom, recess, or passing period
- ☐ Assisting with implementation of IEP goals under the direction of the certified educator
- ☐ Implementing behavior plans developed by the certified educator
- ☐ Supervising students at lunch, passing periods, recess, study hall, bus arrivals and departures, or various activities (field trips, assemblies, and so on)
- ☐ Performing clerical duties such as operating media, maintaining daily logs, or photocopying (Clerical duties should be kept to a minimum, and school leaders should tell the teacher and paraeducators their main purpose is to work with students.)

FIGURE 4.2: Tasks paraeducators can perform.

Visit ***go.SolutionTree.com/specialneeds*** *for a free reproducible version of this figure.*

According to Gerlach (2015), paraeducators also provide related services in the following programmatic areas under the certified educator's supervision.

- Educational programs, including behavior programs
- Physical therapy
- Occupational therapy
- Speech and language therapy
- Early intervention and preschool programs
- Recreation programs
- Social work and case management
- Parent training and child-find programs
- Vocational training programs and job coaching
- Playground, lunchroom, and library
- Computer assistance
- Health assistance
- One-to-one instruction (such as by interpreters)

Often the supervisor is not on campus daily, and the paraeducator must carry out the service without direct guidance. For example, the therapist will create the lesson plans and materials and leave them with the paraeducator, who will provide the service. This means communication between the supervisor and the paraeducator is especially important, and planning time is necessary for this communication.

Confidentiality

To protect the dignity of all students and of the inclusive school, confidentiality is critical. Specific details about a student's education and personal life should be discussed only in professional circles and only with people clearly involved in the specific student case. Students are entitled to confidentiality in matters related to diagnosis; program goals; academic, social, emotional, and physical performance and progress; and personal and family information.

Confidentiality needs to be discussed with the paraeducator, as do school safety procedures (that is, never be alone with a student, and so on). Paraeducators must be specifically told not to publicly discuss test scores, student files, IEPs, 504 information, or behavior. One never knows who is sitting at the next table or on the opposite park bench! Similarly, venting on social media about a particularly challenging day at work or giving details about a student case should be avoided at all costs.

The primary rule is just don't talk about any school-related business in public. In some cases (especially in schools where litigation in this area has been an issue), this appears in the paraeducator contract. When paraeducators receive a rationale, they can carry out their assigned tasks in an efficient manner (Karge et al., 2011). Paraeducators should be told to be cordial to parents; however, it is not their role to engage the parents in a discussion about their child's progress, behavior, or teacher. This is critical not only for confidentiality but also for continuity in voice. The teacher or principal should be the one who speaks to the parent about all education issues.

Action for Administrators

The special or general education teacher is responsible for the direct instruction of all students. The paraeducator's role is to reteach, reinforce, or provide curriculum support. Paraeducators may be called on to implement behavior management. A certified teacher or administrator must supervise them. The IEP should provide the framework for their work.

One-to-One Adult Support

Assigning a paraeducator to a student with a disability in a one-to-one ratio is valuable in that the student has an adult alongside them every step of the way. However, this every-step-of-the-way approach can also cause challenges. Sometimes this relationship leads to isolation of students from their peers. Because these students are exclusively spending time with the paraeducator, they don't have the opportunity to develop deep social connections with peers. The teacher may also feel isolated from the student and may not develop a sense of ownership as the case carrier. On the other hand, the paraeducator can serve as a facilitator to model natural, respectful interactions and friendships with peers.

If your school site has a paraeducator assigned to a one-to-one role, take time to observe and learn what the person is doing. The paraeducator should be available to provide support yet should hold back and wait until the student needs the support or asks for the support. Perceived needs for support are often directly tied to the individual student and the severity of the disability. In these cases, the one-on-one paraeducator must have training related to the disability area. For example, you might ask paraeducators of students with autism to view several resources available at the Ohio Center for Autism and Low Incidence (OCALI) website (https://autisminternetmodules.org). This site has free modules for ideas and supports that paraeducators can use when working with a student with autism.

Action for Administrators

Encourage paraeducators to greet parents and family members appropriately. *Discourage* paraeducators from engaging in lengthy discussions about how a student is doing. Especially when the paraeducator is working in a one-to-one role, the parent might seek the paraeducator's input. Make sure all involved realize the primary communicator should be the teacher. This policy can minimize the potential for legal action.

Tier 2 Intervention and Learning Centers

Many schools use paraeducators to implement Tier 2 intervention. Hiring paraeducators to conduct small-group interventions is a simple solution. If you decide to do this, remember you cannot truly measure the impact without ensuring proper implementation (Arden, Gandhi, Edmonds, & Danielson, 2017). A single training is not enough for paraeducators to implement intervention on their own. Before the program begins, training needs to take place, and someone needs to oversee and continually prompt appropriate strategies and precise implementation. Since paraeducators are not certified teachers, they should not be expected to know how to accommodate or change the intervention strategies to meet student needs. Remember that paraeducators might be applying for these jobs simply because they love children. In my experience in many international schools, people hired as paraeducators are often trailing spouses; this means their spouse is working for an embassy, the military, or a private company, and they also want to work. Sometimes these individuals have education or the equivalent of graduate degrees but are not certified to teach in the country where they are residing.

Ongoing coaching and instruction are necessary for paraeducators to successfully support the implementation of Tier 2 intervention. And as stated previously, fidelity of implementation is essential: "When practices are not implemented with fidelity, improved student outcomes are much less likely" (Arden et al., 2017, p. 275). Paraeducators need professional learning about how to model behavior that respects diversity. They need coaching in using various reinforcement and data-collection strategies as well as proper safety measures for assisting students with daily living skills, such as restroom use, hygiene, and mobility.

Often when schools are designing MTSS programs, they set up a learning center to support Tier 2 intervention. A certified teacher supervises the learning center, which may include several paraeducators employed to work with students in intensive intervention groups, help with or coordinate homework clubs, and work on remedial tasks with individual students. The key to running an effective learning center is having the proper personnel in place. This means a certified teacher who works well with other adults can train paraeducators in the necessary skills, then step back and facilitate as they support students. The following case study demonstrates the successful use of a learning center.

> *Maria was a socially outgoing fourth-grade student with executive function challenges who attended a suburban school in central Arizona. Her second-grade teacher had referred her to the LST two years before. She had been having difficulty meeting the academic demands of second grade, despite many classroom interventions.*
>
> *In second grade, Maria had great difficulty with basic decoding skills, spelling, and memorization of specific mathematics processes. She also had difficulty with concentration, comprehension, and memory skills; she had a hard time working independently and required repeated drills in order to master basic academic concepts. Maria had an IEP and received support from her general education teacher, her special education teacher, and a paraeducator.*
>
> *Maria worked in a small group within her general education class for reading and written language. Her accommodations included a mathematics class taught in a group with an emphasis on mastery and reteaching by a paraeducator in the learning center. The paraeducator taught basic skills with an emphasis on listening to particular information and using manipulatives to solve addition, subtraction, and multiplication problems. Maria repeated the*

reading and written language directions the paraeducator gave, and the paraeducator acted as facilitator to ensure Maria correctly carried out the directions.

At the end of the day, at 2:00 p.m., the learning center was open so students could catch up on their work, get a little extra help, or make up missed assignments from a previous day. Maria attended the learning center approximately twice a week. Here, visual clues along with auditory input enhanced understanding. Classwork and homework assignments were modified or shortened depending on difficulty. After a year of these supports, Maria acquired a year and three months' worth of learning. This was substantial growth.

As a fourth grader, Maria was able to fully participate in instruction and did not need the additional support in reading and mathematics. Her support became focused on her writing. With the guidance of the special education teacher, the paraeducator was teaching Maria writing strategies and systems to help her with initial conceptualization of a writing assignment.

Bilingual Paraeducators

If English is students' second language, bilingual paraeducators can help the students move through complex situations and make needed connections. Tasks that bilingual paraeducators usually perform include doing recess duty and bus duty, translating homework for students and parents, supporting testing of English learners, and working with small groups, sometimes in both the first and second language (depending on the school policy for language instruction).

Bilingual paraeducators are often also certified translators, depending on their background and training. They are able to help teachers with phone calls home as well as written communication. I have worked in international schools where students speak over thirty languages, and many paraeducators are available for various supportive situations. In the United States, first language depends largely on the community. In California, a school may need to accommodate ten different languages or just two.

Paraeducators as Members of the Team

Paraeducators are not certified teachers, yet they are valuable members of the school community. Many paraeducators live in the community and have been at the school for a long time. When they receive the guidance and support they need, they can, in turn, help schools fulfill school-improvement expert Douglas Reeves's (2006) four requirements for effective schools.

1. **Set rigorous standards based on the core curriculum:** Paraeducators need to understand the rationale for rigorous standards based on the core curriculum. If they are not informed, they may unintentionally undermine students' progress by giving them answers or doing the work for the students. Helping paraeducators learn the value of standards-based instruction and the rationale behind the core curriculum will build team capacity.
2. **Frequently use performance assessment to modify instruction:** Paraeducators are often assigned to give formative and summative assessments. They need to be informed of the importance of performance assessment and how it is used to modify instruction. Otherwise, the paraeducators may help students too much on the assessment, resulting in inaccurate test scores. Their best intentions to assist with the assessment may mean that schools receive an erroneous report of student capabilities.
3. **Have teachers collaborate frequently and discuss best practices:** Paraeducators consistently work with students. It is important that the teaching team collaborates and educates paraeducators on best instructional and assessment practices. If the teachers are to supervise the paraeducators and facilitate lesson planning, they need to take time to share their expectations, their rationale for asking the paraeducators to use particular strategies, and how the paraeducators can implement the strategies.
4. **Ensure *everyone* is highly focused on student learning:** This cannot be a hidden agenda. You need to be up-front and clear with all paraeducators. They need to know they are part of a team that is highly focused on student learning. Sometimes educators who lack training in special education have difficulty understanding hidden disabilities (such as learning disabilities, executive function problems, and dyslexia) and why students with these disabilities have such challenges learning. Equally difficult is understanding why students with autism or physical disabilities need to be in inclusive settings. Paraeducators must be coached on and reminded of the purpose of setting schoolwide goals for every student so that the students make progress and acquire knowledge.

Paraeducators need instruction to consistently monitor their own role with individual students, especially if they are working one on one. For example, are paraeducators separating students from their peers? Are students developing a dependence on paraeducators? Are students getting instruction only from paraeducators and not from certified teachers? These are all questions paraeducators need to ask themselves. And paraeducators must be ready to change within the instructional system based on leader or teacher directions so that they allow for peer interaction, student independence, and time with the certified educator.

School leaders have much to consider when bringing paraeducators on board, including the hiring process, evaluation, scheduling, and communication.

Hiring Process for Paraeducators

Districts each have different policies on the hiring of paraeducators. The generic process includes posting a job description, reviewing applications, contacting references, interviewing, reviewing competency exams or transcripts, and negotiating schedules. It is very beneficial to have the inclusion facilitator (that is, the special education teacher) be part of the hiring team. This teacher involvement may seem beyond the scope of traditional responsibilities, yet it will help with establishing a good fit between teacher and paraeducator (Kurth & Gross, 2015). The teacher and paraeducator will be working together, so why not allow the future supervisor a say in developing interview questions and participating in the interview process?

Once new hires are on board, make sure they are introduced to the other employees at the school. This helps new paraeducators feel welcome. Take time to give paraeducators a tour of the school, and include workspaces and classrooms they might use, such as the teacher workroom, the lunchroom, the staff restroom, and the mailboxes. When paraeducators see these things up front, they will feel equipped to begin their new role.

When paraeducators join your team, they may have many questions. Common questions newly hired paraeducators ask include the following.

- "Should I attend school activities such as open house?"
- "Will I receive a district email address for communication?"
- "If I am not able to come to work, whom should I call?"
- "If the teacher I am assigned to is absent, will my role change in any way?"
- "Who gives me my work schedule (including breaks, lunch, and which classroom to be in when)?"

- "Will I be required to work in the lunchroom, on the playground, or on a bus?"
- "Should I attend IEP meetings?"
- "Who is my immediate supervisor?"
- "Will I need to gather data? Who will train me to take data?"
- "If I work in a general education classroom, who will write the lesson plans for me?"
- "Who locks up the classroom each day? Will I have keys?"

You can proactively set up an initial meeting with the new hire and share your responses to these questions.

There are many online resources available to assist you in securing professional learning for and working with paraeducators. For example, the National Resource Center for Paraeducators (https://nrcpara.org) and the Paraprofessional Resource and Research Center at the University of Colorado Denver (https://paracenter.org/helpful-links/professional-organizations) have wonderful sites. As you look at these websites and others, I encourage you to bookmark areas with specific suggestions.

Evaluation of Paraeducators

Like any employees, paraeducators need evaluation. At many schools, this falls through the cracks as there is confusion about who is the primary supervisor and who is the evaluator. Make these decisions upon hiring, and document the process for evaluation. Who is responsible for the formal evaluation of paraeducators? Will the paraeducators receive a copy of the evaluation? Most importantly, what specifically will they be evaluated on?

If paraeducators are assigned to a classroom or a specific teacher, get the input of the persons working with them. However, ultimately, the administrator should conduct the evaluation (the teachers may not be able to participate based on their contracts). During the evaluation, you can inspire and empower paraeducators to be the best they can be. Knowing you understand their job and the processes they deal with daily can play a significant part in team building.

Posted Schedules

I strongly recommend that everyone who works with students with disabilities or students with interventions have access to one another's schedules. Post these schedules, and be sure to include hour-by-hour or class-by-class schedules for students and all adults who support them. Give room numbers and locations. Also include block scheduling or shortened-day scheduling. This is an important way to track all services. It also makes things much easier for your office staff should a parent need to pick up a student early while the student is in a designated service area, not their classroom. If paraeducators need to check in with a teacher or a student, they won't waste time walking the campus to find them. Additionally, the posted schedules can verify legally required duty-free breaks as well as LST, IEP, and staff meetings. Figure 4.3 illustrates what this might look like.

Communication Between Paraeducator and Supervising Teacher

In addition to knowing where everyone is and documenting their own work (as exemplified in figure 4.1, page 86), paraeducators need planning time with their supervising teacher. Typically, the paraeducators and special education teachers are spread across the school and do not always work in the same classroom. They need to plan and have ways to communicate with each other so their process of supporting the students they work with is effective and efficient. Something simple like a communication book (stored daily in a private place) or an electronic document (saved on a secure website) can allow staff to write notes to one another and share details about students. It is very important that this document be only available to people working with the students and that all involved realize the courts can subpoena the notes in the event of litigation. Notes should be factual and useful to each adult working with the student.

Action for Administrators

Teachers are not typically trained to work with other adults. They will need your assistance as they give feedback to paraeducators about their daily work. Educators may be unsure how to do this. Frequently meet and check in with them. You may be the primary contractual supervisor; however, they work with paraeducators day to day and need to develop the proper communication skills to guide the paraeducators with implementation of lesson plans, assessments, and other tasks.

Time	Monday	Tuesday	Wednesday	Thursday	Friday
8:00–8:45 a.m.	Meeting with special education teacher	One-on-one tutoring for student 1	LST meeting	One-on-one tutoring for student 1	Meeting with special education teacher
8:45–9:00 a.m.	Pick up materials.	Pick up materials; quick check-in with special education teacher.	Pick up materials.	Pick up materials; quick check-in with special education teacher.	Pick up materials.
9:00–10:00 a.m.	Small-group instruction in grade 1	Small-group instruction in grade 1	Small-group instruction in grade 1	Small-group instruction in grade 1	Small-group instruction in grade 1
10:00–10:15 a.m.	Recess duty	Recess duty	Recess duty	Recess duty	Recess duty
10:15–10:30 a.m.	Break	Break	Break	Break	Break
10:30–11:30 a.m.	Small-group instruction in grade 2	Small-group instruction in grade 2	Small-group instruction in grade 2	Small-group instruction in grade 2	Small-group instruction in grade 2
11:30 a.m.–12:10 p.m.	Small-group instruction in grade 3	Small-group instruction in grade 3	Small-group instruction in grade 3	Small-group instruction in grade 3	Small-group instruction in grade 3
12:10–1:00 p.m.	Lunch break	Lunch break	Lunch break	Lunch break	Lunch break
1:00–1:30 p.m.	Grade 1 to the library	Grade 2 to the library	Grade 3 to the library	Administer formative assessment designed by special education teacher.	Administer formative assessment designed by special education teacher.
1:30–2:30 p.m.	Small groups in learning center, as assigned by special education teacher	Small groups in learning center, as assigned by special education teacher	Small groups in learning center, as assigned by special education teacher	Small groups in learning center, as assigned by special education teacher	Small groups in learning center, as assigned by special education teacher
2:30–2:45 p.m.	Write in communication journal.	Write in communication journal.	Write in communication journal.	Write in communication journal.	Write in communication journal.

FIGURE 4.3: Example paraeducator schedule.

Conclusion

When paraeducators work in general education classrooms, even for part of the day, the adult-to-student ratio changes, and this can lead to enhanced learning and more on-task behaviors. Paraeducator duties vary according to the student needs at a school site. Regardless of the situation, whether it's one-to-one, small-group, or general education, confidentiality is critical. Professional learning is key. Give paraeducators time to work with specialists and teachers to plan and learn from them. Take the time to give constructive feedback, efficiently manage resources, and provide assistance and direction when needed. This ensures paraeducators are viable, active members of your instructional team.

Paraeducators work alongside general and special education teachers as well as related services personnel. Chapter 5 explains the various related services personnel who will work alongside you to support the students at your site and strengthen your team.

FIVE

COLLABORATING WITH RELATED SERVICES PERSONNEL

The strength of the team is each individual member.
The strength of each member is the team.
—PHIL JACKSON

Builders typically have many subcontractors to assist with constructing a home. They subcontract electricians, plumbers, painters, and others who come together as a team to successfully build the house. Similarly, many related services personnel in special education come together to support students. As the leader, you must know who works on your campus and what services they provide. This chapter describes the various related services personnel who supply designated instructional services (speech and language therapists, occupational therapists, social workers, and many others) and their essential roles in school systems. Some of these individuals are school district employees while others provide their services to the district on a contractual basis. Check with your district office to know the status in your area. Each of these specialists is an important and critical team member who delivers services designed to support equity and equality. These services are invaluable in helping students succeed and achieve academically, socially, emotionally, physically, and mentally.

This chapter discusses the specific roles of the most prominent related services providers along with the additional considerations of including these providers as members of the team. Understanding how these professionals can support your school will help you decide how to encourage their participation.

Each related services specialist is an important and critical team member who delivers services designed to support equity and equality. These services are invaluable in helping students succeed and achieve academically, socially, emotionally, physically, and mentally.

Related Services Personnel Roles

Related services for individual students are documented on the IEP, which indicates when the service will begin, how often and for what amount of time the student will receive it, and where the student will receive it (IDEA, 2004). Always encourage service providers to work in the general education classroom. When specialists provide these services in the general education classroom, students are more easily able to generalize the skills or techniques they acquire. That is, we know from the research that when students are pulled out of their classrooms and receive instruction in segregated settings, they have difficulty generalizing what they learn back in the classroom environment (Packer et al., 2018).

Related services differ depending on the needs of the students. These specially trained professionals may include individuals who provide the following services.

- Counseling
- Interpreting services
- Occupational therapy
- Orientation and mobility services
- Physical therapy
- Psychological services
- Recreation therapy
- School nursing
- Speech and language pathology and audiology services
- Social work

Ideally, leaders would hire or contract these professionals for in-person learning. But in some cases, online therapy may make sense. International and rural schools have used online companies for many years. For example, Specialized Assessment and Consulting (https://specializedassessment.com) and Communication Therapy

Associates (https://comtherapy.com) have many related services personnel available for hire. They also have special education teachers. If you have only one student needing a particular therapy, it may be fiscally efficient to contact a reputable company of highly trained online therapists. I often refer schools to DotCom Therapy (www.dotcomtherapy.com). This company offers a unique service, as it can assess and provide therapy online. The company contracts with the school and assigns a therapist or project manager if more than one provider is necessary. This person becomes a member of the school community, participates in LST and IEP meetings via the internet when requested, and provides online data for students receiving services.

In addition to working with individual student cases, the related services personnel can collaborate to support overall school well-being. The following case study describes how one leader brought her team together to assist with student friendships and relationships.

> *The principal at Friendship School in Southern California began seeing an unwanted pattern of social problems during passing periods and lunch. Bullying, teasing, and foul language were increasing. The nurse's office had repeated referrals by students who experienced no medical issues. Some students appeared isolated; others seemed extremely shy. Attendance was down and days missed were up.*
>
> *As an administrator for fourteen years, the principal knew these behaviors would only increase further if a schoolwide intervention did not take place. She called a meeting of the related services personnel and administrators at the school. In attendance were the psychologist, school nurse, speech and language pathologist, counselor, behavior specialist, data specialist, and assistant principals. Because some of the observed behaviors were from special education students, the principal also invited the special education teachers to attend. The team reviewed both quantitative and qualitative data, and members brainstormed solutions. They decided to implement a schoolwide friendship program. Their goal was for every student to have at least one friend. They set a schoolwide goal for all students to properly engage with a peer, hoping to form friendships so no one felt afraid, unwanted, or alone.*
>
> *Teachers and staff discussed the schoolwide friendship program. Each teacher was asked to refer at least one student for the program. Each related services person also made a referral. The school experienced*

immediate success. For example, Juan, a ninth-grade student with a disability, was connected with peers who were honors students. The peers were members of the Best Buddies program (https://bestbuddies.org) at the school and were recruited to be peer buddies for Juan. They received service hours for participation in the friendship program. Previously, Juan would sit by himself and away from others at lunch because his classmates bullied him. The peers assigned themselves to a day of the week and met Juan at his fourth-period class, walked to lunch with him, and sat with him during lunch. Two of the peers enjoyed their time with Juan so much that they began riding bikes together before and after school. Another peer invited Juan to his birthday party. Juan had new friends.

In addition to this work with individuals, a few parents volunteered to offer students positive alternatives at passing period, nutrition break, and lunch. These were activities that were unavailable at any other time (for example, a yoga class, a hip-hop class, board games, and card games). Soon, referral rates dropped.

Additionally, one of the inclusion facilitators (a special education teacher) was assigned units to work with the Best Buddies program. The teacher met with the peer buddies and introduced peer-directed problem solving. Natural interaction became the norm, and the rates of bullying and teasing went down. Social networks of peers were visible during noninstructional time. The parent volunteers recruited more parents and alternated days and times. General education teachers witnessed the changes and referred other students to the program.

If you are interested in implementing a friendship club, a Best Buddies program, or something similar, I recommend the following six steps.

1. **Establish schoolwide coordination:** Appoint an employee to be the point of contact (coordinator) who organizes the program, calls meetings, follows through with program evaluation, and so on.
2. **Review referrals from teachers:** The coordinator may need to prioritize the referrals. If too many referrals come from certain teachers, ask the coordinator to contact you to meet and decide who will participate based on need.

3. **Collect baseline data to assess needs:** Progress monitoring is important. Work with the LST to establish baseline measurements with preassessments.
4. **Individualize social groups:** Be sure grade-level students are grouped together (so you don't have a first grader with a fifth grader), unless you are using a divided peer model.
5. **Assign and train peers to be social facilitators:** Be present at the trainings, and let the students know you are supportive and thankful for the volunteer work they are providing to the school.
6. **Implement and monitor the program:** Conduct postassessments and bring the LST together to review data and evaluate the overall program.

The friendship club is an example of what can occur schoolwide when all related services providers work with teachers at the school to make a difference. These professionals include the speech and language pathologist, the behavior specialist, the social worker, the counselor, the school psychologist, the occupational therapist, the physical therapist, the adapted physical education teacher, and the nurse.

Speech and Language Pathologist

Speech and language pathologists typically have a master's degree and are certified to work with students to support and enhance communication skills. The American Speech-Language-Hearing Association certification is voluntary; however, most will earn this certification alongside their graduate degree while in training. This certification is also available to educators in Canada.

A speech and language pathologist may work with individuals or small groups on intelligibility issues, such as voice and fluency disorders or articulation. Typically, the speech and language pathologist or a trained paraeducator can enforce and coach both receptive and expressive language skills, including social skills, sentence structure, and basic language processes.

Behavior Specialist

When writing IEPs, the IEP team must include a measurable IEP goal or behavior intervention plan if students exhibit any behavior that impedes their own learning or the learning of others. To fully address the behavior, a certified behavior analyst or behavior specialist might be necessary. The specialist can conduct the initial functional behavioral assessment, develop an appropriate behavior intervention plan, and give specific intervention strategies related to behavior.

Students need additional support to overcome behavior that impedes learning. It is common practice to hire a behavior specialist to provide highly structured therapeutic supports and personalized behavioral supports. The best scenario is to hire a behavior specialist to support any student in need of assistance. This means you should not hire the person with special education funds. If you hire a specialist with general funds, you can have the person conduct behavior observations and assessments and provide Tier 1, 2, or 3 interventions in addition to supporting specific behaviors noted in IEPs at your school.

The behavior specialist should be trained in how to write and implement a behavior intervention plan. A Board Certified Behavior Analyst or a Registered Behavior Technician has specific training in how to manage, support, and minimize behaviors. Specialized Education Services (https://sesischools.com) will come in with cost-effective programming for students at risk for out-of-district placements. Their programs are customized and flexible based on the student needs. The Specialized Education Services staff have experience in eighteen U.S. states (with over six hundred district partners) and a reputation of building districts' capacity to meet IDEA and free appropriate public education mandates.

School leaders are all too aware that problem behavior can negatively impact a student's ability to make progress on educational and functional goals. Knowing what triggers the behavior, knowing how the student reacts in different settings, and analyzing the functions the problem behavior serves for the student are valuable. Therefore, a functional behavioral assessment is important.

All behavior is communicative and functional in nature (Skinner et al., 1990). The basic functions served by behavior are *get* and *escape*. The student is interested in getting something or escaping from doing something. Students are usually after social attention, an object, or some type of activity. Or they want to escape from an assignment, social contact, or stimulation—sometimes known as the *aversive* (Skinner et al., 1990).

Three basic components (the ABCs) of observable behavior can be analyzed to explain the behavior: (1) antecedents, (2) the behavior, and (3) consequences. Often, the event just prior to the behavior (the antecedent or trigger) may be removed. With supports, the student can receive coaching in how to replace the undesirable behavior (behavior or response) with a desirable behavior. Or maybe the desired consequence (feedback) must change to interrupt the functional relationship to the behavior (the consequence—that is, what comes immediately after the behavior; Skinner et al., 1990).

Figure 5.1 features a graphic of the ABCs of functional analysis. The ABC model is the foundation for applied behavior analysis (Cummings, 2021). Note both the arrows point to the behavior.

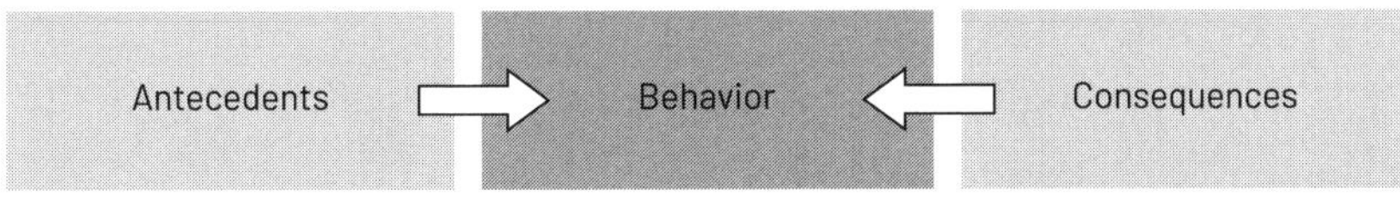

Source: Adapted from Skinner et al., 1990.

FIGURE 5.1: ABCs of functional analysis.

The following exchange that I witnessed between a special education teacher and a student illustrates the ABC model.

- **Antecedent:** The special education teacher said, "It is time to go to the library."
- **Behavior:** The student was doing an activity on the computer and very loudly responded, "No."
- **Consequence:** The teacher requested everyone line up and begin moving toward the library.

The student became outraged, and the teacher called the site administrator and behavior interventionist to assist. Upon analyzing the situation, the behavior interventionist used applied behavior analysis to help the student learn a more appropriate behavior.

- **Antecedent:** The following week, the teacher once again stated, "It is time to go to the library."
- **Behavior:** The student, having been prompted by the behavior interventionist, asked, "Can I have five more minutes?"
- **Consequence:** To this, the teacher responded, "Yes, the class will line up and go to the library in five minutes."

In five minutes, the student stood up and was the first in line for the library. The student had successfully replaced an inappropriate behavior with an appropriate behavior, which is what the concept of applied behavior analysis is all about. A behavior specialist using this approach can truly make a difference in student outcomes.

A behavior specialist will also help put into practice *positive verbal reinforcement*, which is the notion that positive behavior increases with positive attention, a powerful tool in shaping any student behavior (Mantasiah, Yusri, Sinring, & Aryani, 2021).

Positive behavior increases with positive attention (in fact, *any* behavior reinforced either positively or negatively will increase). Providing this attention is as simple as recognizing appropriate behavior and verbally reinforcing that behavior; teachers cannot control students' behavior, but they can reinforce it. Teachers, meanwhile, can control antecedents and consequences. Educators and family members can learn how to give a *prompt*, which, in this context, is additional assistance that will increase the likelihood of a positive response.

A behavior specialist can assist with determining verbal, physical, or visual prompts. The specialist can coach on how to use model, gestural, or positional prompts. Planning and training for all involved allow for the behavior to be adjusted. Systematic data collection and information gathering via the ABC process can minimize behaviors. Therefore, it is critical to have a trained behavior specialist available to support the teacher.

WATCH LISTEN ASK LEARN

Action for Administrators

In a case that goes to mediation or court, a judge may consider it a denial of a free appropriate public education if the school tolerated inappropriate behaviors without teaching appropriate replacement behaviors. A behavior specialist can teach both the teacher and the student how to replace the inappropriate behavior.

Social Worker

Social workers are skilled at communication between families and the school. They may assess the impact of home life on school performance and assist families with support strategies for mental, behavioral, and social issues. They can support families in need or in crisis situations by helping them find community supports. They make referrals for child protective services, mental health help, psychotherapy, or substance abuse treatment. Then they follow up with the various professionals, evaluating whether the treatment was successful. For example, in the case of substance abuse treatment, does the student have the appropriate amount of sobriety (as defined by the state, province, or country where the student lives) to return to school? Social workers also coordinate services related to probation and the juvenile court system. They work with the judge or referral agency from the courts or prison to assist with additional services as needed.

"A social worker is basically an encyclopedia of resources" (K. Parker, personal communication, December 8, 2021). Social workers research and provide resources for a student in need. If you are fortunate enough to have a social worker assigned to your school site, work with the person to learn the various services available in your community. If the school does not have an assigned social worker, reach out to the local medical facility to collaborate and coordinate needed services.

Let's review the case study for DeeDee, a high school student. DeeDee was assigned a social worker, who worked with DeeDee's mom and the school to get both DeeDee and her mom counseling services. The social worker also had DeeDee join an after-school tutoring program to reinforce her school learning and to facilitate homework completion while her mom was at work.

> *DeeDee was fully integrated into general education classes at her Oklahoma high school and received instruction in the core curriculum alongside her peers. She swam on the swim team and tried out for the cheerleading team. DeeDee's father was addicted to drugs and was diagnosed with bipolar disorder. Her mom had left her father when DeeDee was eight years old. The school provided counseling.*
>
> *DeeDee had a brother who was gifted. He was in fifth grade and read better than DeeDee did. It was not unusual for DeeDee to ask her brother what a word was or how to pronounce what a particular road sign said. DeeDee worked with an after-school tutor. Despite having a full-time job and attending night classes herself, DeeDee's mom read at least one magazine story with DeeDee each evening. This suggestion had come from the special education teacher at the school. DeeDee's high school had an open learning center model. This meant that whenever students with disabilities required extra help, they could give a ticket to the general education teacher and go to the learning center. DeeDee was eligible under the specific learning disability category and usually spent about three hours a week in the center.*
>
> *DeeDee saved audio recordings of her health and history classes to assist her in studying for the multiple-choice exams common to health and history. Her exams were read to her, and she recorded her answers as audio files. She knew a variety of strategies, including the paraphrasing strategy and the writing strategy from the University of Kansas (Deshler et al., 2009), and used them in the general education classroom. She applied these on a regular basis in English and*

> *political science. When she did not understand what was going on in the classroom, she used the SLANT strategy (described in chapter 6, page 128; Wulandari, 2014) and later asked her learning center teacher or paraeducator to help her. DeeDee often created her own mnemonics or sang songs to help her remember important details and concepts. She carried a calculator with her to mathematics class.*
>
> *DeeDee continued to have low reading abilities; however, she was very social and enjoyed being in the mainstream of the high school. She was getting passing grades in all her classes. The related services she received helped her be successful.*

As indicated in the case study, the learning strategies of paraphrasing, writing, and SLANT were vital tools for DeeDee's success. The University of Kansas has designed a series of strategies and routines for grades 4–12. The paraphrasing and writing strategies fall under the *strategic instruction model*, an umbrella term that describes content enhancement strategies (teacher focused) and learning strategies (student specific; Deshler et al., 2009). The work represents over forty years of research. For example, DeeDee learned the *RAP* acronym for paraphrasing: *read* the paragraph, *ask* yourself what the main idea and supporting details are, and *put* those into your own words (Schumaker, Denton, & Deshler, 1984). She could adjust this straightforward mnemonic and use it in all her content-area classes. The writing and SLANT strategies used similar mnemonics to focus her executive function and encourage learning.

Counselor

"School counselors are advocates, leaders, collaborators, and consultants who create systemic change by providing equitable educational access and success by connecting their school counseling programs to district mission and improvement" (American School Counselor Association, 2016, p. 1). Ask the counselor assigned to your school what their training is and what they can offer the school. Find out how you can collaborate with them as part of your leadership team.

Some counselors have expertise in specific areas, such as determining a clinical diagnosis, conducting group therapy for high-risk students, facilitating peer-support groups, and working with parents or specific populations (for example, pregnant teens or suicidal students). Whatever their specialization, insist counselors go into every classroom at the beginning of the year (or when they are hired, if that occurs midyear), as you want the students to know who they are. Insist that counselors be visible during recess and passing periods, at lunch, and before and after school.

"This way, if the counselor must talk to a student individually due to a crisis (for example, death in a family) or disruption, the student will know and trust the counselor" (K. Parker, personal communication, December 8, 2021).

The school counselor can also work individually with students to establish systems that can be used both at home and at school. For example, a counselor might help a student with autism write a social story. A *social story* is written from the perspective of the person with autism and can include supports for navigating socially (Gray, 2022). The student can use an assortment of formats—including text, pictures with words, audio, video, photos, or slides—to create the story. Then the student can use the social story at school and at home. Social stories can include social scripts to give the student ideas for conversation starters, responses to questions, or even appropriate phrases to change the topic of conversation. The script gives individuals the language they need to participate appropriately in an identified social situation.

Many high school counselors hold group meetings to teach parents how to advise their children as they move toward higher education, whether that's community college or a four-year institution. For example, students with a current IEP can receive the accommodations in college; however, they must ask for the services and know how to advocate for themselves. Counselors can coach parents in methods for supporting their teens as they move into the adult world.

Often, counselors of large comprehensive schools serve as the administrative designee at IEP meetings. This means they need to know and understand all school resources and placements so as to not cause concerns that might lead to litigation. Counselors are also typically the case carrier for all Section 504 plans. Their role includes ensuring 504 plan implementation and compliance and monitoring accommodation implementation to ensure needs are met.

Elementary school counselors go into the classroom and conduct lessons on social and coping skills, including how to be a friend, how to share, and how to relax when anxious. Counselors can give guidance or model for teachers how to conduct restorative justice circles. *Restorative justice practice* is a relational theory designed to bring students together to restore relationships (Parker & Bickmore, 2021). The idea is that while sitting in a circle and looking at each other, students have a safe place to listen to and talk through potential issues (if the circle is used proactively) or discuss all angles of an event (if the circle is used reactively). Many schools begin the day or end the day with restorative justice circles.

School counselors are crucial to students' making the connection between comprehensive planning and postsecondary decisions. They can assist parents and students with disabilities with relevant tools and online websites and programs (for example, AVID [www.avid.org] and Naviance [https://naviance.com]) that help students navigate their futures and explore occupations. Using resources like personality assessments, ready-to-use college-planning tools, and specific user-friendly websites, school counselors provide support and expertise.

They use inventories and assessments (such as College Board and ACT) and share excellent interactive tools and links to explore and guide student planning. Whether students choose to attend a vocational school, a community college, or a traditional four-year university, they need to know how to search for the best fit for their individual goals and needs.

Most counselors have an advanced degree in counseling, and in many states, they are required to teach prior to obtaining their pupil personnel services credential or certification. All school counselors are familiar with and required to follow the American School Counselor Association's (2016) ethical standards. You can expect the counselor to treat all students with dignity and respect and to maintain confidentiality. They will be trained in the Family Educational Rights and Privacy Act (FERPA, 1974). They will help you promote and maintain a safe learning environment for all involved at the school.

School Psychologist

The primary person trained to conduct standardized assessments is the psychologist. The National Association of School Psychologists (NASP; https://nasponline.org) provides guidance for the skill set of school psychologists. Many are certified by the National School Psychology Certification Board (https://nasponline.org/standards-and-certification/national-certification).

Trained psychologists are qualified to evaluate psychological and cognitive abilities, and they may also do a comprehensive evaluation of academics and social, emotional, physical, and mental health. NASP (n.d.) indicates school psychologists are direct service providers who give intervention support to students, consulting with families, educators, and other service providers. School psychologists help schools improve academic achievement; promote positive behavior and mental health; support diverse learners; create safe, positive school climates; and strengthen family-school partnerships. Furthermore, NASP (n.d.) shares that highly skilled school psychologists can improve schoolwide assessment and accountability and monitor individual student progress in academics and behavior.

Ask school psychologists how they can support your school and what level of participation they can have. This will be based on their contract. Are they at your school every day or just a few days a week or month? Do they want to just do the diagnosis and share these details at the IEP meeting? Or do they want to be the primary point person to coordinate IEP meetings?

Occupational Therapist

Occupational therapists support students' use of upper extremities and fine motor abilities. They help students develop muscle memory and sensory feedback. The occupational therapist will work with the student to improve things needed to perform everyday tasks, such as coloring, handwriting, word processing, or cutting. If specific equipment is necessary, occupational therapists will train students and parents on how to use it. Their primary role is to help students take part in all components of school: classrooms, sports, and activities based on the students' individual potential and unique characteristics.

An *occupational therapy assistant* is a paraeducator who is specifically trained to help students do the various exercises and activities that the occupational therapist designs specially for them.

Physical Therapist

The physical therapist assesses and supports the use of lower extremities and large muscles. Students' motor-ability or motor-skill level can be improved with physical therapy. Physical therapists consult with the LST, parents, and students to understand students' physical condition and any symptoms. After developing and implementing a treatment plan, the physical therapist can work with the family and student to determine whether full restoration of the motor abilities is possible. Physical therapists assess needs and determine the amount of time each individual student requires for muscle manipulation and movement. If necessary, they teach students and parents how to use their specific exercise techniques to provide proper stimulation. If the student needs to use equipment, such as a walker or wheelchair, the physical therapist will show the student proper form for use of the equipment.

Adapted Physical Education Teacher

The adapted physical education teacher coaches students with disabilities during physical education and activities that involve gross motor skills. These teachers are experts in creating accommodations so students can participate in physical education, and they can create various exercises necessary to contribute to students' well-being. It is important that students participate in physical activities at school, and the adapted physical education teacher can create sets of exercises that will lead to the goal of participation.

Nurse

The nurse or health assistant completes vision and hearing screenings. When students require medication, the nurse monitors prescription medicines and works with you and the IEP teams to establish times and locations for students to take their medicines. If students use prosthetic or adaptive devices, the nurse can check the function of these devices and clarify procedures for cleaning them.

Related Services Personnel as Members of the Team

As a leader, you have a great deal of power to ensure that related services personnel feel like true members of the school community, even if they are not full-time employees of the school or district. Just saying they are members is a start, but it's not sufficient. These essential professionals must feel like leaders, teachers, and students value their contributions and honor their expertise. Leaders can make this happen by ensuring that related services personnel have a place on the LST (and the IEP team) when an individual student needs their services, and by building relationships with these personnel. Related services personnel are also vital team members when it comes to extended-school-year services, transition services, and assistive technology.

Related Services Personnel's Input on the LST

All certified related services personnel receive extensive training. When appropriate, invite them to attend LST meetings to provide input and brainstorm support strategies. Having a related services person's expertise on specific strategies directly connected to the IEP goals can be extremely positive for the student with a disability. Curriculum planning is one process in which related services personnel are invaluable. The curriculum-planning form in figure 5.2 uses the tenets of choice theory to assist LST members in determining what types of accommodations the student needs in order to be included in general education.

In his book *The Quality School: Managing Students Without Coercion*, psychiatrist William Glasser (1993) introduces the concept of *choice theory*, which is the notion that educators cannot make students participate or join a group—or do anything, for that matter! But we can influence students to do things that lead to better behavior and increased learning. Glasser (1993) purports that teachers must create an interesting school environment to satisfy students' needs. He concludes that we should view his work not as a system but as a starting point to design a classroom discipline progression that works for the teacher. After hearing him speak earlier in my career, I synthesized his ideas and created the form in figure 5.2, which I have used in my work with great success.

What is everybody doing?

____

____

____

Can _______________ participate just like everyone else?

Yes? Then go have fun!	No? What can we do to include _______________ ?
Can we give _______________ some help from friends? From whom? _______________	Can an adult help _______________ ? Who? _______________

Can _______________ use different materials?

How can they be used?

____

____

____

What can _______________ do that is related to what the class is doing?

____

____

____

Source: Adapted from Glasser, 1993.

FIGURE 5.2: Curriculum-planning form.

*Visit **go.SolutionTree.com/specialneeds** for a free reproducible version of this figure.*

In planning lessons with the LST, the related services person can think about the student and the services needed to fill in the form. A key question the related services person will ask is, "What is everybody else doing?" If the related services person determines that the student can do the same thing, that means the rest of the form does not need to be completed (go have fun!). However, if the student cannot do what everyone else is doing, then related services personnel help teachers move through the form and determine how the student can participate. As the teachers work through the curriculum-planning form, the materials and activities section frequently puzzles them, but the related services personnel can often provide suggestions.

For example, when the team is making decisions about different materials, the occupational therapist might suggest a pencil grip. The speech and language pathologist could suggest a voice reader. Each student is an individual, and it is important to use this form specifically for one student at a time. Thus, the form has places where the LST can put in the student's name—for example, Can *Belinda* use different materials? How can they be used? The spot where the form asks what the student can do that is related to what the class is doing is a perfect place for related services personnel to provide strategies, activities, and materials.

The following case study describes another example of how an LST solved an issue with the help of related services personnel.

> *Tamika was a student with diabetes who received services under Section 504. She had been earning straight As, but during the first reporting period in ninth grade, her grades in every class dropped substantially, and her attendance was very low. Two of her teachers referred her to the LST, and the team tried several interventions. At the end of the second reporting period, her grades had not improved. The principal asked all the related services personnel to join the LST meeting where the team would discuss Tamika (for the second time). No one seemed to know what had happened. The team conducted a comprehensive review of her file. During the brainstorming session, the school counselor suggested she talk to Tamika privately.*
>
> *Tamika had missed many days of school and now had Fs in all her classes. The school counselor and principal called Tamika's parents and drove to her home. Tamika's parents were very discouraged when they learned she had been ditching school. The counselor asked her where she went during the school day. Tamika shared that she just sat in her room at home all day. Her parents worked and had not realized this was happening.*
>
> *The counselor asked her why she had not been attending school. Tamika got very upset and stated, "Everyone makes fun of me." The counselor asked her to give an example. She told the principal and the counselor that the last time she was on campus, she wet her pants in third period because she could not recall that class's bathroom policy. In frustration and between tears, she stated one class had a bathroom pass, another had a bathroom sign-out sheet, and a third had bathroom tickets. She just could not remember which class she was in, so she tried to hold it. Unfortunately, she soiled her clothes.*

She was so embarrassed she left school. In her quest to follow the rules, she wet her pants. She perceived the students would make fun of her, so she did not return.

The LST members met again and debriefed. They discussed that students with diabetes need to use the restroom very frequently. The team had to come up with an appropriate plan. If the team developed a policy that said Tamika could go to the restroom anytime, it might make her feel singled out and reluctant to return. Instead of creating such a policy, the team developed a schoolwide system for using the restroom. Anytime any student had to go to the restroom, that student merely had to sign out, walk to the restroom, and sign back in upon their return. The team developed a sign-out sheet that every classroom would use.

The principal and counselor visited Tamika a second time (at home) and shared the new plan. The next day, she was in school. At the end of the third reporting period, her grades were steady and climbing.

Tamika was fortunate to have a caring group of adults who met and specifically discussed her situation. She was fortunate the related services persons were at the meeting and a trained school counselor went with the principal to talk to her at home. And, notably, the counselor was able to connect with her personally and gain her trust in order to get her to tell the real story, which could not have been easy to talk about with an adult. The system established for all students hugely benefited Tamika. It also benefited other students. Furthermore, the learning services team members realized they needed other schoolwide systems.

Relationship Building With Related Services Personnel

It is not enough to just say the related services personnel are members of the team; everyone needs to believe that they can contribute and that their voice counts. This means that, as a leader, you need to meet with the personnel. Due to the variety of schedules and the fact that some are not full-time school employees (they may be contracted), it will take time. You may need to schedule individual meetings. You may need to coordinate LST meetings so they align with times when most of the related services persons are on campus.

Envisioning inclusive services involves making sure all members of your team are aware of the focus. You can animate the vision by enlisting the ideas, views, and suggestions of the related services personnel. It's necessary to get beyond going through the motions: "To make extraordinary things happen . . . you have to go beyond reason, engaging the hearts as well as the minds of your constituents" (Kouzes & Posner, 2017, p. 119). This begins with discussing and understanding where the individual is. Talk about what is unique about the school, and help the related services personnel see their value and feel as if they are making an extraordinary difference. You can do this by speaking genuinely, practicing positive communication, and sharing your passion and emotions (Kouzes & Posner, 2017). In turn, those extraordinary differences will appear. When they do, take note and provide a compliment. Let the related specialists know you recognize their worth. Trust makes an important difference in feelings of worth.

Action for Administrators

Related services personnel are key members of your staff. Help them feel valued by making sure they have a place to work and a box in the mailroom. When you give small holiday gifts, be sure they are included. If you do something special for Day of the Educator, include them! This sounds so simple, yet leaders often forget these services personnel.

A key way leaders lead is to model learning. As you converse with the related services personnel, take note of their expertise, their strengths, and the types of services they can provide the students and teachers at your school. As you listen, consider innovative ways you can add the new learning to your toolbox. Create value from the relationships.

Communication among leaders, teachers, paraeducators, related services personnel, and parents needs to be strong and consistent to ensure student success. The LST is a key component of this communication. The use of established systems and forms will keep things on track. The more aware you are of what is taking place, the easier it will be to fine-tune communication among the team. The goal is to prevent overlap or contradictory supports and programming from occurring. This can impact student success and parent confidence in the school and the whole community support system.

Extended-School-Year Services

Annually, every student with a disability must be considered for *extended-school-year services*, which are services that extend beyond the normal school year at no cost to the student's parents and in accordance with the student's IEP (IDEA, 2004). The regulation is often misunderstood and confused with summer school (Barnard-Brak & Stevens, 2020). If a student's IEP team determines on an individual basis that services are necessary for the provision of a free appropriate public education, the student must receive extended-school-year services. As the leader, you must be knowledgeable of and comply with the school district's policies and procedures. While you are evaluating an individual case with the IEP team, consider whether the benefits the student gained during the school year will be lost with significant breaks (for example, two months for summer vacation). If you and the team believe that not providing an educational program over the summer would significantly jeopardize the student's learning growth, then extended-school-year services are necessary (Weatherly, 2021). It is important to prevent regression and help students continue to move forward and make progress on IEP goals.

To fully develop the program for the student, you should make extended-school-year service decisions early (by January or February for the upcoming summer). This allows you time to allocate or hire the appropriate staff, remembering that services cannot be denied due to lack of funding (Bateman, 2015). Developing an early extended-school-year program for all your school or district's students on IEPs will give you time to make sure adequate funding and resources are available and scheduled appropriately. However, it is critical to realize parents can reject extended-school-year services, as they are not obligated to send a child to summer school.

Transition Services

IDEA (2004) mandates setting postsecondary goals for each student with an IEP (based on appropriate transition assessments), and services needed to reach the goals provided, by the time the student turns sixteen. This means determining goals ranging from possible employment to training, education (including courses of study), and, when appropriate, independent living skills. Check with your state, as some states have established an earlier date of implementation. This transition plan must be updated each year after the initial plan is written (IDEA, 2004). This may mean administering a career interest inventory or a college and career planning program. See My Next Move (www.mynextmove.org), Naviance (https://naviance.com), or CareerOneStop (www.careeronestop.org) for samples.

As indicated elsewhere, society doesn't have separate banks for students with disabilities, and it doesn't have separate stores. We leaders want all students to live in society as is appropriate for them. Transition services are about planning for inclusion in society.

Transition services are also necessary anytime a student moves from a different school. This includes students transferring between schools within a district as well as students coming into a district for the first time. An example of how litigation can occur when transition services are not provided appears in *R. E. B. v. Hawai'i Department of Education* (2017). The Hawai'i Department of Education violated IDEA when it failed to ensure that the appropriate IEP-incorporated services were delivered to a student with autism to ease the student's transition from a private school to a public school program. There should have been a plan to assist the student in gradually acclimating to the new school.

Assistive Technology

Educational consultant Paula Frederica Hunt (2021) purports that, around the globe, lack of assistive technology is a primary barrier to inclusive services. According to section 602 of IDEA (2004), the definition of *assistive technology device* is "any item, piece of equipment, or product system, whether acquired commercially off the shelf, modified, or customized, that is used to increase, maintain, or improve functional capabilities" of a student with a disability. In turn, *assistive technology services* are services that help students with disabilities choose, acquire, or use an assistive technology device. Assistive technology may be necessary if the IEP team determines that the current placement is appropriate but a student's disability impacts the student's ability to be successful in that environment.

The IEP team should consider the area of need alongside the necessary type of technology. Various types of assistive technology typically carry the terms *low-*, *mid-*, and *high-tech*. Low-tech assistive technology is easy to use, and most schools have the material already. Mid-tech assistive technology generally requires batteries or a plug and requires some maintenance or upkeep. High-tech assistive technology requires specialized training, and it requires high maintenance as well as considerable expense. Figure 5.3 provides a visual comparison of each type and the areas of need that might be connected to the various assistive technologies.

In the United States, every IEP team must assess for assistive technology. As a leader, you must know what assistive technology devices and tools are available and what funds you can access to purchase the necessary tools and devices that will allow students to appropriately access the environment. Students may enter the school already

Area of Need	Low-Tech Assistive Technology	Mid-Tech Assistive Technology	High-Tech Assistive Technology
Writing	Slant board (clipboard)	Assistive writing device (such as an alternative keyboard)	Specialized software
Reading	Book stand	Auditory books	Reader software
Educational access	Preferential seating	Voice output software	Head tracker
Communication	Single switch (a communicator such as a BIGmack switch)	Augmentative or alternative communication device (such as a Go Talk)	High-level augmentative or alternative communication device (such as a speech tablet or a speech watch)
Hearing	Augmentative or alternative communication	Amplifier	Hearing aid
Vision	Large print	Magnifier	Braille
Physical access	Walking stick	Specialized seating	Power chair

FIGURE 5.3: Levels of assistive technology.

using an assistive device. It is vital that young students learn to use and interact with assistive technology as much as possible to ensure the assistive technology use is instinctive and does not create an additional barrier to inclusive services (Tamakloe, 2020).

The following websites provide excellent examples of how to use assistive technology.

- Boardmaker (https://goboardmaker.com)
- Don Johnston (https://learningtools.donjohnston.com)
- AbleNet (www.ablenetinc.com)
- Proloquo2Go (www.assistiveware.com/products/proloquo2go)

Conclusion

Related services personnel are vital members of the LST. It is the leader's responsibility to include them in the culture of the school by getting to know their strengths and what they can offer. Each specialist is highly talented. Ask the specialists to support the LST in various ways, including by making suggestions for the curriculum-planning form.

Part 3 of this book starts off with chapter 6. This chapter adds to your repertoire some ways that you can ensure you include all students as you create your master schedule and provide for extended-school-year, transition, and assistive technology services. It also offers suggestions for how to work with teachers who might be trying to undermine progress toward inclusive practices.

Part 3

HOW TO PROGRESS TOWARD SCHOOLWIDE IMPLEMENTATION OF SUPPORT FOR ALL

SIX

ENSURING THAT INCLUSIVE EDUCATION IS EQUITABLE EDUCATION: ALL MEANS *ALL*

The best way to build trust with another person is to make a commitment and keep it.

—STEPHEN R. COVEY

Making a commitment to inclusive education means consistently valuing all students—and showing it. It means understanding the laws, processes, personnel, and systems of special education that allow students to be included. Parts 1 and 2 of this book have helped prepare you to do that. Now it's time to begin to put those pieces together.

Equity and inclusion are intertwined; this book has hopefully made a good case for that. When educators, students, parents, and community leaders see you are committed to equity for all, they will trust you to move the school (or district) forward. In this process of moving forward, centering equity and inclusion is essential to effectively implement the eleven steps for establishing an inclusive school (chapter 7, page 145). This chapter discusses how to center inclusion and equity. While they are weighty topics with entire books devoted to them, discussion here is warranted if you are committing to inclusion.

School leaders are responsible for creating the climate at their schools. When you talk about equity and inclusion daily, those ideas will permeate your school climate. But talking about them isn't enough; inclusion won't truly be part of the climate unless you are intentional about it day in and day out. Some ways you can help ensure you are centering inclusion and equity include keeping them in mind while creating the master schedule, prioritizing social inclusion during both instructional time and noninstructional time, staying on top of progress monitoring, navigating the possible negative attitudes among staff, engaging with parents of students with disabilities, addressing the needs of gifted and talented and twice-exceptional students, and aligning inclusion with other initiatives.

When you talk about equity and inclusion daily, those ideas will permeate your school climate. But talking about them isn't enough; inclusion won't truly be part of the climate unless you are intentional about it day in and day out.

The Master Schedule and Equity

The master schedule is critical for delivering curriculum for every school. It's a juggling act to determine when things will occur, who will teach what classes, and how athletics, music, the arts, the science fair, and numerous other events and clubs will fit into one calendar and one schedule. When developing the master schedule, consult with the LST, and place the students with disabilities in classes or periods first (schedule them before athletics and the arts). This may seem different from or even go against what you learned in administration courses or educational leadership trainings. But I firmly believe that if you are serious about establishing an inclusive school, it begins with the master schedule. Starting here allows you to build on the notion that equality and equity are different. When everyone receives the same schedule, resources, and accommodations, you create equality. However, equity recognizes that every student has different needs and situations that cause you to allocate the exact resources or class time slots to reach an equal outcome for all.

Second, take into consideration co-teaching opportunities, and make sure planning time is available for co-teaching teams (meaning the co-teaching planning is scheduled at the same time). If an IEP says a student with a disability needs to be in a co-taught algebra class, and you have only two sections, that student needs to be placed first and the co-teachers identified. Do not place more than 20 percent of students with disabilities in any one classroom.

Third, schedule your intervention providers, related services personnel, and paraeducators. When possible, schedule these professionals in general education classrooms instead of in segregated environments. If the speech and language therapist is on campus only two days a week, the students with speech and language on their IEPs need scheduled time on those two days. Scheduling can get tricky when you have paraeducators with different but equivalent full-time assignments from human resources.

Plan to create the schedule in the spring of the prior year. Talk to your feeder schools and find out how many students with IEPs will transition to your school and what their IEP services will look like.

When possible, schedule meetings ahead of time. Add LST and faculty meetings to the master schedule. Consider placeholder times for IEPs, knowing you will need to include them eventually. Do you need specific intervention time in the schedule for Tier 1, 2, or 3 of MTSS? Are you planning professional learning activities or trainings (learning walks, book club, movie club, research club, and so on)? They need time slots allocated to them as well. At the beginning of the year, take time to review the schedule with all teachers and specialists to make sure, ahead of time, that it is free of conflicts.

Social Inclusion

The best real-life practicum for college, career, and a successful adult life is social inclusion (Steinbrenner & Watson, 2015). Furthermore, if it is important for students with disabilities to function in society, at parties, while shopping, at sporting events, and in all the other places and situations to live full lives, we must give them time while in school to be with general education students. This is a critical philosophy of social inclusion (Dillenburger, McKerr, Jordan, Devine, & Keenan, 2015). Sadly, the research shows students with learning disabilities and behavior disorders are often socially excluded (Krull, Wilbert, & Hennemann, 2014). When contemplating social inclusion, educators should consider both instructional and noninstructional time.

Instructional Time

Having a physical seat allows the student a place in the general education classroom. However, social inclusion is what opens the door for interaction with peers, feelings of belonging, and chances to have friends and be part of a learning community (Burke & Karge, 2022). To enhance social inclusion and build on learning outcomes for all students with disabilities, educators need to coordinate mixed-ability groups and facilitate engagement during instructional time (Dillenburger et al., 2015). Ask all educators at the school to include grouping activities in their teaching to encourage social inclusion. For example, team-pair-solo (Karge, 2014) is a strategy that allows for a student with a disability to work with a team of four students on an assignment, pair with one team member to do the same activity, and, finally, work solo on the assignment. This gives students with disabilities two opportunities to go over the assignment, see how others do it, and then work on their own. It also encourages social inclusion, as the students must interact and exchange information.

The general education teachers I work with consistently mention that students who act out pose a key challenge as they integrate and help students with social inclusion. Something we have found successful is to teach students with a disability the *sit* up, *lean* forward, *activate* thinking, *note* key ideas, and *track* the talker (*SLANT*) strategy (Wulandari, 2014). The idea is that students use SLANT if they don't understand what is going on. This way, they are not acting out, and they have something to do. Then, later, they can ask the teacher to explain what was going on or to share the information in a way they will understand. The version of SLANT we use is the same one that doctoral student Sintia Ayu Wulandari (2014) used in her work with high school students for her dissertation. The five steps in SLANT include the following.

1. **Sit up straight:** When students are confused, anxious, or not sure what to do during teacher-directed instruction or group time, they often slouch or put their heads on their desks. When they do this, the classroom teacher may incorrectly assume that they are misbehaving. To avoid this perception, students with disabilities can react to their feelings by sitting up straight. This means they put their bottom in the chair, back against the chair, and feet on the floor.
2. **Lean forward:** When students are sitting up straight and lean forward just a little bit, it appears they are paying attention. In actuality, students have told me that when they lean forward, they do tend to pay better attention and try to figure out what is going on.
3. **Activate your thinking:** Students are encouraged to focus on thinking about what the teacher or their peers are saying.
4. **Note key ideas:** Hand in hand with *activate your thinking* is to note key ideas. This is a cue to students to remember (or take notes on) the big ideas (the items that seem the most important).
5. **Track the talker:** In the United States, it is polite to look at the person who is speaking. In this final step, students should look at and track the teacher or peer who is speaking (move their head back and forth).

Inclusion facilitators (special education teachers, counselors, and so on) will need to teach social skills. Figure 6.1 is a sample of a social skills session that I created based on the work of my doctoral student Elizabeth Ann Burke (2021).

Description	Skill Development
Students take turns sharing one item; it can be something from the current or previous day. Students label emotions (for example, "Today, I was frustrated when my mom was rushing me this morning").	Students practice speaking and listening skills. Students show that they're thinking of others by turning their body toward the speaker and keeping their eyes on the speaker. Students keep the spotlight on the speaker (listening without commenting). Eventually, students will practice *reflecting and mirroring*—thinking about what was shared and sharing back, such as, "Sounds like you were upset when you didn't get to go." Students are encouraged to share experiences and relate comments outside of group time or during social time at the end of the session.

Source: Adapted from Burke, 2021.

FIGURE 6.1: Sample social skills session.

Noninstructional Time

A typical day at school means repeated social navigation, and this can be exhausting for students with disabilities. Interacting with the teacher, working in groups with peers, and sharing space are examples of common classroom scenarios where social navigation is important. Instructional time like this has its challenges, but the social rules are predictable and navigable. On the other hand, noninstructional time, which includes the unstructured times of recess, passing periods, lunchtime, and assemblies, can cause multiple difficulties for students with disabilities as they don't always know how to navigate the social interactions they may encounter. Typically, these noninstructional times consist of large unstructured areas—hallways, auditoriums, lunchrooms, and so on. These provide space where students can roam around, engage in group games without explicit rules, and use social language. How overwhelming!

Understand that implicit or unstated social rules make a hidden curriculum for many students with disabilities, especially students with autism or challenges related to executive function or attention. Students who violate these rules may be teased, bullied, or ostracized. This may result in inappropriate behavior. These are times the administrator can step in and lead in a supportive way.

Establishing schoolwide rules and policies supports all students and helps everyone know what is expected. When dealing with challenges related to social skills and responding to overwhelming or stressful situations, students with disabilities find the social-behavior learning strategy *SODA* (*stop*, *observe*, *deliberate*, *act*) useful (Hurlbutt-Eastman & O'Malley, 2015). This strategy consists of the following steps.

1. **Stop:** Students find a place to stand to observe and ultimately learn about the social situation before jumping in. They use self-questioning to decide what to do when they encounter a challenging situation. This self-questioning consists of a series of questions that helps them develop an organizational schema for the setting (that is, "Where should I go to observe? What is the lunchroom arrangement?").
2. **Observe:** The primary purpose of this step is to identify what others are doing. Students observe the various social cues other students are using in the setting. They listen to what people are talking about and watch what other students are doing in the situation. Hearing various conversations can help students understand what behavior is appropriate in this setting. Viewing students carrying lunch trays and sitting down to eat or watching how other students ask to join a game can preteach the appropriate behavior. When teaching this step, make sure students understand they should not be eavesdropping on private conversations or staring in such a way that someone might see them as suspiciously loitering.
3. **Deliberate:** Students ask themselves the question, "What do I need to do to successfully participate in this setting?" This encourages them to identify anything that might be problematic and figure out ahead of time what strategies they can use to address it.
4. **Act:** During the final step, students use the ideas from the *deliberate* step and join the activity.

The process of SODA is designed to help the student know how to interact with others appropriately. When administrators or leaders observes a challenging social navigation situation, they can direct the student to use SODA. Remember, too much adult control can be a deterrent for both the student and their peers. Too much adult control can inhibit learning and interactions. It is important to facilitate the use of SODA, step back, and allow the students to interact. Leaders can introduce SODA schoolwide as a strategy for solving problems and a tool for interpreting behavior. Educators can also use it in individual classrooms, at a schoolwide assembly, and in various other learning environments. If educators effectively teach the meaning of the acronym, they can help minimize many situations and diminish behaviors that might otherwise escalate.

Action for Administrators

Consider implementing schoolwide systems such as the SODA strategy to help all students with social interactions and self-efficacy. Brainstorm with your staff which schoolwide systems will work best at your site.

Progress Monitoring and Data

I have discussed data elsewhere in this text. However, using data to monitor student progress warrants further conversation. If students are not making progress, something needs to change. Your role as a leader includes maintaining progress monitoring for every student at the school site (or district if you are a district-level administrator). Yes, IEPs require annual review, but waiting an entire year to view progress is inefficient. The data days suggested in chapter 2 (page 44) are a good opportunity to check in on students.

Data build efficacy. When educators see students making academic progress and improving behavior, it is highly motivational (Knight, 2022). Development of a strong MTSS for academics, behavior, and mental health is key to progress monitoring, as was covered in chapter 2 (page 35). If the data are not reviewed in a consistent, strategic manner, the value of the MTSS tiers goes unnoticed as students can fall through the cracks. Successful student outcomes tie directly to progress monitoring of your multitiered system of support. The following examples of progress monitoring all come from schools I have worked with.

- A preschool director in Eastern Europe has a cohesive approach for individualization for every student. Every other week when the early learner teachers send their reports to parents, they also send the reports to the director. The director looks at each one, and if there are any indications of below-average performance, a meeting takes place in which the teacher and director make suggestions for intervention. Early intervention is such a critical component, and every leader should be able to evaluate and know where every student is on the learning continuum.

- A principal at an elementary school in Los Angeles holds team meetings every Monday morning. These meetings include the administration team (principal, assistant principal, counselor, and testing coordinator). The purpose of the meetings is to review student data at the school. The team members look at one class per week, and if they receive a special request of a student with a significant dip in scores, they analyze those data.
- At a middle school in Africa, the head of the school meets with the LST coordinator and the assistant principals monthly. They review the student standardized assessments in alphabetical order. The week prior to their meeting, team members provide the school staff with the names of the students to be reviewed and ask the staff for formative and summative assessments from any subject area, before- or after-school clubs, and sports activities. This comprehensive review continues all school year. Typically, each student at the school is reviewed at least four times a year.
- A high school in Canada has an assistant principal specifically designated to conduct progress monitoring of all students with disabilities at the school. This person is also the administrator designated to attend IEP meetings, make team decisions, and sign all IEPs. There are several ways to track and monitor student services and progress online; this high school uses the Brolly program (https://brollyed.com). Brolly is an easy way to track data with interactive data dashboards and a custom reporting center. The application has a strong progress-monitoring component to track all data that special education teachers and related services providers need to make informed decisions.

As leaders view data and see improvement, they can keep schools progressing by building momentum based on the smaller successes (individual student achievements) and the larger ones (successful schoolwide policies; Grissom et al., 2021). Professional learning administrator Nader I. Twal (2022) states, "Measure what you treasure" (p. 11). When they use data to measure inclusive services and supports, schools can begin to treasure the measured practices by celebrating the successes and focusing on future practices.

Educator Attitudes

Even when all the supports, tools, and strategies are in place, educator attitudes can create a negative vibe toward inclusive practices. People who don't believe in inclusion can bring others down. If you have persons like this on your staff, consider using the following analogy at your next faculty meeting: Think back on a time when you felt left out or excluded as a child or teen. Perhaps you were not invited to a party or you had to sit alone at lunch. How did that feel? Now contemplate a time when you felt included. Maybe you were in the school band, on a sports team, or part of the local scout troop. Maybe friends invited you to sit with them at lunch. How did it feel? When educators provide a safe place and positive attitudes toward students with disabilities, it allows the students to truly belong to the class and the school and to feel accepted.

School leaders are change agents. True implementation of inclusive practices comes when you shift the culture for all staff members through the support necessary to change how they view students with disabilities. Equity is key to the future of learning. Attitudes and beliefs of the staff are critical to make the change to equity. Effective leadership improves and sustains effective teaching and learning for all students (Karge, Stephens, & Abu Zaineh, 2019).

In the words of one superintendent:

> It is evident that successful inclusion programs exist because of the hard work put into them by school sites. First, teachers must be willing to allow for changes within their own teaching practices and classroom environment. Next, the administrators must create designs of positive inclusion models and work with teams to monitor the progress of the students. It is also vital to have constant evaluation of the model in place to address any concerns or problems that need to be addressed. Lastly, understand that parents are a valuable resource; they provide us with the whole picture and allow the school to witness the benefits of inclusion through their discussions and sharing within the community. (L. Davis, personal communication, December 7, 2021)

Helping general education teachers see that they are an important piece of the solution for supporting every student can be extremely effective. Figures 6.2 (page 134) and 6.3 (page 135) describe support processes for moving students from general education classrooms (where initial challenges were recognized) to additional supports designed to include the students and support their learning.

Charles Duhigg (2014) provides a strategy called the *golden rule of habit change* in his book *The Power of Habit*. He purports a habit-based philosophy used by the award-winning National Football League coach Tony Dungy. Duhigg (2014) says extinguishing a habit is not something people typically do with success; however, they can *change* the habit. The concept of the golden rule of habit change is to use the same cue, provide the same reward, but change the routine. In the football analogy he shares, he states Coach Dungy used the same cue (hut) and the same

<table>
<tr><td colspan="3">After parent and teacher collaboration has been implemented without significant improvement, the classroom teacher requests a meeting with the principal and special education teacher to review an individual student concern.</td><td rowspan="11">LST
Student's teachers
Special education teacher
Guidance counselor
Outside specialists
Principal</td></tr>
<tr><td colspan="3">The classroom teacher requests a parent conference to discuss concerns. (The special education teacher participates.)</td></tr>
<tr><td colspan="3">The classroom teacher implements strategies for improvement, documenting the interventions and recording progress for a minimum of four weeks.</td></tr>
<tr><td colspan="2">The concern warrants further intervention.</td><td>The concern does not warrant further intervention.</td></tr>
<tr><td colspan="3">A parent meeting is held to further discuss concerns and to develop a plan of action. The parent is requested to sign permission for observation or informal assessment conducted by International School of Florence professional staff. The LST may also recommend outside evaluation for related services (such as occupational therapy, physical therapy, speech therapy, and mental health services) at this meeting.</td></tr>
<tr><td colspan="2">The parent consents.</td><td>The parent chooses to withhold consent.</td></tr>
<tr><td colspan="2">The LST conducts observations and consultations, and records results.</td><td>The case is referred to International School of Florence administration for further action.</td></tr>
<tr><td colspan="2">Needs are identified.</td><td>No needs are identified.</td></tr>
<tr><td colspan="2">A recommendation for formal educational or psychological evaluation and medical diagnosis documentation is made. (The parent is given information on accessing evaluations.)</td><td>No further action is taken by the LST.</td></tr>
<tr><td colspan="2">Formal educational or psychological evaluation and medical diagnosis documentation are completed and shared with the International School of Florence.</td><td>The parent declines formal educational or psychological evaluation.</td></tr>
<tr><td>Services are warranted: The LST meets with the parent for consent to serve and proceeds with IEP referral procedures.</td><td>Intervention is unwarranted: The student remains in the general education program.</td><td>The case is referred to International School of Florence administration for further action.</td></tr>
</table>

Source: © 2019 International School of Florence. Adapted with permission.

FIGURE 6.2: Sample LST procedures from the International School of Florence.

The LST applies a strengths-based problem-solving process to address the intervention needs of students who are exhibiting significant difficulties in academics, behavior, social-emotional learning, or attendance. The LST stipulates a team approach that provides for greater cohesiveness, coordination, and instructional continuity and complements existing curriculum and instructional programs.

Procedures

1. A teacher, a parent, or both identify a significant concern or issue related to the student.
2. The referring teacher makes contact with the parent through a phone or personal conference to develop interventions to address the area of concern.
3. The referring teacher documents baseline data related to the concern as well as initial interventions and goals for improvement on the district intervention log.
4. The referring teacher reviews and documents progress of the student toward the improvement goal after an initial period of intervention.
5. If the student has made limited or no progress toward the goal based on gathered data, the referring teacher consults with the grade-level or department team and support personnel to obtain additional strategies or ideas. Then the referring teacher adjusts the intervention to help the student make more significant progress toward achieving the goal. The referring teacher documents the new strategies on the district intervention log and also records the date of the consultation on the log.
6. The referring teacher completes a written request for an LST meeting if the student continues to show little or no response to previous interventions. The request is submitted along with the district intervention log, which must show documentation of all interventions, data, and actions taken by the teacher.
7. The LST coordinator schedules an initial team meeting only after receipt of the fully completed written request and intervention log.
8. The LST meeting must include the following members.
    - Referring teacher
    - Teachers (all if possible; if not, the teachers of the classes the student is having challenges in)
    - Parent
    - Student
    - Other LST members
    - Coordinator, administrator, or both
    - Recorder
    - Counselor, psychologist, or social worker (optional based on the case)
    - Others as deemed appropriate
9. At the initial LST meeting, participants develop a holistic action plan, which addresses both the strengths and the concerns of the student. The team uses data to identify the primary area of concern and to develop a specific, goal-based action plan to address the concern. All stakeholders share responsibility for implementing the actions of the team. The plan should include school and home actions as well as specific interventions and short-term goals that identify how the success of the plan will be measured. A follow-up meeting is scheduled at the end of the initial meeting, allowing enough time between meetings for the implementation and evaluation of interventions agreed on by the student success team (approximately four to six weeks).
10. After a specified intervention period, the team reconvenes to review student outcomes based on data gathered as part of the agreed-on interventions. At the follow-up meeting, the team again makes a decision based on data. Every initial LST meeting requires the scheduling of a follow-up meeting to ensure accountability for actions agreed on by the team. At the follow-up meeting,

FIGURE 6.3: Sample districtwide LST procedures. continued →

participants review the student's progress toward the initial goals and provide any new information needed to address any continuing areas of concern. During this meeting, the team may ponder the following options.

- Close the case (the student has successfully met the goal).
- Adjust the LST plan to address current or new student concerns.
- Consider a referral to alternative programs or services.
- Consider a possible referral for special education services.

If the team suspects a possible disability, special education support staff should be invited to any follow-up meetings to assist the team in determining any need for a formal referral for special education consideration. The team may also determine that the student may potentially have a disability under Section 504 of the Rehabilitation Act of 1973. In this case, the team may need to schedule a 504 eligibility meeting.

11. LST coordinators, administrators, or both are responsible for tracking LST cases. Instructional coaches can be called on to support classroom instruction.

reward or goal (touchdown) while coaching, but he changed the routine. He taught his players new plays and new ways to run and catch the ball. He taught them new positions and new strategies (as cited in Duhigg, 2014).

Similarly, you can use the golden rule of habit change with your veteran teachers since we leaders know habits are difficult to change, and established systems are often comfortable for educators who might see inclusion as just one more initiative. These teachers might not take the philosophy seriously. So, keep the basic cues (the standards, the curriculum, and so on) and the reward (the goal of student progress, student outcomes, and student improvement). And change the routine by establishing a multitiered system of support and an LST and taking time to really support the students at the school who struggle, are diagnosed with a disability, or have second language issues.

Action for Administrators

Take time to think about your staff at your site, considering their attitudes and beliefs. What will it take to help them see the value of inclusive practices?

Engagement With Parents of Students With Disabilities

When leaders achieve sensitive and careful engagement with parents and caregivers, they can make equitable education a reality. Parents know their children better than anyone else does. Extending a collaborative hand to parents is key to sustaining quality relationships. As has been discussed throughout this book, parent involvement in the LST and IEP process and in special education services is critical. But for parents of students with disabilities, acceptance of the disability is sometimes hard to come by (Baugh, 2009). School leaders can fill a supportive and compassionate role here.

A period of time may pass before parents understand and accept their own children. Research shows that when parents first learn their child has a diagnosed disability, they often go through the same stages one goes through when losing a loved one (Fernańdez-Alcántara et al., 2016). These stages include different details. However, the series of simplistic stages that psychiatrist Elisabeth Kübler-Ross (1969) developed in her work with terminally ill people have been regularly applied to explain the process that families of children with disabilities go through in learning to accept their child. Researcher Manuel Fernańdez-Alcántara and his colleagues (2016) apply these stages to families of children with disabilities.

1. **Denial:** When in denial, parents try to understand the *why* (for example, "It is difficult to believe that a child with disabilities was born to *me*"). Fernańdez-Alcántara and colleagues (2016) recommend that leaders not pressure parents to make critical decisions about their children during this stage. Helping parents locate resources provides the beginning of a support system. One critical source of support is other parents of students with disabilities. For example, in California, the local community advisory committee meets periodically to establish a forum for parent involvement and to review all aspects of special education. For specific examples of what this looks like, see the Community Advisory Committee Guidelines (https://bit.ly/3v0k9Mg) or the Whittier Area Cooperative Special Education Program's website (www.wacsep.org/domain/58). Additionally, parent organizations exist for many disability areas. For example, the Learning Disabilities Association of America (https://ldaamerica.org) and the National Down Syndrome Society (https://ndss.org) advocate for and support individuals with disabilities and their families.

2. **Guilt:** Parents contemplate the reality of what they believe they are responsible for and must develop a sense of control. When working with parents who are clearly in this stage, show empathy and be a good listener. Parents need to think about and talk through their feelings in order to move into stage 3.
3. **Depression:** This stage is a common reaction to any loss—the feeling of defeat, limited strength, or both. People who work with parents of students with disabilities should help them develop supportive relationships with other such families in order to avoid any tendency toward isolation. Introduce parents to other parents in your school community, and have opportunities for them to talk. Host small parent groups for dialogue, and encourage all parents to attend parent-teacher association events.
4. **Anger:** As parents emerge from depression, they often feel very angry and frustrated. Sometimes they take these emotions out on the educators trying to assist them. This is a time when many legal issues arise. It is critical to allow upset parents time to express their emotions and concerns and to share their anger. Be a good listener and recognize that most anger can later be translated into positive energy.
5. **Anxiety:** At this stage, the reality of redefining and reprioritizing parental responsibilities sets in, which can feel overwhelming. This is a time to really make parents feel welcome by reminding them to strike a balance between family responsibility and care for a child with a disability. Parents are ready to listen and learn and will begin the long process of acceptance.
6. **Acceptance:** Parents come to value the masterpiece and the gift of raising a child with a disability. For many families, this becomes a time of reaching out to others and sharing their personal journeys. Sadly, not every family reaches this stage of peace.

Action for Administrators

Anger is the stage educators are often dealt, causing much frustration and angst. Help all school personnel involved realize it is part of the whole process of evolving. Take time to role-play and discuss how to listen and respond to angry parents to assist them through the grief process.

Psychology researchers Ingrid Rentinck, Marjolijn Ketelaar, Marian Jongmans, Eline Lindeman, and Jan Willem Gorter (2009) developed an assessment tool known as the *reaction to diagnosis interview* to investigate parental reactions following a diagnosis of cerebral palsy. This instrument is useful with any parent or any disability group to assess their grief stage. Understanding these stages can go a long way when building relationships with parents. Encouraging smiles, reassuring body language, and positive comments build trust and help families know you have their children's best interests at heart (Sears et al., 2021).

I encourage educators, as a call to action, to be aware of the support networks that are available in their area for the families they serve. Seek out and make connections with businesses, nonprofits, and other organizations willing to support families and students in your community. Advocate for community support.

Action for Administrators

Understand that sometimes parents of students with disabilities are experiencing various stages of grief. Treat these parents as you would someone who has experienced significant loss. Make time to listen to them and hear about their frustrations and challenges.

Gifted and Talented and Twice-Exceptional Students

Gifted and talented students do have needs that differ from those of their peers, and school leaders should think about the kinds of special services and supports that they can provide to respond to their gifts and talents. Inclusion means *all.* In their book *Exceptional Learners*, Daniel P. Hallahan, James M. Kauffman, and Paige C. Pullen (2019) write at great length about the nature of giftedness and how it affects the individual's social and emotional adjustment as well as educational and psychological needs in school. In the United States, gifted is not one of the thirteen categories of disability; however, gifted students can be "disabled" by the school system and attitudes from the community. That is, when their needs are not met and equitable education is not offered, gifted students may not progress.

Professor of special education Ibrahim A. El-Zraigat (2012) reminds us that students with gifts are significantly different from the norm; they are considered exceptional learners (that is, learners with special needs), and they need special provisions and counseling services in order to respond to their unique needs. El-Zraigat's (2012) work comes from inclusive schools in Jordan. These international schools have found provisions for alternative instructional formats to meet student interests; they apply instructional activities that encourage thinking skills and accommodate gifted students.

If your school does not have a gifted program, consider adding gifted resources; for example, the Gifted Education Research, Resource and Information Centre (https://gerric.arts.unsw.edu.au) in New South Wales, Australia, provides many resources for students who are gifted. It might also be appropriate to consider a program for students who, for example, want to expand their science knowledge and have some fun.

Other examples include the World Scholar's Cup (https://scholarscup.org), Knowledge Bowl (https://bit.ly/3nRWOYu), NASA Space Place (https://spaceplace.nasa.gov), Academic Decathlon (www.usad.org), Destination Imagination (https://destinationimagination.org), and my favorite, Odyssey of the Mind (www.odysseyofthemind.com). Odyssey of the Mind is an international educational program that provides creative problem-solving opportunities for students from kindergarten to college. Team members apply their creativity to solve problems that range from building mechanical devices to presenting their own interpretation of literary classics. They then bring their solutions to competition at the local, state, and world levels. Thousands of teams from throughout the United States and from about twenty-five other countries participate in the program.

Odyssey of the Mind is about creativity, an often-overlooked element in many students' growth and development. Students are rewarded more for how they apply their knowledge, skills, and talents than for whether they come up with the right answer. In fact, Odyssey of the Mind problems don't have one right answer. Ever.

The term *twice exceptional* is used when a student with a disability is also diagnosed in the area of gifted and talented (an actual diagnosis—just not in the disability category). In the United States, the services often fall under special education since gifted is not one of the thirteen categories under IDEA. And it is left up to the special education teacher to creatively develop the proper supports.

Alignment With Other Initiatives

Inclusion has a place in the mission, vision, values, and strategic plan for any school, district, or organization. It should never be "the program over in special education." Inclusion needs to align with other initiatives at the school. This may mean rethinking work that is ongoing to make sure equity and inclusion are centered.

In his book *Ambitious Instruction: Teaching With Rigor in the Secondary Classroom*, author Brad Cawn (2020) introduces *problems of practice groups* as a way for teachers to work together on an area of interest. Similar to the various clubs discussed in chapter 3 (page 73), the problems of practice groups are organized around instructional priorities. If inclusion is a priority and the goal is to achieve equitable education while being mindful of other initiatives, teachers need time to process and practice the concepts and ideas put forth in this book. They can do this processing and practicing by using Cawn's (2020) problems of practice groups (figure 6.4).

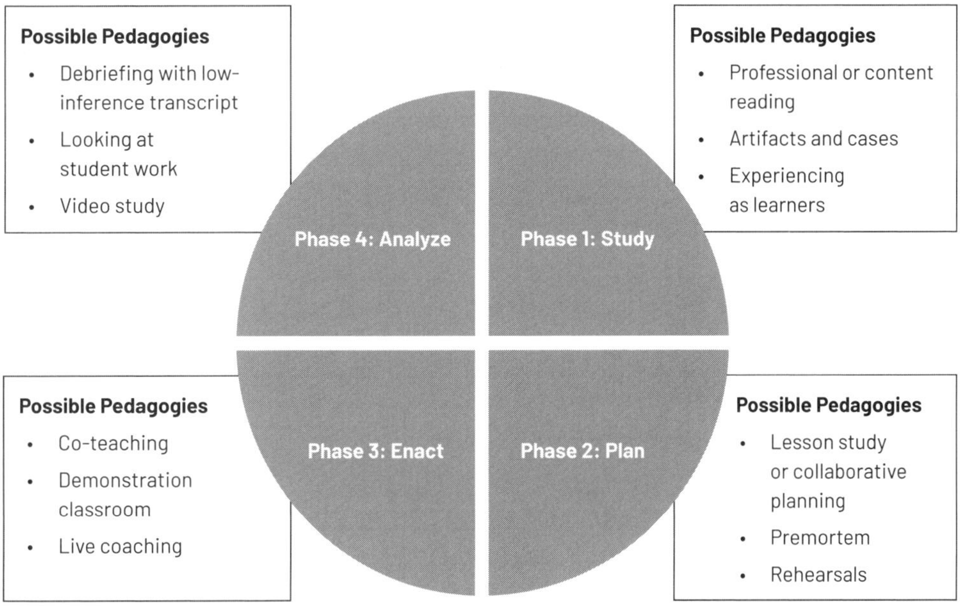

Source: Cawn, 2020, p. 165.

FIGURE 6.4: Problems of practice groups inquiry cycle.

Cawn (2020) suggests beginning with a simple know, want to know, learn (KWL) chart before engaging with the inquiry cycle (Ogle, 1986). To put this into action, group members could brainstorm what they know about inclusion and what they want to know. Taking the time to pose questions about what information they need, what they need to know about inclusion, and which questions they need to answer first will get things started. Once the priority questions are on the table, they can review readings on inclusion (either from the reference list of this book or from their own resources). When the group members come back together for a discussion after doing the readings, that is the time to share figure 6.4 and explain they are participating in an intentional cycle of inquiry. The knowledge they bring to the group begins phase 1 (study). Then the answers to the questions they've asked help them with phase 2 (plan for implementation), and phase 3 asks them to take action to observe one another. And finally, phase 4 is about analyzing the results.

Teaching optimum topic exploration is crucial when processing how inclusion impacts all content areas (Karge & Moore, 2015). The most noteworthy element that influences academic achievement gains is quality instruction (Johnson, 2012). Students with disabilities benefit as educators dive into inclusion strategies and brainstorm how to enhance the teaching of reading, writing, mathematics, and other content areas.

In a *Harvard Business Review* article on leadership, leadership and strategy expert Sydney Finkelstein (2018) reminds us that great leaders are great teachers. Leaders model and build relationships one at a time. As you meld inclusive practices into the other school initiatives you are working on, model inclusive language and highlight inclusive resources to support the initiative. As Finkelstein (2018) notes, cognitive psychologists and educational consultants have long known the value of personalized, intentional coaching. Offer tips and explain how a student with a disability can be part of the schoolwide initiative. Make it personal. Your staff will see your passion and follow suit.

Conclusion

The National Center for Education Statistics (2021) reports that in the fall of 2019, 95 percent of the students with disabilities in the United States, ages six to twenty-one, were enrolled in general education schools. Of this group, 65 percent spent 80 percent or more of the school day in general education classrooms. Researchers Sandi Cole, Hardy Murphy, Michael Frisby, Teresa Grossi, and Hannah Bolte (2019) followed a cohort of students with disabilities from third grade to eighth grade and found that students who spent 80 percent or more of their time in general education made substantial academic growth over other students with disabilities who spent less time in general education settings. Using triangulation in research methods, including state and district standardized assessments, the researchers found that students with disabilities from 340 schools in Indiana that used inclusive practices showed academic gains (Cole et al., 2019). These data show greater certainty that inclusion is the correct choice.

What began in the 1980s has become a mainstay in education. Students with disabilities can successfully receive special education services in general education classrooms and on the general education school grounds. This is possible with the leadership of an administrator who believes all students can and should be successful and who is willing to ensure every student has an opportunity to succeed. When all students are elevated and encouraged to succeed, and educators receive the necessary tools under a strong administration's leadership, everyone benefits. Equity is woven all the way through what educators do on a daily basis (Curren-Preis, Garcia, & Shaughnessy, 2022).

Strong school leaders build a supportive and empathetic climate for the educators at their school (Grissom et al., 2021). There are many ways you can prepare yourself to lead an inclusive school that successfully supports all students and educators.

- Create a positive and energetic learning environment.
- Let the educators and parents know how much you value their opinions and expertise.
- Resolve conflicts with a listening ear.
- Be innovative, think creatively, and explore options presented.
- Compliment team members and find ways to show appreciation.
- Celebrate successes.

As simple as this may sound, when implemented consistently and sincerely, your leadership will be appreciated and valued. Take the initiative, state the goal of developing an inclusive school, and set the tone. You will be viewed as a visionary and will inspire inclusive practices across all programs. In the next chapter, we'll put everything together and go through the specific steps necessary to implement inclusive practices in a school.

SEVEN

ESTABLISHING AN INCLUSIVE SCHOOL IN ELEVEN STEPS

Leadership is the capacity
to translate vision into reality.
—WARREN BENNIS

The term *inclusion* means all students at the school site are valued, supported, and serviced in the most effective, equity-based way possible to achieve academic, social, and emotional success. Canada, India, Hong Kong, Singapore, Australia, Europe, and the United States have civil rights laws protecting their citizens embedded in national policies. These rights extend to children, and international organizations such as the United Nations Educational, Scientific, and Cultural Organization (UNESCO, 2009) and the World Health Organization (2011) have advocated for student rights.

These beliefs build on the fundamental principles of respect for human diversity and the right to equitable education opportunities for all students. On January 22, 2019, the United Nations published *Empowering Children With Disabilities for the Enjoyment of Their Human Rights, Including Through Inclusive Education* as an overview of the legal framework and practical measures to support students with disabilities.

All means *all* and every means *every* student at the school. Remember, it is the job of every adult at the school site to support every student. As the leader, ensure that conversations about student needs include deliberate thought toward the needs of students with disabilities; this way, you can help ensure those needs are met equitably. If the goal is for every student to achieve success, then that goal must be stated and discussed in a way that all involved believe and see the vision.

All means all *and every means* every *student at the school. Remember, it is the job of every adult at the school site to support every student. As the leader, ensure that conversations about student needs include deliberate thought toward the needs of students with disabilities; this way, you can help ensure those needs are met equitably.*

As previous chapters have established, all students have the right to be in the same educational space—educated in the general education classroom (Cobley, 2018; Florian, Black-Hawkins, & Rouse, 2017; Hehir et al., 2016). Inclusive education increases academic and social opportunities for students both with and without disabilities (Cooper, Smith, & Russell, 2017).

Successful inclusive education requires that school systems take time to go through a transformation. This is a design-focused process, *not* a resource-intensive process. When implemented correctly, inclusive services are very cost-effective (Banks & Polack, 2013). Measuring the success of inclusive education goes far beyond just counting how many English learners or students with disabilities are in general education classrooms; school quality outcomes we must measure include but are not limited to student achievement. There are three implementation factors that are foundational to the eleven steps of establishing an inclusive school.

1. School review and planning
2. Professional learning and support for all teachers on inclusive practices
3. Support for school leaders to enact an inclusive vision for their schools

WATCH LISTEN ASK LEARN

Action for Administrators

The term *inclusion* has been around since the 1980s. Inclusion is not a bandwagon approach. You can accomplish it with careful planning and without a great deal of funds.

Whole-school restructuring approaches lead to inclusion. The goal is a schoolwide approach in which students are not removed from general education classrooms and all supports and services are provided to enhance the learning of *all* students (Karge & Lasky, 2007). In this chapter, I first highlight a case study that describes how one school used the eleven steps to fully implement inclusive education. Then I go into detail on all the steps and how to put them into practice in your school using everything you have learned so far.

One School's Progression to a Sustainable Inclusive Program

The following case study describes a yearlong planning process that led a school to adopt a successful, long-term inclusion model. Without planning and attention to detail, this school would not have been successful. Based on the experience of this school and many others around the globe with similar stories, I created the eleven steps for establishing an inclusive school. These steps assist school leaders in guiding successful school transformation that will support not just students with disabilities but every student at a school site.

> *Inclusive Elementary School is in a suburban area approximately forty-five miles from Los Angeles. There were 807 students who attended the school, and 306 of those students had IEPs. The school staff consisted of forty-two certified staff and twenty-six classified employees. The LST included one principal, one assistant principal, six special education teachers, two speech and language teachers, ten upper-grade teachers, and twenty-two primary-grade teachers. The teachers represented every grade in the school, K–6. The classified employees included instructional paraeducators, playground supervisors, day-care personnel, a bilingual clerk, office workers, cafeteria staff, and custodial personnel.*
>
> *For several years, a sprinkling of parents requested inclusion in general education grade-appropriate classrooms as the placement of choice. The faculty and staff recognized the successes of these students and decided to explore options to provide more inclusive efforts at the site. They believed it was the inclusive environment that led to both the academic and social successes they witnessed.*
>
> *The principal set out to facilitate the staff as they designed a plan. In the spring, the school leadership team visited several model schools*

that provided excellent inclusive services to students with disabilities. One of the sites the school leadership team visited had a collaborative partnership with a member of a local university. The school leadership invited the university consultant to its school site to present an overview of inclusion to the entire school staff. This was the beginning of a yearlong planning process.

In August, the school leadership team formed a site leadership committee to plan steps in the school transition process. The committee examined full-inclusion literature and began a library of resources at the school. In October, grade-level teams held meetings to discuss the impact of inclusion and share the pros and cons as perceived by the staff. In November, the leadership team met to review the grade-level notes. Team members created a chart on what the school site was already doing with regard to inclusive and special education services and what the next steps would be if the team were to provide more inclusive services.

A common theme emerged: student success. In every case, grade-level teams had discussed and provided examples of the excellent progress of students who were currently included. And grade-level teams had talked about the what if*—that is, "What if every student could have this inclusive experience? What if we set up an equitable system where every student could be successful? What if we did away with segregated classes?" The progress of the students who were already included motivated team members to continue researching and exploring models that might work at their school.*

January brought time to visit several additional model sites. The university facilitator led a whole-staff professional learning session providing an overview of special education laws, different models of fully included sites, and many successes witnessed at the sites where inclusive programs were implemented. A follow-up meeting was held for special education staff only. In February, a similar follow-up meeting took place for general education staff. And in March, a meeting for classified staff took place. At each of these meetings, teachers and paraeducators had the opportunity to address their specific concerns in relation to their classes and programs and the changes an inclusive model might create.

In March, the LST attended an inclusion showcase conference. A showcase conference is a day of exhibits by school districts already involved in inclusive practices. The school team came back from the conference with an important message for the other team members: "We already do a lot of this." All personnel who were already working with at least one full-inclusion student met for a half-day meeting. Individuals had the opportunity to communicate the positives and negatives they personally experienced when a student was fully included in their classroom. The team agreed that the successes far outweighed the challenges and the school should continue its planning and set the goal for beginning a new and improved inclusive program in the fall.

Teams of roving substitutes were brought to campus to cover classes while grade-level teachers again met with team members, administration, and the university facilitator (consultant) and discussed the students receiving special education services in their classrooms. Every student with an IEP was discussed. The team documented each student's strengths, weaknesses, and education requirements. At the end of the day, the team noted whether a student appeared ready to spend more time in the general education classroom and looked in depth at the types of supports and services the student would need to be successful in an inclusive setting. For example, did one student need her social studies text read to her or recorded as an audio file because her reading level was below that of the rest of the class? What is special about special education is the individualized support; this team did not want to lose this! Team members wanted to ensure more supports would be provided and each student's IEP goals and objectives were taken into consideration.

In April, a Saturday brainstorming and planning meeting took place. The meeting was scheduled on a Saturday morning so that any staff member could be present (the team would not have to worry about covering classrooms), and the meeting was optional. Almost everyone attended. The evening prior, one second-grade teacher had a brainstorm that emerged as the triangle plan. *She shared the plan with all in attendance, and the group refined the proposal. The triangle plan addressed the placement of students into ten classrooms and the establishment of collaborative support teams. The day concluded with a list of needs to be shared with the district and some proposed ideas for staff support for the inclusion teams.*

The LST visited several additional model sites in May, and a staff meeting was held to discuss potential challenges with implementation of the triangle plan; final summer plans were made to move forward with the implementation phase. Many IEP meetings and parent meetings took place to explain the options. At the May staff meeting, specific strengths, challenges, IEP goals and objectives, and test scores for all students with disabilities who attended the school were reviewed. Grade-level teachers gave input on potential challenges and what they believed was needed to set the students up for success the following year.

The summer was a busy one! The principal, in consultation with team members, spent many hours designing the enrollment plan, setting up classrooms, scheduling support staff, and scheduling parent meetings. A new assistant principal was hired, and the special education staff had opportunities to attend more training. The upper-grade special day classroom was reassigned to a general education teacher, as it had been decided that the upper-grade special day classroom students and teacher would all be fully included. Co-teaching teams met to collaboratively plan a scope and sequence for the year. The upper-grade special day classroom special education teacher and the resource specialist special education teacher established the learning center with their teacher desks and small work areas. Two part-time school counselors were hired to assist with behavior challenges and other supports necessary for the inclusive program to be successful.

In August, the welcome-back staff meeting began with training on differentiated instruction. When school opened, inclusion was built into the vocabulary, the literature, and most importantly, the organizational structure and operations of the school. All students were accepted and supported. This school went on to receive many recognitions and awards (including Blue Ribbon School, the Schwab Foundation Social Innovation Award, and an inclusive technology award, to name a few) for its inclusive efforts, and it has successfully maintained the inclusive program since 2005.

Having a strong and cohesive parental support system is vital to the benefits of inclusion. Parents become more active members when given opportunities. For example, each year, this school hosts a parent university night, where parents attend thirty-minute presentations designed to inform them of what is going on at the school. When new families join the school, a parent mentor is assigned to greet them and share ideas and methods for supporting the school and ultimately their own children's education.

When asked why this school has a successful inclusive program, the principal noted, "The first few years were spent changing the culture. We had to change the general education teachers' hearts and minds to welcome all students with a positive attitude." (A. Taylor, personal communication, May 4, 2015)

Much has been written on school governance and inclusive practices. In my experience, inquiries about how to implement these practices always arise; the people I work with often laugh and ask for a recipe for successful inclusion. I used to laugh along and share there was not a clear recipe. However, as more and more schools globally asked me the same question, I began to realize there were steps I could suggest. I created the following eleven steps to establish and maintain inclusive education based on my work with schools. I do not believe you must implement the steps in sequence to accomplish inclusion. However, I do believe you must master each step to achieve equitable, inclusive education. My work as a college professor is deeply rooted in research, thus the detail and numerous citations in this text!

1. Review current practices.
2. Involve the leadership team.
3. Do some action planning.
4. Conduct professional learning.
5. Read the research.
6. Encourage family engagement.
7. Design and implement an inclusion plan.
8. Implement data-collection measures.
9. Monitor implementation.
10. Revise and adjust.
11. Celebrate and share successes.

Action for Administrators

Include all members of the school staff as you plan and implement inclusive practices. When *all* members have buy-in, they are more likely to focus and work as a team to support *all* students.

Eleven Steps for Establishing an Inclusive School

School leadership is critical for the successful implementation of inclusive education (Shogren, McCart, Lyon, & Sailor, 2015; Villa & Thousand, 2017). Leaders who lead with vision, inclusive values, motivation, autonomy, and trust in school staff are the most effective (Sherab et al., 2015). Figure 7.1 provides a simple form for administration teams to use as a guide for the eleven steps to develop an inclusive school community.

Leaders can use these steps to judge the state of a school or district and develop a gap analysis of where to go in the leadership and learning journey. The eleven steps are key to any inclusion audit. Educational consultant Lauren Porosoff (2022) describes an *inclusion curriculum audit* as a way of assessing whether historically marginalized groups are integrated into the school system. I recommend you establish your LST and task it as the team to support the progression of the steps.

The following sections more fully explore each of the eleven steps.

Step 1: Review Current Practices

All general education teachers must realize that it is within their professional roles to include all students in their classrooms; this concern is not just the domain of the specialist or support staff (Bhatnagar & Das, 2014; Forlin & Chambers, 2011; Sharma, Simi, & Forlin, 2015). Teachers need to understand that they *do not* have the right to say no to inclusion of *any* student.

Every school has different systems for reviewing current practices. An effective one is for the school leader to begin by asking every staff member to complete a climate survey. This survey typically asks respondents to answer questions such as the following.

Step Toward Inclusion	Activities	Who (List which team members were involved.)	When (Record when the step was discussed.)
1. Review current practices.			
2. Involve the leadership team.			
3. Do some action planning.			
4. Conduct professional learning.			
5. Read the research.			
6. Encourage family engagement.			
7. Design and implement an inclusion plan.			
8. Implement data-collection measures.			
9. Monitor implementation.			
10. Revise and adjust.			
11. Celebrate and share successes.			

FIGURE 7.1: Form for implementation of the eleven inclusion steps.
*Visit **go.SolutionTree.com/specialneeds** for a free reproducible version of this figure.*

- Do you believe your school mission statement supports all students?
- Have you had any training on or experience with inclusive education?
- Do you have experience co-teaching?
- What do you think the biggest challenges are as we look to move toward more inclusive practices?
- What professional learning is essential for you to be successful in an inclusive environment?

Prompts should include items that leadership wants to know more about to review current practices at the school. Remember, there is not one model for inclusion.

Every school must review its current practices and create its own plan for moving forward to support all students at the site.

Figure 7.2 features a sample inclusion climate survey.

Check *yes* or *no* for the following questions.

☐ Y ☐ N Do you believe your school mission statement supports all students?

☐ Y ☐ N Have you had any training on or experience with inclusive education?

☐ Y ☐ N Are you familiar with Universal Design for Learning?

☐ Y ☐ N Do you use grouping strategies in your classroom?

☐ Y ☐ N Do you have experience co-planning?

☐ Y ☐ N Do you have experience co-teaching?

☐ Y ☐ N Do you believe the current referral system is effective?

☐ Y ☐ N Do you know all the related services persons at the school?

Write your answers in the spaces provided.

Define inclusive education.

How comfortable do you feel working with students with disabilities?

How comfortable do you feel working with students who are gifted?

How confident are you with using differentiation strategies in your classroom?

Give two examples of differentiation.

Give two examples of accommodations.

What do you think the biggest challenges are as we look to move toward more inclusive practices?

What professional learning is essential for you to be successful in an inclusive environment?

What else would you like to share with the LST?

FIGURE 7.2: Sample inclusion climate survey.

Visit ***go.SolutionTree.com/specialneeds*** *for a free reproducible version of this figure.*

Using data from the survey, analyze current school practices and the school climate. Where are the students with IEPs currently receiving services? What is the general staff culture related to services provided to support *all* learners? What do your school mission and vision say? You really can't compartmentalize. That is, inclusion can't just be one part of the strategic plan; it must inform the whole plan. It cannot be an initiative that is carried out by a few. It must be schoolwide, and for that reason, administration must be involved. In reviewing current practices, also keep in mind that if a gifted and talented education expert is on the school staff or in the district, it would be beneficial to bring that professional into the LST for brainstorming sessions, IEP meetings, and professional learning. This expert can help make sure that twice-exceptional and gifted and talented students receive the support they need as well.

Step 2: Involve the Leadership Team

Most schools have a leadership team already established. If your school needs to create such a team, I suggest including a representative of every grade level or content area.

The leadership team should analyze the eleven steps and determine the school's progress throughout the entire implementation. As the school leader, you may make the decision to have the LST serve in this role. Sometimes these steps do not go in the exact order as listed here. However, all of them are necessary in a school where students with both gifts and disabilities, as well as typical students, are effectively supported.

Recall that the Education for All Handicapped Children Act of 1975 was reauthorized in 1990, with its name changed to the Individuals With Disabilities Education Act (IDEA). The name change was directly related to how we refer to individuals with disabilities. All are people first, and secondary is the disability. This is known as *person-first terminology*. To focus on the person is more inclusive. Instead of saying "that autistic student," we say "the student with autism." The leadership team members should adopt this person-first language and model it for others at the school site. If they use person-first language consistently, others will follow.

Step 3: Do Some Action Planning

As the inclusive model is planned and rolled out, everyone must know, talk about, and accept the concept and procedures of the learning support specialist working in classrooms alongside or as a consultant to general education teachers (Karten, 2013). *Action planning* is the process of assigning roles and procedures to carry out the plan (creating the actual plan comes along at step 7). If the school does not have an MTSS, that would be an action item. Take some time to think through what actions are needed to begin and implement the inclusive process at your school. A primary component of the MTSS includes a multilevel prevention and intervention system composed of screening, progress monitoring, and data-based decision making (discussed in chapter 2, page 35). Contained in the plan should be an avenue for general education and special education teachers or general education and English language arts teachers to collaborate and possibly co-teach.

Co-teaching involves two teachers working together in a classroom with groups of students, sharing the planning, organization, delivery, and assessment of instruction as well as the physical space (discussed in chapter 2, page 51). Both teachers are actively engaged in all aspects of instruction (Bacharach, Heck, & Dahlberg, 2010). If co-teaching is to be implemented, the plan needs to have professional learning opportunities embedded in it.

Another component of planning is asking all teachers to review their classrooms with inclusive practices in mind. The United Nations Educational, Scientific, and Cultural Organization International Bureau of Education (UNESCO-IBE; n.d.) suggests that teachers review their classrooms to make certain of the following eight factors.

1. Teaching is planned with all students in mind.
2. Lessons encourage the participation of all students.
3. Students are actively involved in their own learning.
4. Students are encouraged to support one another's learning.
5. Support is provided when students experience difficulties.
6. Classroom discipline is based on mutual respect and healthy living.
7. Students feel that they have somebody to speak to when they are worried or upset.
8. Assessment contributes to the achievement of all students.

Include parents and past students in the planning process. It is up to each individual school how involved to make this step; you can informally gather feedback from a few parents and past students, or you can conduct a wider survey. Ask the question, "What will our school look like in three to five years?" Parents and past students may have very different perspectives than the LST members do.

Step 4: Conduct Professional Learning

As discussed in chapter 3 (page 73), professional learning gives individuals an opportunity to participate in trainings, events, clubs, or other activities that enhance their personal learning and develop them as educators. In this context, this step is a chance for the LST to strategically plan some schoolwide professional learning opportunities centered on inclusive practices.

Teachers can learn a lot from the Swedish model, where staff reveal an inclusive school culture in how they collaboratively interpret situations, express thoughts and criticism, discuss learning strategies and problems, support students with gifts and disabilities, and propose justification for actions (von Ahlefeld Nisser, 2017). The LST can accomplish this by holding professional learning sessions (such as school function teams), having book club readings, or sharing literature with staff a bit at a time. Schools that function as professional learning communities, because they focus on collaboration, are well prepared for these conversations. The cycle of inquiry for lifelong learning in the teaching profession is based on the plan, teach, reflect, apply cycle (California Commission on Teacher Credentialing, 2018). Teachers need professional learning sessions to help them understand that as they plan, they need to be thoughtful about supporting *all* students. In my experience, in order for schools to embrace inclusion, they must have professional learning opportunities centered on Bloom's (1956) taxonomy and its Anderson and Krathwohl (2001) update, the difference between accommodation and modification, schoolwide differentiation, Universal Design for Learning, and the thirteen disability categories.

BLOOM'S (1956) AND ANDERSON AND KRATHWOHL'S (2001) TAXONOMIES

Research in effective teaching has validated that students with disabilities often need teachers to introduce a concept in various ways in order to remember it (Karge & Moore, 2015).

Figure 7.3 (page 158) includes two pyramids. The pyramid on the left is Benjamin Bloom's (1956) taxonomy. Lorin W. Anderson and David R. Krathwohl (2001) revised it to reflect relevance to the 21st century (the pyramid on the right). Many teaching experiences leave the topic after the lower three levels, rarely pushing it up into the upper tier, where problem solving is required. Teaching is hard work! Effective teachers must explore the topic, understand it, and be willing to shift the responsibility of learning from themselves to learners (Crockett, Jukes, & Churches, 2011). The teacher becomes the facilitator of learning, not the guardian of knowledge (Karge & Moore, 2015).

THE DIFFERENCE BETWEEN ACCOMMODATION AND MODIFICATION

Professional learning needs to include a review and reemphasis of the difference between appropriate accommodations and modifications (Karge & Lasky, 2009; see figure 7.4, page 158).

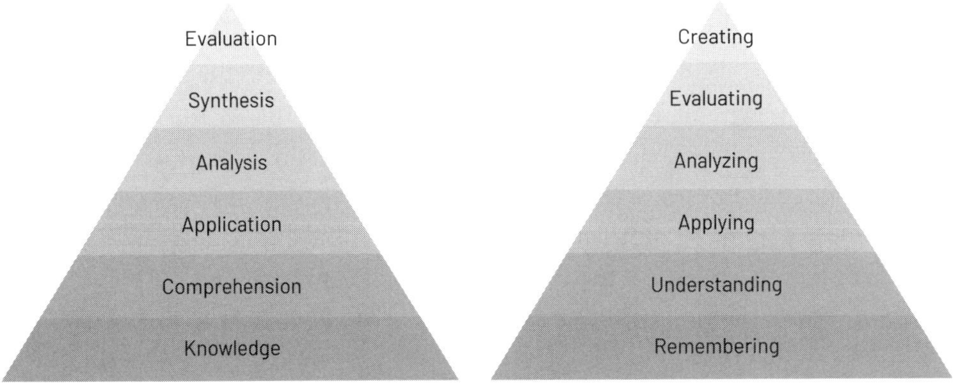

Source: Anderson & Krathwohl, 2001; Bloom, 1956.

FIGURE 7.3: Bloom's (1956) and Anderson and Krathwohl's (2001) taxonomies considered.

Accommodations change *how* a student learns the material.	Modifications change *what* a student is taught or expected to learn.
The teacher has a student verbally answer questions on a test.	The teacher rewords test questions using simpler language.
The teacher provides an outline before a lecture.	The teacher provides alternative books or materials on the same theme.

FIGURE 7.4: Examples of accommodation and modification.

WATCH LISTEN ASK LEARN

Action for Administrators

Understanding the difference between the terms *accommodation* and *modification* is paramount as you work with parents to provide a maximal inclusive learning experience for their children.

An *accommodation* changes how a student accesses information to create an equitable opportunity for that student to demonstrate knowledge and skills. The assignment, test, or project is the same as for the other students in the class. The accommodation is the how. Accommodations do not change the instructional level, content, or performance criteria for meeting the standards; they are designed to level the playing field (Scarpati, Wells, Lewis, & Jirka, 2011).

A *modification*, on the other hand, is an actual change in what a student is expected to learn or demonstrate. Modifications adjust what is being taught. Teachers make these changes to provide meaningful opportunities for students to participate. When modifications are discussed in the United States, they are typically included in the IEP.

DIFFERENTIATION AS A SCHOOLWIDE INITIATIVE

In an article discussing barriers to inclusive education, Jayne Renee Pivik (2010) notes the most frequently reported barrier to full-inclusion implementation is a lack of staff (general education teacher) understanding of how to support students with different needs in the typical classroom. The article provides the examples of teachers giving inappropriate substitute work when they are too busy to adapt the curriculum and excluding students with different needs from certain class activities without stating a reason. All teachers need to understand how to accommodate and differentiate instruction for all students, which requires professional learning on effective differentiation.

Carol Ann Tomlinson (2014) is often denoted as the one who coined the term *differentiation*, which simply refers to "providing consistent and robust plans in anticipation of and in response to student learning differences" (p. 9). However, despite years of writing on the topic, there is only limited congruence between beliefs and practices. There is little evidence of teacher educators, K–12 educators, and others in the field actually using a comprehensive model of differentiation (Osborne, 2019; Santangelo & Tomlinson, 2012). This is concerning. Perhaps this deficit relates to insufficient understanding of the basic principles of differentiation. Figure 7.5 is a simple visual for lesson planning based on the work of educational consultant Wendy Conklin (2011). Use of this visual may be helpful as teachers implement inclusive lesson planning.

How	Why
Vary the Content (What is taught)	**Readiness** (Students are not at the same academic level.)
Vary the Process (How it is taught)	**Learning Preferences** (Students prefer different ways of learning.)
Vary the Product (What students produce)	**Interests** (Students have different passions.)

Source: Adapted from Conklin, 2011.

FIGURE 7.5: The how and why of differentiation.

All students deserve appropriate differentiated curriculum and accommodations to support their individual learning. For example, a professional learning session or series should address how to differentiate for English learners without and with disabilities. English learners need guided oral practice to enhance academic discourse. I recommend that discussions take place on how an effective lesson scaffolds information through language frames to provide students the academic language they need to demonstrate mastery of the content objective. Thus, encourage teachers to ask questions as they develop and plan lessons. For example:

- "What responses do I anticipate that would demonstrate understanding for every student?"
- "Which scaffolds will I provide to support less proficient and more proficient students in accomplishing academic tasks?"
- "Am I differentiating for every student in my class or just one or two students?"

All students can learn; it is our role to differentiate to accommodate the learning. Giving teachers a place to ask questions and learn about differentiation will build your team and your program.

Different Places, Different Needs

Following is a list of considerations for teachers when establishing a classroom environment to meet the needs of all students. Are there places for students to be part of a group and places to be alone? Use the following list to assess the classroom environments in your school.

Places to be part of a group	Places to be quiet
Places to be alone	Places to be messy
Places to be taken care of	Places to have one's own things
Places to be on one's own	Places to share with others
Places to be free and move	Places to be creative
Places to be noisy	

What is your environment like?

UNIVERSAL DESIGN FOR LEARNING

It is my experience that many schools in the United States are now structuring classrooms and learning spaces based on the principles of Universal Design for Learning (UDL; Rose & Meyer, 2002). UDL is a framework for designing instruction based on individual learners at the planning stages. Universal design originated in the architectural field. The design of an accessible building is thought through from the planning stages. The ramps, elevators, electronic doors, and special lighting are all established at the design stage, and anyone can use the features. For example, someone pushing a stroller might use the electronic doors, and someone carrying something large and heavy might choose to take the elevator.

The framework of universal design is intended to be a guide for teaching and learning that educators can customize and adjust to meet individual needs (CAST, n.d.). The best resource for the use of UDL in education planning, instruction, and assessment is CAST (www.cast.org). According to CAST (n.d.), the UDL framework provides three guiding principles.

1. **Engagement (why):** Recruit interest, sustain effort and persistence, and provide options for self-regulation. Are there multiple ways to help students remain engaged in the lesson? Is the teacher providing ideas and supports for how the students can take ownership of their learning and organize information for recall in a way that makes sense to them (Murawski & Scott, 2017)? What are the students' feelings about the topic?
2. **Representation (what):** Provide options for perception, language and symbols, and comprehension. How is the teacher representing the concepts, skills, or strategies that students must learn? What are the various ways the teacher can present material so students can easily recall the material at a later date? How do students gather and organize material?
3. **Action and expression (how):** Provide options for physical action, expression and communication, and executive function. Allowing students to take control and express their learning in a way that makes sense to them is critical to retention of knowledge acquired. What formats and options are allowed? How will the teacher allow students to show what they know? Can they create a video, record an answer, or write a poem instead of an essay?

When educators think about the why, what, and how of learning related to engagement, representation, and action and expression, they inevitably conclude students must have access to lessons, materials, and required homework. Universal design allows for flexible ways of accessing materials, as well as consideration for student autonomy, flexibility, and interest. It allows for educators to provide information in more than one format. When this is the case, students with exceptional needs have the opportunity for successful attainment of content and learning.

Universal design should be a mainstay in every inclusive classroom. Professional learning on how to implement it will be critical as teachers begin collaborating, co-teaching, and designing inclusive lesson plans.

DISABILITY CATEGORIES

During this professional learning stage, it is wise to review the disability categories and talk about the areas in which educators feel they need more information or ideas on how to support students with disabilities. The label is much less important than how teachers guide and provide the student with support. For example, students with ADHD have a very difficult time with simple social interactions. They often struggle to read facial expressions or body language. Generally, comments tend to be impulsive; these students may interrupt others continuously and struggle to fit in with peers. At times, they may talk too much or not at all. Simple resources such as table 7.1 give educators suggestions for how to shift their thinking about these traits. The professional learning does not necessarily have to go into great detail; however, it does need to focus on research-based strategies and techniques for understanding students on the ADHD spectrum and providing them with effective instruction.

TABLE 7.1: ADHD Traits and More Positive Views on Them

ADHD TRAIT	MORE POSITIVE VIEWS
Talkative	Friendly, chatty, articulate, vocal, communicative
Hyperactive	Busy, fast, quick, energized, motivated, lively
Bossy	Skilled in leadership, take-charge, organized
Dreamy	Creative, artistic, resourceful, imaginative, inventive

Educators will need professional learning on the following broad areas of need and ideas for how to support these needs.

- Cognitive and learning difficulties (dyslexia, dyscalculia, executive function challenges, and other specific learning disabilities)
- Social, emotional, and mental health (depression, ADHD, eating disorders, anxiety, and so on)
- Communication and interaction needs (speech, language, and communication needs; autism; social inclusion; and so on)
- Sensory and physical needs (visual impairment, hearing impairment, multisensory impairment, physical disability, and so on)

Step 5: Read the Research

Once students fall behind, they are likely to stay behind, and the gap is likely to widen unless immediate intervention takes place. In most cases, this means the students need exposure to general education curriculum and intervention in general education in order for them to effectively generalize what they learn. For example, if students learn a writing strategy in the general education classroom, they are more likely to generalize the strategy to other content areas in general education. If they learn the strategy in a self-contained environment, they might not know how to use it or even how to recall it when they go back into a general education setting. This is why all teachers need a solid research foundation. For inclusive practices to succeed, educators need to read research, and not just research about special education, to see what is happening in other areas beyond their immediate classroom.

Numerous studies verify the academic achievement value for all students when inclusion is properly implemented. For example, Rita Brusca-Vega, Kathleen Brown, and David Yasutake (2011) report exemplary student achievement in science with high-level inquiry methods. Evidence demonstrates that students with intellectual disabilities gain far more in inclusive classrooms than in segregated ones (Dessemontet, Bless, & Morin, 2012). The research clearly supports inclusive practices raise achievement in students with disabilities and their peers globally (Choi, Meisenheimer, McCart, & Sailor, 2017; Dyssegaard & Larsen, 2013; Florian, 2014; Gunarhadi, Anwar, Andayani, & Shaari, 2016; Kefallinou, 2016; UNESCO, 2020). To find current research, search for keywords, such as *inclusion*, and the current year in Google Scholar (https://scholar.google.com). This will immediately give you a few research-based, peer-reviewed articles to read and review. Also, bookmark the What Works Clearinghouse (https://ies.ed.gov/ncee/wwc), which always updates its site with the most current research.

Sometimes educators feel mere exposure to general education settings is a waste of a student's time that could be better spent in a self-contained or more segregated classroom. They do not understand that the research is clear: exposure stimulates learning and builds self-esteem for students with disabilities, especially those who feel ashamed of their needs. It allows students to hear content discussions and listen to their peers' interactions. These small but mighty interactions activate learning. Additionally, the inclusion of students with disabilities does wonders to strengthen relationships between the school and parents.

Sweden's international schools have managed to create an inclusive school culture by adopting strategies based on values and attitudes instead of on external educational models that pull students out of classrooms (or what some refer to as having a school within a school). The Swedish school system is renowned for its vision of creating an inclusive school for all (Magnússon, 2020). This is what is possible when educators explore, read, and implement research schoolwide. As the LST discovers and absorbs the research, be sure to design ways to convey the information to the rest of the school, and as faculty and staff access research directly, keep an avenue open for them to share with the entire school community.

Step 6: Encourage Family Engagement

Historically, families are strong advocates for inclusive services (Smith & Tyler, 2014). As the school moves to plan and implement a new program or expand an existing system of service, it is important to include the families of all students. Families want to feel valued and know their voices are heard (Fallah, Murawski, & Moradian, 2018). Families feel mutual support by authentically working side by side with the school faculty and staff (Avendano & Cho, 2020). Get their ideas and inform families of the research related to the structure your school is selecting. Consider hosting grade-level family focus groups and asking parents for their ideas for how all student needs can be met in inclusive environments. This is not a one-size-fits-all endeavor; the schools that I have seen achieving the most success come up with creative ways to engage with their students' families.

Step 7: Design and Implement an Inclusion Plan

Chances are, even as you have discussed some of the other steps (many of which focus on gathering knowledge), your schoolwide planning has begun. Ultimately, your role as the leader is to decide who actually designs your school plan. I suggest that the LST take on this role with schoolwide buy-in. Every school is going to be different, as you base your plan on your staff, your students, and your resources.

Design a plan that you can implement schoolwide; build on the previous steps, and always focus on the students' needs. Keep in mind that organizations like the World Health Organization (2011) and UNESCO (2020) both advocate for national policies protecting students' and families' civil rights. The concept of a safe environment is discussed in depth in Twiggy Chan and Mantak Yuen's (2015) case study of inclusive education in Hong Kong. Your school needs to have a common understanding of inclusive education and the concept of working together to deliver a differentiated curriculum with flexible teaching and assessment accommodations. The curriculum and the teaching and learning processes must closely match the needs and talents of individual students (Tomlinson & Imbeau, 2010), and teachers should vary their strategies for presentation and student engagement in lessons (Karge, 2014). Remember, *student needs may dictate changes each year*! That is why, once the inclusion plan has been designed and implemented, leaders should plan to meet annually to revise it (see step 10, page 174). Flexibility is the key.

I suggest using the following eight school function areas as tools for schoolwide inclusion (Karge, Stephens, & Abu Zaineh, 2019; Karge, Stephens, Widener, & Poda, 2019; Stephens, Widener, & Karge, 2019). These areas and the questions they include can act as a blueprint for your schoolwide inclusion plan.

1. Vision, mission, and school values:
    a. Were parents represented in the teams that developed the vision and mission?
    b. Is the word *inclusion* in the vision statement?
    c. Is the language in the mission all-inclusive?
2. Leadership, faculty, and staff human capital management systems:
    a. Have you developed workable schedules for staff, including planning time?
    b. Are all educators trained in inclusive practices?
    c. Do you need to consider other related services or online therapy?
3. Management of organizational structure and operations:
    a. Do students with disabilities have access to all areas on campus?
    b. Are students with disabilities grouped in age-appropriate settings?
    c. Are all management systems driven by data?
4. Leadership for instruction and school improvement:
    a. Does the LST meet on a regular basis (at least once a month)?
    b. Are all involved knowledgeable about local, state or provincial, and federal or national policies?
    c. Are parents aware of the school-improvement procedures in place?
5. Teaching, learning, and assessment:
    a. Do teachers use Universal Design for Learning to prepare lessons?
    b. Are teachers using differentiation to support all learners?
    c. Do teachers see instruction of all students as a collective responsibility?
6. School climate, equity for students, and cultural responsiveness:
    a. Do class rosters reflect the natural proportion of students with disabilities?

   b. Are learning areas integrated?
   c. Do students with disabilities have access to extracurricular activities?

7. Professionalism, ethics, and professional conduct:
   a. Does professional learning include information on disability categories?
   b. Is it the norm to use person-first language (for example, *the student with autism*, not *the autistic student*)?
   c. Is there evidence of shared roles and responsibilities of co-teachers?

8. Communication and collaboration with families and stakeholders:
   a. Does the team write IEPs that focus on general education goals, curricula, and settings?
   b. Are school board members aware of the inclusion plans, procedures, and implementation?
   c. Do parents and caregivers feel they are part of the school community?

The school function areas are explained in much greater depth in the book *Thinking That Matters for Schools: School Function Areas From Challenge to Change* (Stephens et al., 2019). The areas are used in analyzing the school's effectiveness and efficiency as a means for determining plans of action. Depending on each individual school, questions beyond those in the preceding list will certainly arise. For example, area 2 focuses on *staff human capital management systems*. Does the school have the appropriate staff to execute the inclusion plan? Will you need to hire another paraeducator to carry out your plan?

WATCH LISTEN ASK LEARN

Action for Administrators

Use inclusive terminology in the school mission and vision statements. During strategic planning, keep inclusive practices front and center.

Step 8: Implement Data-Collection Measures

The scientifically based practice of progress monitoring is used to assess student academic performance and evaluate the effectiveness of instruction (Fuchs & Fuchs, 2001; Gesel & Lemons, 2020). You can use the decision-making cycle depicted in figure 7.6 to collect data about and monitor the progress of your school's or district's inclusion plan on data days. This schoolwide process takes place at the individual class and student levels and is designed to help teachers make more informed instructional decisions and document student progress for accountability purposes. Progress monitoring provides for efficient communication with educators and families and helps the school determine whether students are making progress and whether the inclusive plan is effective.

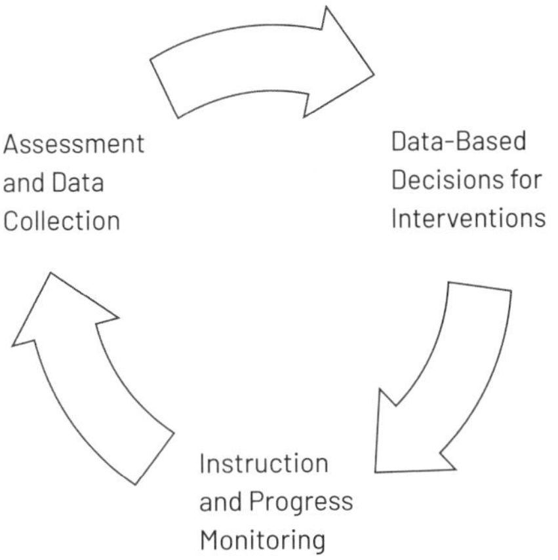

FIGURE 7.6: Decision-making cycle for data collection.

Figure 7.7 (page 168) documents the progress and tremendous growth of the students in the special education program at Inclusive Elementary School (see the case study on page 147).

The improvements the school saw by using inclusion are clear. With faithful data collection and tracking, it is possible to provide incontrovertible visual proof that educators' efforts are making a real, positive difference for their students.

The following case study, which follows Leadership School, provides an example of transformational leadership for instruction and school improvement in which data take a front-row seat. Professor of communication Peter Guy Northouse (2019) describes *transformational leadership* as a "process whereby a person engages with others and creates a connection that raises the level of motivation and morality" (p. 164). This case study reveals the power of engagement in

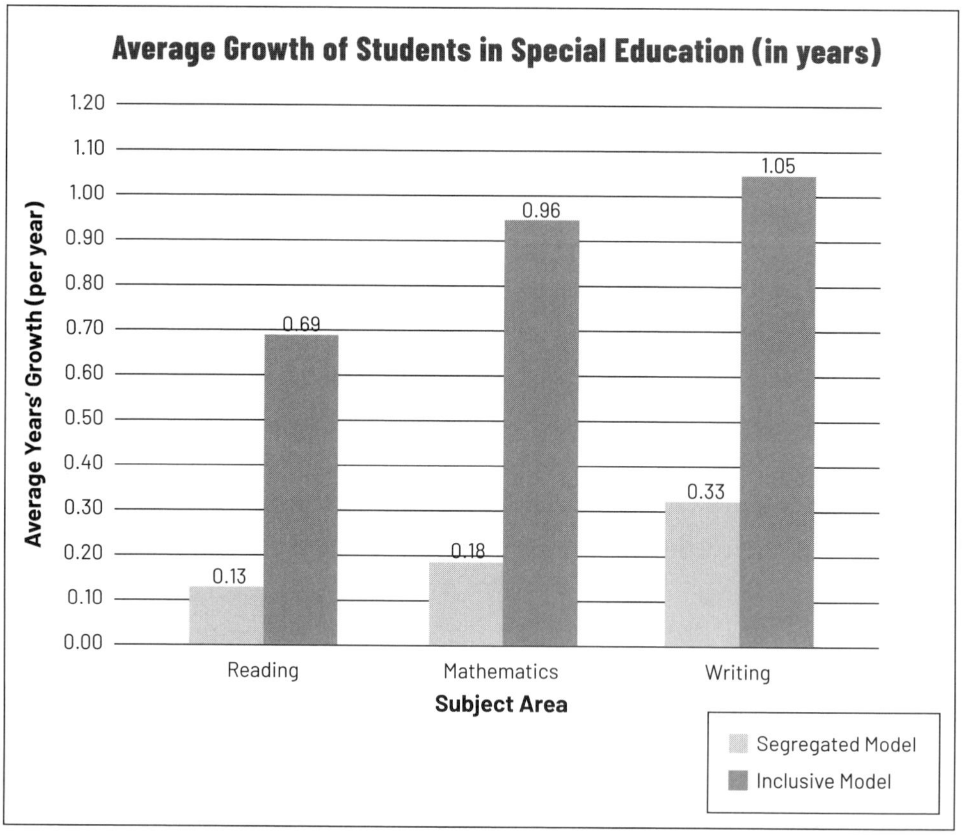

FIGURE 7.7: Academic growth of Inclusive Elementary School students enrolled in the special education program.

a variety of ways to improve instruction and ultimately lead to schoolwide reform whereby all students are supported and make progress.

Leadership School is a K–6 school located in an urban area of California. The principal of Leadership School was recognized as the state's principal of the year for her outstanding leadership abilities. School function area 4 (leadership for instruction and school improvement) discusses the importance of a schoolwide focus on research and continuous data-based decision making (Stephens et al., 2019). In the interest of closing the achievement gap at Leadership School, the principal created a school function team for the single purpose of exploring student data. Under the guidance of the principal, the teachers worked together to recognize where all students were academically and teach them from that point in their learning. Teachers used students' individual performance as a compass to guide instruction, intervention, assessment, and, if needed, acceleration.

The goal was to provide interventions and motivating programs that would empower Leadership School students to succeed.

By putting faces to the data, the school function team asked, "What is fair to expect for each student?" Fair is not the same for every student. Educators kept in mind the crucial difference between equality and equity; equality means each student receives the same lesson or the same instruction, while equity recognizes each student's different circumstances and allocates the exact resources, lessons, and instructional opportunities necessary to reach an equal outcome. It is this focus on every student that drove the team's decisions on what programs to implement and what systemic changes to make.

Every trimester, the leadership team reviewed Where We Are charts, using progress monitoring to consistently know whether each student was at, above, or below English language arts and mathematics standards. Checking achievement and social-emotional learning goals and standards for students (step 9, monitor implementation) and taking the details and revising and adjusting implementation (step 10, revise and adjust) provided a focus that continually served as a needs assessment for each student, propelling teachers to redefine and rethink interventions.

Leadership School teachers and staff knew their students, including their behavior, academic ability, and social and character development. With consistent and effective communication from school to home, they provided parents valuable and timely feedback on how their children were progressing. With the powerful information of Where We Are charts, report cards, and multiple end-of-year measures and benchmarks, Leadership School made goals for interventions. Leadership School determined which students needed intervention, in-depth instruction, or acceleration. The question then became how to find the right programs and strategies for all.

Key intervention programs made a substantive change for students at Leadership School, helping to close the achievement gap. These programs included the following three approaches.

1. ***Research-based computer and technology programs:*** *Many interventions included visual conceptualization, from web-based computer programs to state-of-the-art electronic keyboards in the computer lab.*

2. ***Bell-to-bell interventions throughout the school day:*** *In addition to new technology, Leadership School implemented interventions or acceleration opportunities for students. As a result of the school function team, Leadership School added flexible small-ability groups, station rotations, and project-based learning to existing best practices. When scheduling students in classes, Leadership School determined that it could cluster students with disabilities, those with gifts, and English learners, focusing on differentiation. Leadership School welcomed into classrooms paraeducators who had a repertoire of diverse strategies for at-risk students. Leadership School students switched classrooms daily for specific leveled instruction. This clustering of students led to a more in-depth focus for teachers and greater student results. In addition, the teachers served as mentors for student teachers. Student teachers assisted Leadership School teachers with at-risk students, shared new strategies in the classroom, and helped meet students' diverse needs.*

3. ***Supplemental instructional services program:*** *This weekly before-and-after-school intervention program aligned with grade-level standards. Most significantly, the program enabled teachers to meet students where they were academically, meaning students could learn at their own pace. Leadership School saw great growth in standardized test scores and significant subgroup results.*

Although many students achieved at academic proficiency, Leadership School needed a systemic change to hold itself accountable for all students schoolwide. It scheduled daily and weekly interventions for students. Leadership School also added technology programs to excite and actively engage the students in academic subject areas. And the school function team shifted the focus from how educators teach to how students learn.

Leadership School was awarded Innovative School of the Year in Science, Math, and Technology by the state even as it continued to look for effective, research-based interventions and acceleration strategies to propel every student toward academic proficiency. These systematic interventions provided ongoing computer-generated reports, from which teachers and the leadership team could analyze students' progress. They proved efficient in the goal of closing the achievement gap.

Leadership School experienced a dichotomy: a generation of students who did to learn were taught by educators who learned to do. Leadership School students were digital natives from birth, yet many educators were learning technology as a second language. Therefore, professional learning was crucial for effective implementation of any new technology programs. As they were competing in a fast-paced world of technology and information, educators faced the challenge of how to make academic subject material relevant to the lives of Leadership School students, particularly students with disabilities. Whether intervention or acceleration was necessary, the teachers learned they must check for understanding and monitor progress toward academic proficiency. Continually, the school leadership team met to assess what tools to use to engage students as active participants in their learning.

Literature has documented that principals' attitudes and their leadership as change agents greatly affect schoolwide reform (Lasky & Karge, 2006; Northouse, 2019). Through the school function team, professional learning was provided on all programs brought to the school. In addition, all certified and classified staff meetings focused on student needs. With valuable input from staff, students, parents, and community partners, Leadership School created a shared vision as a team. Parents and partners were informed about new programs and technology through websites, school messenger emails and phone calls, the parent-teacher association, the school site council, back-to-school night, open house, spirit ceremonies, parent conferences, visitations, and the principal's newsletter. In addition, pertinent articles were sent home in Monday packets that taught the parent community about new programs.

While Leadership School couldn't attribute all academic success to any one intervention, the leadership team believed the three key programs made a big difference. All student subgroups made significant growth on standardized assessments. On the California progress-monitoring system, each demographic made the following gains: Asian students up 9 points to 987, Hispanic students up 44 points to 874, White students up 24 points to 924, socioeconomically disadvantaged students up 59 points to 816, and English learners up 46 points to 934. Leadership School English learners outperformed the English-only students. The students with disabilities increased 41 points to 712. Although achievement gaps continued to challenge the school, all subgroups showed great progress.

Interventions and acceleration for the Leadership School's inclusive model evolved over time and continued to be works in progress, positively affecting student learning before, during, and after school. Tangible results included student progress toward proficiency of academic standards and 21st century skill–based learning. The ability to show concepts visually helped all students. As digital natives, Leadership School students successfully used the technology and hands-on approach of the music lab, mathematics lab, and previously mentioned interventions. These programs brought forth positive gains and curricular connections that transferred into academic success in the classroom. Intangible results were more qualitative in nature, and were expressed through smiles; the gratitude of the staff, students, and parent community; and an excitement to come to school.

These improved practices elicited positive outcomes, and the computer-generated reports allowed educators to communicate with students and parents on individual goals. Results of these education supports showed that the school provided scaffolds for struggling learners, challenges for excelling learners, and high standards and expectations for all. The process of the eleven steps to inclusive programming was very effective at this site.

The principal at Leadership School made it very clear to all involved that the vision of high-quality teaching and learning was the focus (Fullan & Quinn, 2016). She knew she played a key role in student achievement (Goldring et al., 2018), and she did not shy away from keeping instruction for *all* students front and center (Hattie, 2015).

Step 9: Monitor Implementation

When they experience an inclusive environment, students are nurtured in a holistic setting. Students are challenged to be the best they can be and to learn all they can about academics while participating as fully as they are capable in creative arts, spirituality, athletics, and cocurricular activities. The world does not have banks for people with disabilities or stores for people with disabilities; therefore, there should not be separate places of education for people with disabilities. Equity and diversity in society include people who are learning a language, are gifted, and have various disabilities. LST monitoring of data collection, student progress, and teacher beliefs about the process will enhance movement toward schoolwide inclusion.

For example, monitoring data at Leadership School provided value and research to improve not only that school but also a sister campus in the same district. A longitudinal study compared thirty students from Leadership School and thirty students from a neighboring school in the same district that did not have an inclusive program and instead provided services to students with disabilities in a segregated special education classroom (Miller & Karge, 2015). The study used several data tools and took place over six years, following the students from first grade to sixth grade. The graph in figure 7.8 shows the average change in standard scores between initial and subsequent administrations of the Woodcock-Johnson achievement tests given between first and sixth grade for Leadership School's and the neighboring school's students.

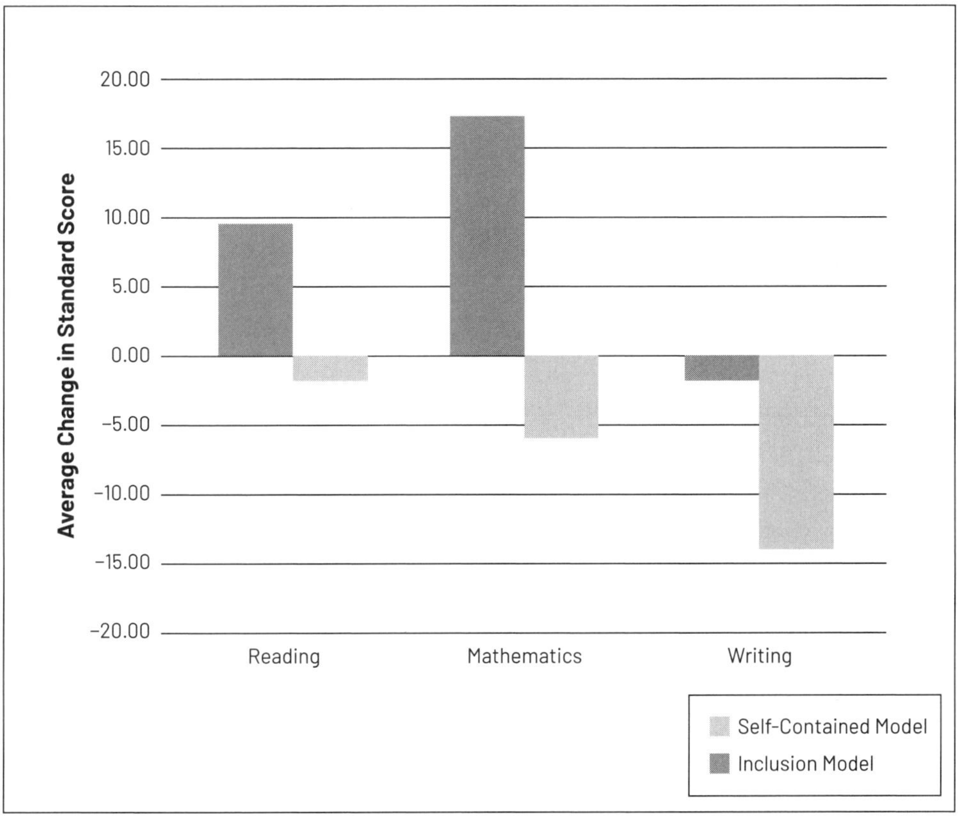

Source: Miller & Karge, 2015. Used with permission.

FIGURE 7.8: Achievement test data from Leadership School versus a noninclusive school.

The students enrolled in the inclusive school program experienced tremendous growth, while students who received their special education services in segregated classrooms flatlined in both reading and mathematics. The researchers hypothesized this was because the students in the inclusive school received all the core content instruction and specially designed services in the general education classroom (Miller & Karge, 2015). In contrast, the segregated classroom, taught by a very talented special education teacher, merely focused on IEP goals, and the students did not have access to the core content instruction. It is also important to note that when the principals of both schools and the superintendent saw the data on writing, they formed a think tank, and the following year, they implemented a writing process program districtwide to increase writing scores. Thus, they implemented multiple monitoring initiatives.

Step 10: Revise and Adjust

As indicated in figure 7.6 (page 167), the decision-making cycle for data collection is continuous. The LST should monitor and adjust the inclusion plan based on results, student needs, and the school- or districtwide vision. For example, a high school district in California used these eleven steps to determine how it could improve on providing inclusive practices. When the LST reached step 10, it realized from the data it gathered that it needed to go back and conduct more professional learning on differentiation and engagement strategies (Karge, 2014).

In another example, during the revise and adjust stage, a California middle school district learned it needed to address some of the general education teachers' fears and feelings about working with students with disabilities. This meant adjusting the professional learning time to be more focused on discussing the various disabilities at the school; the behavior specialist spent time with the staff describing some of the behaviors and how they had been minimized. The site administrator saw discussing discomfort or potential discomfort as "stepping into vulnerability." That administrator writes, "After taking the daring step of really talking about the individuals and their needs, we were able to go back through steps 3 through 10 and eventually celebrate successes we never dreamed possible" (H. Cunningham, personal communication, November 12, 2021). The process this middle school principal used was what lecturer and author Brené Brown (2018) refers to as "daring leadership" because the staff went through a process of "talking straight" and "taking action" (p. 110).

Transparent discussions and reflections related to the data cycle provide for future planning to take place and adjustments to be made. Each year, different students enroll and new data emerge. The inclusion plan is always in implementation mode!

Step 11: Celebrate and Share Successes

When schools see progress and students are achieving, it is critical to celebrate and share successes. There are countless ways to do this. The principal could plan a school success hour and celebration as a school. Bring special treats or goodies to faculty meetings. Let the local businesses know what you are doing. You may be able to obtain donations for the celebration. One school I worked with gave teachers a day to write personal notes to every student in their class or on their caseload. These were handed out at the same time during school success hour.

At another school where I worked, when the leadership team learned of the substantial progress all students made in the high school's co-taught English class (see figure 7.9), it brought in pizza for the class to celebrate.

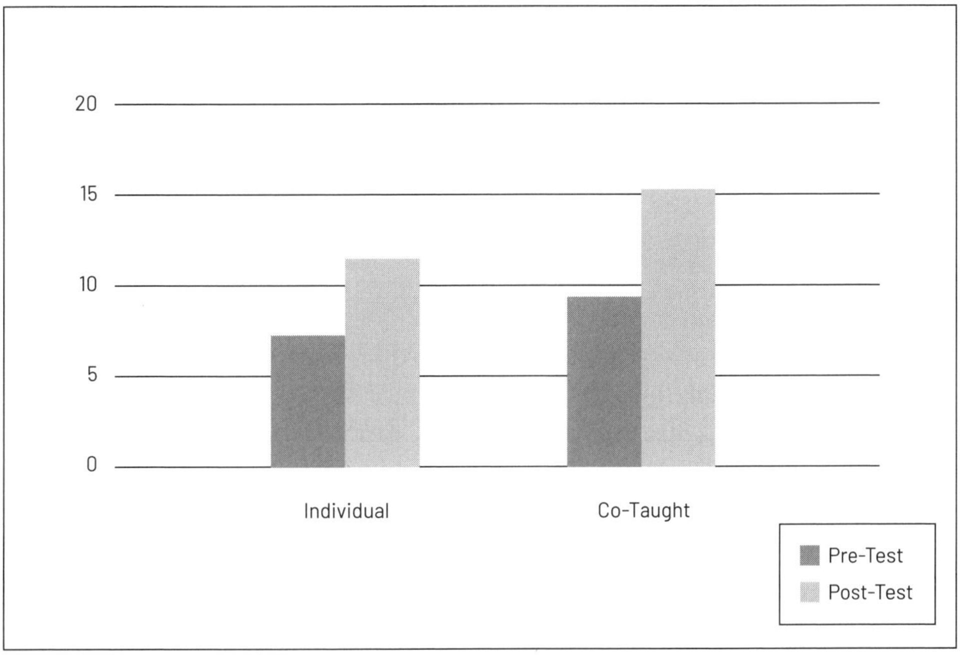

FIGURE 7.9: Pre- and post-test scores in individual and co-taught high school English classes.

During the celebration, the administrators asked the students why they believed their test scores had improved so much during one term; many students indicated having two teachers in the room was the reason. Others talked about the different ways the two teachers taught and the value of each when the students needed to understand a certain concept, vocabulary word, or book view. This school had just started to implement inclusive practices and had begun by placing all students with disabilities in co-taught classes. The individually taught class in the figure did not have any students with disabilities in it; five of thirty students in the co-taught class had disabilities. The exact same pre- and post-tests were used in each class, and the tests were all administered on the same day (just different class periods). Something intriguing to keep in mind about these data is that the general education teacher was the same for both classes. A similar study compared pre- and post-test scores in mathematics. Brian A. Bottge and his colleagues (2017) found that when the special education teacher was in the mathematics classroom providing the specially designed instruction, the students with disabilities scored higher and made fewer errors than peers in other settings.

Conclusion

Inclusion should be a cycle, an ongoing process of review and planning. When leaders are prepared to coach their leadership teams using the eleven steps, a clear path for success is in view. Remember, the steps do not always occur in order. As education specialists Jal Mehta, Max Yurkofsky, and Kim Frumin (2022) assert, leadership toward continuous improvement is not a linear process. There is no one way to establish an inclusive school. However, the data are clear. Ample evidence shows students with disabilities gain academic and social benefits from inclusive settings (Hehir et al., 2016). The underlying principle is that all students receive a chance to be successful, to be supported, and to achieve in their own right. In her book *Dare to Lead*, Brown (2018) writes, "We need braver leaders and more courageous cultures" (p. 6).

A strong school leader builds a supportive and empathetic climate for the educators at the school (Grissom et al., 2021). My best advice for school leaders is to watch, listen, ask, and learn. If you do this consistently, you will create an inclusive environment for students with disabilities. Effective leadership combined with proper vision and implementation using the eleven steps to an inclusive school will lead to a successful inclusive climate.

Appendix

The following resources and templates can make the school's path toward becoming more inclusive a smoother one.

At-a-Glance Review of IDEA (2004)

IDEA is the primary legal reference for supporting the free appropriate public education of students with disabilities.

There are six primary principles of IDEA.

1. **Zero reject:** No child may be denied an education. Specifically, the Fourteenth Amendment gives specific rights to a *free appropriate public education*. The most common way we note free appropriate public education is progress on IEP objectives.

2. **Free appropriate public education:** All students with disabilities have the right to a free education that is specifically designed to meet their unique needs. *Appropriate* is defined through IDEA and case law as "meaningful gain" and "some educational benefit." Without an *appropriate* education, a school is violating a student's rights under IDEA.

3. **Least restrictive environment:** To the *maximum extent appropriate*, students with disabilities (from birth to their twenty-second birthday) must be educated with students without disabilities. If the least restrictive environment cannot confer a free appropriate public education, then the continuum of services must be available.

4. **Due process:** *Procedural due process* is provided to citizens to allow them to challenge the government's intrusion on their liberties. Students placed in special education programs have the same right of *due process* to ensure that at the time of placement, and at least annually thereafter, this environment is and continues to be the *least restrictive* and offers *appropriate education*.

5. **Parent participation:** Parent rights are called *procedural safeguards*. Parents have the right to participate in every decision related to identification, evaluation, and placement of their children suspected of having or already identified as having a disability. Parents are the experts on their own children and should be consulted and considered members of the education team.

6. **Nondiscriminatory evaluation:** To assess a student, two or more assessment instruments must be used, and the instruments must be administered in the student's native language.

Reference

Individuals With Disabilities Education Improvement Act of 2004, Pub. L. No. 108-446 § 300.115 (2004).

Sample Learning Services Team Referral Form

Student Background Information

Full name: ______________________________

Date of birth: ______________ Preferred pronouns: __________ Age: ____

School: ____________ Grade: ________ Current teacher: ______________

Parent or guardian: ____________ Home phone or cell phone: ____________

Address: ________________________ Email: ______________

Primary language: ______________________________

Date enrolled: __________ School history or retention: ______________

Student Medical Information

Vision: ______________

Hearing: ______________

Medication: ______________

Any relevant family information: ______________________

____

Attendance: ☐ Good ☐ Fair ☐ Poor

Days missed this year: __________

Referral Information

Referral date: ______________

Referral initiator: ______________

Reason for referral or summary of primary concerns: ______________

____

Areas of Concern

Check all that apply.

Academic Performance	Study Skills	Language Skills
☐ Mathematics performance	☐ Comprehension	☐ Articulation
☐ Reading recognition	☐ Homework	☐ Command of English
☐ Language arts or writing	☐ Organizational skills	☐ Oral vocabulary
☐ Reading comprehension	☐ Classwork	☐ Comprehension
☐ Content-area knowledge	☐ Assignment completion	☐ Grammar
☐ Electives	☐ Time on task	☐ Social interactions with peers

Attendance	Behavior or Social Skills	Health
☐ Tardiness	☐ Self-concept	☐ Suspected vision problem
☐ Skipping of certain classes	☐ Peer relationships	☐ Suspected hearing problem
☐ Physical education attendance	☐ Depression or mood swings	☐ Mobility issue
☐ Number of sick days	☐ Classroom conduct	☐ Broken bone
☐ ________________	☐ Attention	☐ Other health factors
☐ ________________	☐ Motivation	☐ ________________
☐ ________________	☐ Attitude	☐ ________________

Answer the following questions.

1. What are the student's strengths?

2. What are the teacher's concerns—academic, behavioral, or both? Describe them.

3. Describe the interventions you have tried and the duration for which you have tried them. Check all that apply.

Teaching Techniques	Teaching Environments	Teaching Assignments
☐ Vary your voice volume.	☐ Change the classroom setting.	☐ Simplify the assignment.
☐ Lower the amount or degree of stimulation.	☐ Create more physical space.	☐ Shorten the assignment.
☐ Circulate around the room.	☐ Reduce physical distractions.	☐ Use a notebook recording system.
☐ Repeat instructions the same way.	☐ Reduce the student's physical space.	☐ Use advanced organizers.
☐ Use visual or auditory aides.	☐ Create study carrels or "offices."	☐ Have the student copy directions.
☐ List assignments on the board.	☐ Rearrange the seating.	☐ Change the assignment structure.
☐ Write directions on the board.	☐ Use centers.	☐ Extend the time allowed.
☐ Use behavior modifications; provide modeling.	☐ Use parent or volunteer aides.	☐ Use a daily progress report.
☐ Teach study skills.	☐ Use study buddies.	☐ Use weekly progress reviews.
☐ Limit oral instructions.	☐ Assign cross-age tutors.	☐ Confer with specialist personnel.
☐ Use hand or shoulder contact.	☐ Create a special study area.	☐ Keep work samples or portfolios.
☐ Provide concrete examples.	☐ Take the class or group outdoors.	☐ Review past achievement tests.
☐ Use a tape recorder.	☐ Team-teach with another teacher.	☐ Review cumulative folder.
☐ Use a computer.	☐ Change groups.	☐ Have parent contacts or conferences.
☐ Use diagnostic materials.	☐ Form variable groupings.	☐ ____________________
☐ Keep a graphic or chart of progress.	☐ Form groups with one or more other classes.	☐ ____________________
☐ Have the student repeat directions.	☐ ____________________	☐ ____________________

Sample Parent Notice of a Learning Services Team Meeting

Print this on school letterhead.

Date: ____________________

Dear parent/guardian of ______________________________,

As discussed with your student's teacher, a learning services team (LST) meeting has been set up to discuss concerns regarding ________________. Our goal is to discuss academic, social-emotional, or attendance interventions that will provide your student with opportunities to find success at _____________.

The meeting will be held on ____ at ______________________ in room #_______. If you cannot attend this meeting, please contact me at ______________________ to reschedule as soon as possible. All LST meetings have a follow-up meeting to check on progress and determine additional actions that may be required. The follow-up meeting will be held on __________________________________ at _____________ in room #_______.

Items we will discuss are:

- Areas of student strengths and weaknesses in academic skills, classroom behavior, social interactions, or attendance
- The specific concerns that are the reasons for the referral
- A specific plan to assist the student in finding success at school

Please think about the preceding topics and be ready to discuss them at the meeting.

You are an essential part of this process, and we look forward to working with you.

Sincerely,

____

Student Response Form for the Learning Services Team

Directions: Complete the following sentences.

Name: ______________________________

The school activities I really enjoy are: ______________________________

____

The activities I enjoy the most outside of school are: ______________________________

____

I would like more help with the following classes and subjects in school: __________

____

If I had a chance, the change I would want to make in my classes is: __________

____

I learn best when: ______________________________

What I do best in school is: ______________________________

When I finish school, I would like to have one of the following jobs.

1. ______________________________
2. ______________________________
3. ______________________________

The person I like to talk to the most is: ______________

The person who helps me learn is: ______________

My goals for this year are:

1. ______________________________
2. ______________________________
3. ______________________________

In order to achieve my goals, I plan to: ______________________________

____

____

____

Learning Services Team Log Sheet

Student Name	Referral Date	Reason for Referral	Learning Services Team Meeting Date	Student Disposition
1.				
2.				
3.				
4.				
5.				
6.				
7.				
8.				
9.				
10.				

Learning Services Team Summary Form

Date of initial learning services team meeting: ______________________

Student: ______________________ ID: ______________

Grade: ______________ Date of birth: ______________________

Primary language: ______________ School: ______________________

Student Strengths

Known Information and Monitoring Data (Reference the intervention data log.)	Interventions Attempted	Progress-Monitoring Data (Fill this in following interventions attempted.)
Standardized test scores and common assessment data		
Other pertinent information (samples or examples of classroom work)		

page 1 of 2

Concerns (Be specific—based on data.)		
Questions (Seek clarification.)		
Strategies based on student strengths (Brainstorm.)		
Actions: frequency, duration, and intensity (Prioritize.)	**Who?**	**By what date?**

Follow-up meeting date: ____________ Additional participants?: ________________

Team Members' Signatures

- **Student:** ____
- **Parent or guardian:** ______________________________________
- **Learning services team coordinator:** ______________________
- **Administrator:** ____
- **School psychologist:** _____________________________________
- **Referring teacher:** _______________________________________
- **Team member:** ____
- **Team member:** ____

page 2 of 2

Sample Special Education Referral Form

Student name: ________________________ Date of birth: ______________________

IEP date: ______________________

Grade: _______

Parent or legal guardian: ___________________________ Phone: __________________

Address: ____

City: ____________________________ State or province: _______ Zip: ____________

Person making referral: ____________________________ Title: __________________

Date parent notified of intent to refer: ______________________

Method of notifying parent of intent to refer:

☐ Conference ☐ Phone call ☐ Written communication

Parent's native language or other primary mode of communication if other than English: _______________

Student's native language or other primary mode of communication: ____________

Primary concern regarding student: ____

Specific reasons for referral:

☐ Reading ☐ Written language ☐ Hearing ☐ Attention

☐ Mathematics ☐ Self-help skills ☐ Vision ☐ Social-emotional skills

☐ Spelling ☐ Fine motor skills ☐ Health ☐ Cognitive functioning

☐ Gross motor skills ☐ Speech or language

☐ Other: ____

General education intervention attempts: If this referral is by an educational representative, describe the interventions attempted prior to this referral, and attach documentation. (Please attach all LST meeting referrals and summaries.)

____

____

For District Use Only

Date received: __________________ Date assessment plan due: __________________

Received by ____________________ Forwarded to ____________________

Case manager: ____________________

General Education Student Information Form

Dear ______________________________,

As a member of the LST, I am sharing that ______________________________ will be in your general education class this year. The student has an active IEP.

The IEP goals include the following. (List goals.)

1. ______________________________
2. ______________________________
3. ______________________________

This student will need the following accommodations in order to be successful. (List accommodations.)

1. ______________________________
2. ______________________________
3. ______________________________

It has been determined the least restrictive environment for this student is your classroom with the following supports. (Check the required services, and add the names of the personnel the teacher will be working with to ensure the services are met.)

- ☐ With a consult from ______________________________
- ☐ With paraeducator ______________________________
- ☐ With specialized academic instruction from ______________________________
- ☐ With related services provider ______________________________
- ☐ With co-teaching from ______________________________

If you have any questions, please contact me at ______________________________.

Sincerely,

____

LST member

References and Resources

Abu Zaineh, S., & Karge, B. D. (2019). Learning about mentoring from professions outside of education. *The Chronicle of Mentoring and Coaching, 3*(12), 123–126.

American School Counselor Association. (2016). *ASCA ethical standards for school counselors.* Alexandria, VA: Author. Accessed at https://schoolcounselor.org/getmedia/f041cbd0-7004-47a5-ba01-3a5d657c6743/Ethical-Standards.pdf on March 29, 2022.

Anderson, K. P. (2020). The relationship between inclusion, absenteeism, and disciplinary outcomes for students with disabilities. *Educational Evaluation and Policy Analysis, 43*(1), 32–59. Accessed at https://doi.org/10.3102/0162373720968558 on August 10, 2022.

Anderson, L. W., & Krathwohl, D. (Eds.). (2001). *A taxonomy for learning, teaching, and assessing: A revision of Bloom's taxonomy of educational objectives.* Boston: Allyn & Bacon.

Anderson, N., & Karge, B. (2020). Meaningful mentorship and its impact on the efficacy of secondary music teachers. *The Chronicle of Mentoring and Coaching, 1*(13), 467–473.

Archer, A. L., & Hughes, C. A. (2010). *Explicit instruction: Effective and efficient teaching.* New York: Guilford Press.

Arden, S. V., Gandhi, A. G., Edmonds, R. Z., & Danielson, L. (2017). Toward more effective tiered systems: Lessons from national implementation efforts. *Exceptional Children, 83*(3), 269–280. https://doi.org/10.1177/0014402917693565

Avendano, S. M., & Cho, E. (2020). Building collaborative relationships with parents: A checklist for promoting success. *TEACHING Exceptional Children, 52*(4), 250–260.

Bacharach, N. L., Heck, T. W., & Dahlberg, K. (2010). Changing the face of student teaching through coteaching. *Action in Teacher Education, 32*(1), 3–14.

Banks, L. M., & Polack, S. (2013). *The economic costs of exclusion and gains of inclusion of people with disabilities: Evidence from low and middle income countries.* London: Christian Blind Mission. Accessed at https://cbm.org/fileadmin/user_upload/Publications/Costs-of-Exclusion-and-Gains-of-Inclusion-Report.pdf on March 29, 2022.

Barnard-Brak, L., & Stevens, T. (2020). Criteria for determining eligibility for extended school year services. *The Journal of Special Education, 55*(1), 3–12. https://doi.org/10.1177/0022466920911468

Bartz, C. A. (2017). *The special ed administrator's personal trainer for strengthening leadership, relationship and management skills.* Palm Beach Gardens, FL: LRP.

Bateman, D. (2015). What all school principals know about special education. In *Council of Administrators of Special Education (CASE) essential series.* Manhattan, KS: The Master Teacher.

Baugh, B. (Director). (2009). *To save a life* [Film]. Samuel Goldwyn Films.

Berkeley, S., Scanlon, D., Bailey, T. R., Sutton, J. C., & Sacco, D. M. (2020). A snapshot of RTI implementation a decade later: New picture, same story. *Journal of Learning Disabilities, 53*(5), 332–342.

Bhatnagar, N., & Das, A. (2014). Attitudes of secondary regular school teachers toward inclusive education in New Delhi, India: A qualitative study. *Exceptionality Education International, 24*(2), 17–30.

Billingsley, B., & Bettini, E. (2019). Special education teacher attrition and retention: A review of the literature. *Review of Educational Research, 89*(5), 697–744. https://doi.org/10.3102/0034654319862495

Blackburn, B. R., & Witzel, B. S. (2018). *Rigor in the RTI and MTSS classroom: Practical tools and strategies.* New York: Routledge.

Bloom, B. S. (Ed.). (1956). *Taxonomy of educational objectives: The classification of educational goals; Handbook I: Cognitive domain.* New York: McKay.

Board of Education of the Hendrick Hudson School District v. Rowley, 458 U.S. 176 (1982).

Bogdanovich, P. (Director). (1985). *Mask* [Film]. Universal Pictures.

Bottge, B. A., Cohen, A. S., & Choi, H.-J. (2017). Comparisons of mathematics intervention effects in resource and inclusive classrooms. *Exceptional Children, 84*(2), 197–212. https://doi.org/10.1177/0014402917736854

Bradshaw, C. P., Pas, E. T., Bottiani, J. H., Debnam, K. J., Reinke, W. M., Herman, K. C., et al. (2018). Promoting cultural responsivity and student engagement through double check coaching of classroom teachers: An efficacy study. *School Psychology Review, 47*(2), 118–134.

Brown, B. (2018). *Dare to lead: Brave work, tough conversations, whole hearts*. New York: Random House.

Brown v. Board of Education of Topeka, 347 U.S. 483 (1954).

Brusca-Vega, R., Brown, K., & Yasutake, D. (2011). Science achievement of students in co-taught, inquiry-based classrooms. *Learning Disabilities: A Multidisciplinary Journal, 17*(1), 23–31.

Buffum, A., Mattos, M., & Malone, J. (2018). *Taking action: A handbook for RTI at Work*. Bloomington, IN: Solution Tree Press.

Burke, E. (2021). *The benefit of a social learning intervention to increase self-efficacy, engagement and social inclusion for students with autism* (Publication No. 28094903) [Doctoral dissertation, Concordia University Irvine]. ProQuest. Accessed at www.proquest.com/openview/790bf414e5ee94cd0caaae33931ddec3/1?pq-origsite=gscholar&cbl=18750&diss=y on May 30, 2022.

Burke, E., & Karge, B. D. (2022). Increased engagement, self-efficacy, and social inclusion in students with autism. In F. Reza (Ed.), *Diversity and inclusion in educational institutions* (pp. 49–80). Newcastle Upon Tyne, UK: Cambridge Scholars.

Burt, J. L., & Whitney, T. (2018). From resource room to the real world: Facilitating generalization of intervention outcomes. *TEACHING Exceptional Children, 50*(6), 364–372.

California Commission on Teacher Credentialing. (2018). *California Teaching Performance Assessment guide: Single subject directions and rubrics, instructional cycle 1—Learning about students and planning instruction*. Sacramento, CA: Author. Accessed at www.csusm.edu/soe/currentstudents/caltpa_c1_guide_ss.pdf on July 12, 2022.

Callender, W. A. (2014). *Using RTI in secondary schools: A training manual for successful implementation*. Thousand Oaks, CA: Corwin Press.

Canadian Human Rights Act, R.S.C. 1985, c. H-6 (1985).

Carver-Thomas, D., Burns, D., Leung-Gagné, M., & Ondrasek, N. (2022, January). *Teacher shortages during the pandemic: How California districts are responding*. Palo Alto, CA: Learning Policy Institute. Accessed at https://learningpolicyinstitute.org/sites/default/files/product-files/Teacher_Shortages_During_Pandemic_REPORT.pdf on July 12, 2022.

Carver-Thomas, D., & Darling-Hammond, L. (2017, August). *Teacher turnover: Why it matters and what we can do about it.* Palo Alto, CA: Learning Policy Institute. Accessed at https://learningpolicyinstitute.org/sites/default/files/product-files/Teacher_Turnover_REPORT.pdf on July 12, 2022.

CAST. (n.d.). *About Universal Design for Learning.* Accessed at www.cast.org/impact/universal-design-for-learning-udl on July 1, 2022.

Cawn, B. (2020). *Ambitious instruction: Teaching with rigor in the secondary classroom.* Bloomington, IN: Solution Tree Press.

Champion, M. (2015). *Qualitative phenomenological study exploring instructional practices that contribute to academic success for public elementary school English language learners* (Publication No. 1106) [Doctoral dissertation, Liberty University]. Liberty University Doctoral Dissertations and Projects. Accessed at http://digitalcommons.liberty.edu/doctoral/1106 on July 18, 2022.

Chan, T., & Yuen, M. (2015). Inclusive education in an international school: A case study from Hong Kong. *International Journal of Special Education, 30*(3), 86–97.

Choi, J. H., Meisenheimer, J. M., McCart, A. B., & Sailor, W. (2017). Improving learning for all students through equity-based inclusive reform practices: Effectiveness of a fully integrated schoolwide model on student reading and math achievement. *Remedial and Special Education, 38*(1), 28–41.

Christensen, J., Roberston, J. S., Williamson, R., & Hunter, W. C. (2013). Preparing educational leaders for special education success: Principals' perspectives. *The Researcher, 25*(1), 94–107.

Cobley, D. (2018). *Disability and international development: A guide for students and practitioners.* New York: Routledge.

Cole, S., Murphy, H., Frisby, M., Grossi, T., & Bolte, H. (2019). *A longitudinal study to determine the impact of inclusion on student academic outcomes* [Executive summary]. Bloomington: Indiana University Center on Education and Lifelong Learning. Accessed at https://iidc.indiana.edu/cell/what-we-do/pdf/Inclusion-study-handout.pdf on March 30, 2022.

Conklin, W. (2011). *Higher-order thinking skills to develop 21st century learners.* Huntington Beach, CA: Teacher Created Materials.

Cook, B. G., & Odom, S. L. (2013). Evidence-based practices and implementation science in special education. *Exceptional Children, 79*(3), 135–144.

Cook, L., & Friend, M. (1995). Co-teaching: Guidelines for creating effective practices. *Focus on Exceptional Children, 28*(3), 1–16. Accessed at https://pdfs.semanticscholar.org/31ca/3592c18acdd238ce488cd7184017b904b646.pdf on July 12, 2022.

Cooper, K., Smith, L. G. E., & Russell, A. (2017). Social identity, self-esteem, and mental health in autism. *European Journal of Social Psychology, 47*(7), 844–854. https://doi.org/10.1002/ejsp.2297

Cordingley, P., Higgins, S., Greany, T., Buckler, N., Coles-Jordan, D., Crisp, B., et al. (2015). *Developing great teaching: Lessons from the international reviews into effective professional development* [Project report]. London: Teacher Development Trust.

Cornelius, K. E., Rosenberg, M. S., & Sandmel, K. N. (2020). Examining the impact of professional development and coaching on mentoring of novice special educators. *Action in Teacher Education, 42*(3), 253–270.

Cortiella, C., & Horowitz, S. H. (2014). *The state of learning disabilities: Facts, trends and emerging issues* (3rd ed.). New York: National Center for Learning Disabilities. Accessed at https://ncld.org/wp-content/uploads/2014/11/2014-State-of-LD.pdf on March 30, 2022.

Council of Administrators of Special Education. (1999). *Section 504 and the ADA promoting student access: A resource guide for educators* (2nd ed.). Albuquerque, NM: Author. Accessed at https://files.eric.ed.gov/fulltext/ED436899.pdf on March 30, 2022.

Crockett, L., Jukes, I., & Churches, A. (2011). *Literacy is not enough: 21st century fluencies for the digital age*. Thousand Oaks, CA: Corwin.

Cummings, E. (2021). *Understanding the antecedent behavior consequence (ABC) data model.* Accessed at www.behaviorist.com/antecedent-behavior-consequence-abc-data on July 12, 2022.

Curren-Preis, M., Garcia, N., & Shaughnessy, M. (2022). Why classroom equity strategies aren't always equal. *Educational Leadership, 78*(5), 55–59.

Darling-Hammond, L. (2017). Teacher education around the world: What can we learn from international practice? *European Journal of Teacher Education, 40*(3), 291–309.

Deshler, D. D., Schumaker, J. B., Lenz, B. K., Bulgren, J. A., Hock, M. F., Knight, J., et al. (2009). Ensuring content-area learning by secondary students with learning disabilities. *Journal of Education, 189*(1–2), 169–181.

Dessemontet, R. S., Bless, G., & Morin, D. (2012). Effects of inclusion on the academic achievement and adaptive behavior of children with intellectual disabilities. *Journal of Intellectual Disability Research, 56*(6), 579–587.

Diana v. State Board of Education, Civ. Act. No. C-70-3, N.D. Cal. (1970).

Dillenburger, K., McKerr, L., Jordan, J. A., Devine, P., & Keenan, M. (2015). Creating an inclusive society . . . How close are we in relation to autism spectrum disorder? A general population survey. *Journal of Applied Research in Intellectual Disabilities, 28*(4), 330–340. https://doi.org/10.1111/jar.12144

Disability Discrimination Act 1992, No. 135 (2015).

Douglas, S. N., Uitto, D. J., Reinfelds, C. L., & D'Agostino, S. (2019). A systematic review of paraprofessional training materials. *The Journal of Special Education, 52*(4), 195–207.

DuFour, R., DuFour, R., Eaker, R., Mattos, M., & Muhammad, A. (2021). *Revisiting Professional Learning Communities at Work: Proven insights for sustained, substantive school improvement* (2nd ed.). Bloomington, IN: Solution Tree Press.

Duhigg, C. (2014). *The power of habit: Why we do what we do in life and business.* New York: Random House Trade Paperbacks.

Dyssegaard, C. B., & Larsen, M. S. (2013). *Evidence on inclusion.* Copenhagen, Denmark: Danish Clearinghouse for Educational Research. Accessed at https://edu.au.dk/fileadmin/edu/Udgivelser/Clearinghouse/Evidence_on_Inclusion.pdf on March 30, 2022.

Eagle, J. W., Dowd-Eagle, S. E., Snyder, A., & Holtzman, E. G. (2015). Implementing a multi-tiered system of support (MTSS): Collaboration between school psychologists and administrators to promote systems-level change. *Journal of Educational and Psychological Consultation, 25*(2–3), 160–177.

Eastman, B., & Rasmussen, A. (2021). *Authentic literacy instruction: Empowering secondary students to become lifelong readers, writers, and communicators.* Bloomington, IN: Solution Tree Press.

Education for All Handicapped Children Act of 1975, Pub. L. No. 94–142, 20 U.S.C. § 1401 (1975).

Eggers, D., & Calegari, N. C. (2011, April 30). The high cost of low teacher salaries. *The New York Times.* Accessed at www.nytimes.com/2011/05/01/opinion/01eggers.html on July 12, 2022.

El-Zraigat, I. A. (2012). Counseling gifted and talented students in Jordanian inclusive schools: Conclusion and implication. *International Journal of Special Education, 27*(2), 57–64.

Endrew F. v. Douglas County School District, 137 S. Ct. 988 (2017).

Fallah, S., Murawski, W. W., & Moradian, Z. (2018). The importance of developing cultural competence in working with families of students with disabilities from the Middle East, North Africa, and Southwest Asia. *The Journal of Special Education Apprenticeship, 7*(1), 1–28.

Family Educational Rights and Privacy Act, 20 U.S.C. § 1232g (1974).

Farris-Berg, K., & Dirkswager, E. J. (2013). *Trusting teachers with school success: What happens when teachers call the shots.* Lanham, MD: Rowman & Littlefield Education.

Feller, T. R., Jr., Myers, E., & Smith, A. (2022). Communities of practice empower teachers to tackle thorny problems. *The Learning Professional, 43*(1), 24–29.

Fensterwald, J. (2013, August 12). Common Core poses big challenge for students, big opportunity for teachers. *EdSource.* Accessed at https://edsource.org/2013/common-core-poses-big-challenge-for-students-big-opportunity-for-teachers/37065 on March 30, 2022.

Fernańdez-Alcántara, M., García-Caro, M. P., Pérez-Marfil, M. N., Hueso-Montoro, C., Laynez-Rubio, C., & Cruz-Quintana, F. (2016). Feelings of loss and grief in parents of children diagnosed with autism spectrum disorder (ASD). *Research in Developmental Disabilities, 55,* 312–321. https://doi.org/10.1016/j.ridd.2016.05.007

Fiedler, C. R. (2009). *Making a difference: Advocacy competencies for special education professionals* (2nd ed.). Austin, TX: PRO-ED.

Finkelstein, S. (2018, January–February). The best leaders are great teachers. *Harvard Business Review.* Accessed at https://hbr.org/2018/01/the-best-leaders-are-great-teachers on March 30, 2022.

Fisher, D., & Frey, N. (2014). Using teacher learning walks to improve instruction. *Principal Leadership, 14*(5), 58–61.

Florian, L. (2014). What counts as evidence of inclusive education? *European Journal of Special Needs Education, 29*(3), 286–294.

Florian, L., Black-Hawkins, K., & Rouse, M. (2017). *Achievement and inclusion in schools* (2nd ed.). New York: Routledge.

Forlin, C., & Chambers, D. (2011). Teacher preparation for inclusive education: Increasing knowledge but raising concerns. *Asia-Pacific Journal of Teacher Education, 39*(1), 17–32. https://doi.org/10.1080/1359866X.2010.540850

Friend, M. (2019). *Co-teaching strategies to improve student outcomes* (2nd ed.) [Laminated guide]. Port Chester, NY: National Professional Resources.

Friend, M., & Barron, T. (2016). Co-teaching as a special education service: Is classroom collaboration a sustainable practice? *Educational Practice and Reform, 2.* Accessed at https://journals.radford.edu/index.php/EPR/article/download/55/29 on March 30, 2022.

Fuchs, L. S., & Fuchs, D. (2001). *What is scientifically-based research on progress monitoring?* Washington, DC: National Center on Student Progress Monitoring. Accessed at https://files.eric.ed.gov/fulltext/ED502460.pdf on July 12, 2022.

Fullan, M., & Quinn, J. (2016). *Coherence: The right drivers in action for schools, districts, and systems.* Thousand Oaks, CA: Corwin Press.

Fuller, F. F. (1969). Concerns of teachers: A developmental conceptualization. *American Educational Research Journal, 6*(2), 207–226.

García, E., & Weiss, E. (2019). *The role of early career supports, continuous professional development, and learning communities in the teacher shortage.* Washington, DC: Economic Policy Institute. Accessed at https://files.epi.org/pdf/164976.pdf on March 30, 2022.

Gerlach, K. (2015). *Let's team up! A checklist for teachers, paraeducators and principals.* Port Chester, NY: National Professional Resources.

Gerlach, K. (2017). *The paraeducator's survival guide* [Laminated guide]. Port Chester, NY: National Professional Resources.

Gesel, S. A., & Lemons, C. J. (2020). Comparing schedules of progress monitoring using curriculum-based measurement in reading: A replication study. *Exceptional Children, 87*(1), 92–112. Accessed at https://journals.sagepub.com/doi/full/10.1177/0014402920924845 on July 12, 2022.

Glasser, W. (1993). *The quality school: Managing students without coercion.* New York: HarperCollins.

Goldring, E. B., Grissom, J. A., Rubin, M., Rogers, L. K., Neel, M., & Clark, M. A. (2018). *A new role emerges for principal supervisors: Evidence from six districts in the Principal Supervisor Initiative.* New York: Wallace Foundation. Accessed at www.wallacefoundation.org/knowledge-center/Documents/A-New-Role-Emerges-for-Principal-Supervisors.pdf on July 12, 2022.

Grasley-Boy, N. M., Gage, N. A., & Lombardo, M. (2019). Effect of SWPBIS on disciplinary exclusions for students with and without disabilities. *Exceptional Children, 86*(1), 25–39.

Gray, C. (2022). Social stories. In N. Grove (Ed.), *Storytelling, special needs and disabilities: Practical approaches for children and adults* (2nd ed., pp. 152–158). New York: Routledge.

Grissom, J. A., Egalite, A. J., & Lindsay, C. A. (2021, February). *How principals affect students and schools: A systematic synthesis of two decades of research.* New York: Wallace Foundation. Accessed at www.wallacefoundation.org/knowledge-center/Documents/How-Principals-Affect-Students-and-Schools.pdf on March 30, 2022.

Gunarhadi, S., Anwar, M., Andayani, T. R., & Shaari, A. S. (2016). The effect of cluster-based instruction on mathematic achievement in inclusive schools. *International Journal of Special Education, 31*(1), 78–87.

Habib, D. (Director). (2007). *Including Samuel* [Film]. LikeRightNow Films.

Habib, D. (Director). (2012). *Who cares about Kelsey?* [Film]. LikeRightNow Films.

Hagaman, J. L., & Casey, K. J. (2018). Teacher attrition in special education: Perspectives from the field. *Teacher Education and Special Education, 41*(4), 277–291.

Haines, R. (Director). (1986). *Children of a lesser god* [Film]. Paramount Pictures.

Hall, G. E., & Hord, S. M. (2015). *Implementing change: Patterns, principles, and potholes* (4th ed.). Boston: Pearson.

Hallahan, D. P., Kauffman, J. M., & Pullen, P. C. (2019). *Exceptional learners: An introduction to special education* (14th ed.). New York: Pearson.

Hamdan, A. R., Anuar, M. K., & Khan, A. (2016). Implementation of co-teaching approach in an inclusive classroom: Overview of the challenges, readiness, and role of special education teacher. *Asia Pacific Education Review, 17*(2), 289–298.

Hande, M., & Karge, B. D. (2021, October 10–12). *Developing self-regulation behavioral strategies for elementary students through the use of mindfulness* [Conference presentation]. Clute International Academic Conferences, Las Vegas, NV.

Hannigan, J. D., & Hannigan, J. E. (2021). *The MTSS start-up guide: Ensuring equity, access, and inclusivity for all students*. Thousand Oaks, CA: Corwin Press.

Hattie, J. (2015, February). High-impact leadership. *Education Leadership*, *72*(5), 36–40.

Hehir, T., Grindal, T., Freeman, B., Lamoreau, R., Borquaye, Y., & Burke, S. (2016, August). *A summary of the evidence on inclusive education*. Cambridge, MA: Abt Associates. Accessed at https://abtassociates.com/sites/default/files/2019-03/A_Summary_of_the_evidence_on_inclusive_education.pdf on March 30, 2022.

Herek, S. (Director). (1995). *Mr. Holland's opus* [Film]. Hollywood Pictures; Interscope Communications; PolyGram Filmed Entertainment.

Hiebert, E. H. (2015). Changing readers, changing texts: Beginning reading texts from 1960 to 2010. *Journal of Education*, *195*(3), 1–13. Accessed at www.bu.edu/journalofeducation/files/2015/11/Vol.195.No_.3.Hiebert.pdf on July12, 2022.

Hoover, J. J., Baca, L., Wexler-Love, E., & Saenz, L. (2008). *National implementation of response to intervention (RTI): Research summary*. Alexandria, VA: National Association of State Directors of Special Education. Accessed at www.researchgate.net/publication/228931288_National_implementation_of_response_to_intervention_RTI_Research_summary on July 12, 2022.

Huberman, M., Navo, M., & Parrish, T. (2012). Effective practices in high performing districts serving students in special education. *Journal of Special Education Leadership*, *25*(2), 59–71.

Hunt, P. F. (2021). Inclusive education: The case for early identification and early intervention in assistive technology. *Assistive Technology*, *33*(sup1), S94–S101.

Hurlbutt-Eastman, K., & O'Malley, L. (2015). Using SODA (stop, observe, deliberate, act) with a small group of elementary students on the autism spectrum. *Good Autism Practice*, *16*(1), 18–26.

Hussar, B., Zhang, J., Hein, S., Wang, K., Roberts, A., Cui, J., et al. (2020). *The condition of education 2020* (NCES 2020-144). Washington, DC: National Center for Education Statistics. Accessed at https://nces.ed.gov/pubs2020/2020144.pdf on July 12, 2022.

Individuals With Disabilities Education Improvement Act of 2004, Pub. L. No. 108-446 § 300.115 (2004).

Johnson, J. F., Jr. (2012, September 13). *High-quality instruction that promotes learning and achievement for African American male students* [Webinar]. WestEd. Accessed at https://wested.org/resources/high-quality-instruction-that-promotes-learning-and-achievement-for-african-american-male-students/# on March 30, 2022.

Karge, B. D. (2014). *Engage 11: Strategies to promote student engagement in Common Core lessons.* Vista, CA: The Discovery Source.

Karge, B. D. (2015). *Engage co-teach: Eleven co-teaching strategies—A teaching tool in the Engage 11 series.* Vista, CA: The Discovery Source.

Karge, B. D. (2021). *Engaging every student in inclusive classrooms: Now is the time!* [Slideshow presentation]. Bishop Mackenzie International School, Lilongwe, Malawi.

Karge, B. D., & Lasky, B. (2007). Embracing the concept of inclusion. *The Ladder, 8,* 18–19.

Karge, B. D., & Lasky, B. (2009). Spotlight on special education. *Journal of Staff Development, 30*(3), 49–52. Accessed at https://learningforward.org/wp-content/uploads/2009/06/karge303.pdf on March 30, 2022.

Karge, B. D., & Lasky, B. (2012, January). *Tools for principals: Enhancing knowledge of special education* [Slideshow presentation]. Hawai'i International Education Conference, Honolulu, Hawai'i.

Karge, B. D., & McCabe, M. (2014). Quality alternative certification programs in special education ensure high retention. *Journal of the National Association for Alternative Certification, 9*(2), 24–43.

Karge, B. D., McClure, M., & Patton, P. L. (1995). The success of collaboration resource programs for students with disabilities in grades 6 through 8. *Remedial and Special Education, 16*(2), 79–89.

Karge, B. D., & Moore, R. K. (2015). Common Core: Teaching Optimum Topic Exploration (TOTE). *Contemporary Issues in Education Research, 8*(1), 45–48.

Karge, B. D., Pierson, M., & Robinson, S. (2011). Alternative certification teachers: Building partnerships with paraprofessionals. *Journal of the National Association for Alternative Certification, 6*(2), 3–10. Accessed at https://files.eric.ed.gov/fulltext/EJ1053489.pdf on March 30, 2022.

Karge, B. D., & Reitman, G. C. (2016). *AIMS Scholars Program, U.S. Department of Education Transition to Teaching program, California State University, Fullerton* [Evaluation Report PR No. U350A1110044]. Fullerton, CA: U.S. Department of Education TTT Programs.

Karge, B. D., Ringlaben, R. P., & Schwartz, S. E. (1996). *Human diversity: A guide for understanding.* New York: McGraw-Hill.

Karge, B. D., Stephens, C. E., & Abu Zaineh, S. (2019). Reflecting on school function areas (SFAs) to enhance leadership. *The Chronicle of Mentoring and Coaching, 3*(12), 238–240.

Karge, B. D., Stephens, C. E., Widener, M. K., & Poda, J. (2019). Elevated educators making the LEEAAPS for school improvement. *Childhood Education, 95*(2), 13–19.

Karten, T. J. (2013). *Inclusion coaching for collaborative schools.* Thousand Oaks, CA: Corwin Press.

Karten, T. J., & Murawski, W. W. (2020). *Co-teaching do's, don'ts, and do betters.* Alexandria, VA: ASCD.

Kefallinou, A. (Ed.). (2016). *Raising the achievement of all learners in inclusive education* [Literature review]. Odense, Denmark: European Agency for Special Needs and Inclusive Education.

King-Sears, M. E., Stefanidis, A., Berkeley, S., & Strogilos, V. (2021). Does co-teaching improve academic achievement for students with disabilities? A meta-analysis. *Educational Research Review, 34*(1), 100405.

Kise, J. A. G. (2021). *Doable differentiation: Twelve strategies to meet the needs of all learners.* Bloomington, IN: Solution Tree Press.

Knight, J. (2022). *The definitive guide to instructional coaching: Seven factors for success.* Alexandria, VA: ASCD.

Kouzes, J. M., & Posner, B. Z. (2017). *A coach's guide to developing exemplary leaders: Making the most of the leadership challenge and the leadership practices inventory (LPI)* (2nd ed.). Hoboken, NJ: Wiley.

Kritzer, J. B. (2012). Comparing special education in the United States and China. *International Journal of Special Education, 27*(2), 52–56.

Krull, J., Wilbert, J., & Hennemann, T. (2014). The social and emotional situation of first graders with classroom behavior problems and classroom learning difficulties in inclusive classes. *Learning Disabilities: A Contemporary Journal, 12*(2), 169–190. Accessed at https://eric.ed.gov/?id=EJ1047460 on July 11, 2022.

Kübler-Ross, E. (1969). *On death and dying.* New York: Macmillan.

Kurth, J. A., & Gross, M. (2015). *The inclusion toolbox: Strategies and techniques for all teachers.* Thousand Oaks, CA: Corwin.

Lane, K. L., Menzies, H. M., Oakes, W. P., & Kalberg, J. R. (2019). *Developing a schoolwide framework to prevent and manage learning and behavior problems* (2nd ed.). New York: Guilford Press.

Larry P. v. Riles, 495 F. Supp. 926, N.D. Cal. (1979).

Lasky, B., & Karge, B. D. (2006). Meeting the needs of students with disabilities: Experience and confidence of principals. *NASSP Bulletin, 90*(1), 19–36.

Lee, A., & Gage, N. A. (2020). Updating and expanding systematic reviews and meta-analyses on the effects of school-wide positive behavior interventions and supports. *Psychology in the Schools, 57*(5), 783–804.

Levinson, B. (Director). (1988). *Rain man* [Film]. United Artists; Guber-Peters Company; Star Partners II.

Lipsky, D. K., & Gartner, A. (2012). *Inclusion: A service, not a place—A whole school approach* (Rev. ed.). Port Chester, NY: National Professional Resources.

Love, T. S., & Love, Z. J. (2022). The teacher recruitment crisis: Examining influential recruitment factors from a United States technology and engineering teacher preparation program. *International Journal of Technology and Design Education, 32.*

Maggin, D. M., Hughes, M. T., Passmore, A., Kumm, S., & Scaletta, M. (2020). School administrators' perspectives on special education teacher leadership. *Journal of Special Education Leadership, 33*(2), 78–89.

Magnússon, G. (2020). Inclusive education and school choice lessons from Sweden. *European Journal of Special Needs Education, 35*(1), 25–39.

Mantasiah, R., Yusri, Sinring, A., & Aryani, F. (2021). Assessing verbal positive reinforcement of teachers during school from home in the COVID-19 pandemic era. *International Journal of Instruction, 14*(2), 1037–1050. Accessed at https://doi.org/10.29333/iji.2021.14259a on August 10, 2022.

Marzano, R. J. (2017). *The new art and science of teaching.* Bloomington, IN: Solution Tree Press.

Master, B., Loeb, S., & Wyckoff, J. (2014, January). *Learning that lasts: Unpacking variation in teachers' effects on students' long-term knowledge* [Working Paper No. 104]. Washington, DC: National Center for Analysis of Longitudinal Data in Education Research.

Maxwell, J. C. (2009). *How successful people think: Change your thinking, change your life.* New York: Center Street.

McIntosh, K., & Goodman, S. (2016). *Integrated multi-tiered systems of support: Blending RTI and PBIS.* New York: Guilford Press.

McLeskey, J., Barringer, M., Billingsley, B., Brownell, M., Jackson, D., Kennedy, M., et al. (2017). *High-leverage practices in special education: Foundations for student success.* Arlington, VA: Council for Exceptional Children.

McLeskey, J., Waldron, N. L., Spooner, F., & Algozzine, B. (Eds.). (2014). *Handbook of effective inclusive schools: Research and practice.* New York: Routledge.

Mehta, J., Yurkofsky, M., & Frumin, K. (2022). Linking continuous improvement and adaptive leadership. *Educational Leadership, 79*(6), 36–41.

Menéndez, R. (Director). (1988). *Stand and deliver* [Film]. American Playhouse.

Miller, D., & Karge, B. D. (2015). *The value of inclusion* [Unpublished thesis]. California State University, Fullerton.

Mills v. Board of Education of District of Columbia, 348 F. Supp. 866 (D.D.C. 1972).

Mitchell, B. S., Bruhn, A. L., & Lewis, T. J. (2016). Essential features of Tier 2 and 3 school-wide positive behavioral supports. In S. R. Jimerson, M. K. Burns, & A. M. VanDerHeyden (Eds.), *Handbook of response to intervention* (2nd ed., pp. 519–538). New York: Springer.

Murawski, W. W., & Scott, K. L. (2017). *What really works with exceptional learners.* Thousand Oaks, CA: Corwin.

National Association of School Psychologists. (n.d.). *Who are school psychologists.* Accessed at www.nasponline.org/about-school-psychology/who-are-school-psychologists on July 8, 2022.

National Center for Education Statistics. (2021). *Mathematics performance: Condition of education*. Washington, DC: U.S. Department of Education. Accessed at https://nces.ed.gov/programs/coe/indicator_cnc.asp on March 30, 2022.

National Governors Association Center for Best Practices & Council of Chief State School Officers. (2010a). *Common Core State Standards for English language arts and literacy in history/social studies, science, and technical subjects*. Washington, DC: Authors. Accessed at www.corestandards.org/assets/CCSSI_ELA%20Standards.pdf on March 30, 2022.

National Governors Association Center for Best Practices & Council of Chief State School Officers. (2010b). *Common Core State Standards for mathematics*. Washington, DC: Authors. Accessed at www.corestandards.org/assets/CCSSI_Math%20Standards.pdf on March 30, 2022.

Navo, M., & Williams, A. (2022). *Demystifying MTSS: A school and district framework for meeting students' academic and social-emotional needs*. Bloomington, IN: Solution Tree Press.

Nolan, C. E. (2017). *Build rapport, inspire feedback, celebrate success, and exceed results (BICE): A leadership program to increase administrative support and retention of beginning secondary teachers* (Publication No. 3334) [Doctoral dissertation, Concordia University Irvine]. CUI Digital Repository. Accessed at https://cui.dspacedirect.org/handle/11414/3334 on July 12, 2022.

Nordick, S., Putney, L. G., & Jones, S. H. (2019). The principal's role in developing collective teacher efficacy: A cross-case study of facilitative leadership. *Journal of Ethnographic and Qualitative Research, 13*(4), 248–260.

Northouse, P. G. (2019). *Leadership: Theory and practice* (8th ed.). Thousand Oaks, CA: SAGE.

Ogle, D. M. (1986). K-W-L: A teaching model that develops active reading of expository text. *The Reading Teacher, 39*(6), 564–570.

Ondrasek, N., Carver-Thomas, D., Scott, C., & Darling-Hammond, L. (2020, February). *California's special education teacher shortage*. Stanford, CA: Policy Analysis for California Education. Accessed at https://learningpolicyinstitute.org/sites/default/files/product-files/PACE_Special_Education_Teacher_Shortage_REPORT.pdf on March 30, 2022.

Osborne, J. (2019, April 3). *How "differentiation" became a dirty word to teachers*. Accessed at https://medium.com/age-of-awareness/how-differentiation-became-a-dirty-word-to-teachers-dbf4f3c176a3 on July 11, 2022.

Oswald, D. (2005). An encyclopedia of autism interventions. *PsycCRITIQUES, 50*(28).

Packer, C., Gao, K., Kos, J., Krähenbühl, P., Koltun, V., & Song, D. (2018). *Assessing generalization in deep reinforcement learning.* Accessed at https://arxiv.org/pdf/1810.12282.pdf on July 12, 2022.

Parekh, G., & Brown, R. S. (2019). Changing lanes: The relationship between special education placement and students' academic futures. *Educational Policy, 33*(1), 111–135. Accessed at https://doi.org/10.1177/0895904818812772 on August 10, 2022.

Paris, L. F. (2013). Reciprocal mentoring: Can it help prevent attrition for beginning teachers? *Australian Journal of Teacher Education, 38*(6), 136–158.

Parker, C., & Bickmore, K. (2021). Complexity in restorative justice education circles: Power and privilege in voicing perspectives about sexual health, identities, and relationships. *Journal of Moral Education, 50*(4), 471–493. https://doi.org/10.1080/03057240.2020.1832451

Pennsylvania Association for Retarded Children (PARC) v. Commonwealth of Pennsylvania, 334 F. Supp. 1257 (E. D. Pa. 1971).

Pivik, J. R. (2010). The perspective of children and youth: How different stakeholders identify architectural barriers for inclusion in schools. *Journal of Environmental Psychology, 30*(4), 510–517.

Plotinsky, M. (2020). *Getting it right the first time: Why good first instruction matters.* Accessed at www.educationworld.com/teachers/getting-it-right-first-time-why-good-first-instruction-matters on July 12, 2022.

Porosoff, L. (2022). Which curriculum audit is best for your school? *Educational Leadership, 79*(4), 66–67.

Przekwas, J. M. (2021). *Minnesota principal knowledge and support of special education and special education teacher job satisfaction* (Publication No. 76) [Doctoral dissertation, St. Cloud State University]. The Repository at St. Cloud State. Accessed at https://repository.stcloudstate.edu/edad_etds/76 on July 12, 2022.

R. E. B. v. Hawai'i Department of Education, No. 14–15895. (9th Cir. 2017).

Reeves, D. B. (2006). *The learning leader: How to focus school improvement for better results.* Alexandria, VA: ASCD.

Rehabilitation Act of 1973, 29 U.S.C. § 794 (1973).

Reitman, G. C. (2018). *Reflecting with teachers who were highly supported in their first years of teaching: What strategies helped them remain in the profession* (Publication No. 3348) [Doctoral dissertation, Concordia University Irvine]. CUI Digital Repository. Accessed at http://hdl.handle.net/11414/3348 on July 12, 2022.

Reitman, G. C., & Karge, B. D. (2019). Investing in teacher support leads to teacher retention: Six supports administrators should consider for new teachers. *Multicultural Education, 27*(1), 7–18.

Rentinck, I., Ketelaar, M., Jongmans, M., Lindeman, E., & Gorter, J. W. (2009). Parental reactions following the diagnosis of cerebral palsy in their young child. *Journal of Pediatric Psychology, 34*(6), 671–676.

Ridgeway, T. R., Price, D. P., Simpson, C. G., & Rose, C. A. (2012). Reviewing the roots of response to intervention: Is there enough research to support the promise? *Administrative Issues Journal: Education, Practice, and Research, 2*(1), 83–95.

Rodriguez, J. A., & Murawski, W. W. (2022). *Special education law and policy: From foundation to application.* San Diego, CA: Plural.

Rogers, K. (2020). *Grouping for excellence* [Presentation]. U.S. Department of State Office of Overseas Schools International Certificate Program, Bulgaria.

Rose, D. H., & Meyer, A. (2002). *Teaching every student in the digital age: Universal Design for Learning.* Alexandria, VA: ASCD.

Rothstein, L., & Johnson, S. F. (2021). *Special education law* (6th ed.). Thousand Oaks, CA: SAGE.

Santangelo, T., & Tomlinson, C. A. (2012). Teacher educators' perceptions and use of differentiated instruction practices: An exploratory investigation. *Action in Teacher Education, 34*(4), 309–327.

Scarpati, S. E., Wells, C. S., Lewis, C., & Jirka, S. (2011). Accommodations and item-level analyses using mixture differential item functioning models. *The Journal of Special Education, 45*(1), 54–62. https://doi.org/10.1177/0022466909350224

Scheetz, J., Waters, F. H., Smeaton, P., & Lare, D. (2005). Mentoring in a PDS program: What's in it for me? *Kappa Delta Pi Record, 42*(1), 33–37. Accessed at https://files.eric.ed.gov/fulltext/EJ724906.pdf on March 31, 2022.

Schumaker, J. B., Denton, P. H., & Deshler, D. D. (1984). *The paraphrasing strategy: Instructor's manual.* Lawrence: University of Kansas Center for Research on Learning.

Scruggs, T. E., Mastropieri, M. A., & McDuffie, K. A. (2007). Co-teaching in inclusive classrooms: A metasynthesis of qualitative research. *Exceptional Children, 73*(4), 392–416.

Sears, J. A., Peters, B. L., Beidler, A. M. S., & Murawski, W. W. (2021). Using relationships to advocate with, for, and to families. *TEACHING Exceptional Children, 53*(3), 194–204.

Sharma, U., Simi, J., & Forlin, C. (2015). Preparedness of pre-service teachers for inclusive education in the Solomon Islands. *Australian Journal of Teacher Education, 40*(5). Accessed at https://ro.ecu.edu.au/cgi/viewcontent.cgi?article=2660&context=ajte on August 10, 2022.

Sherab, K., Dorji, K., Dukpa, D., Lhamo, K., Thapa, R., & Tshomo, S. (2015). *Opportunities and challenges of implementing inclusive education in Bhutanese schools: A case study.* Thimphu: UNICEF Bhutan. Accessed at https://researchgate.net/publication/303661279_Title_Opportunities_and_Challenges_of_Implementing_Inclusive_Education_in_Bhutanese_Schools_A_Case_Study on March 31, 2022.

Sheridan, J. (Director). (1989). *My left foot* [Film]. Ferndale Films; Granada Films; Raidió Teilifís Éireann.

Shogren, K. A., McCart, A. B., Lyon, K. J., & Sailor, W. S. (2015). All means all: Building knowledge for inclusive schoolwide transformation. *Research and Practice for Persons With Severe Disabilities, 40*(3), 173–191.

Sierra, H., & Karge, B. (2020). Data from a California teacher induction mentoring program. *The Chronicle of Mentoring and Coaching, 1*(13), 515–520.

Skinner, B. F. (1945). The operational analysis of psychological terms. *Psychological Review, 52*(5), 270–277.

Skinner, E. A., Wellborn, J. G., & Connell, J. P. (1990). What it takes to do well in school and whether I've got it: A process model of perceived control and children's engagement and achievement in school. *Journal of Educational Psychology, 82*(1), 22–32.

Smith, D. D., & Tyler, N. C. (2014). *Introduction to contemporary special education: New horizons.* Boston: Pearson.

Sprick, M. (2021). *The parallel universe, season 1: Implementation basics staff manual.* Eugene, OR: Ancora. Accessed at https://thethirdquest.com/wp-content/uploads/2021/06/Staff-Manual-Implementation-Basics.pdf on April 1, 2022.

Steinberg, M. P., & Lacoe, J. (2017). What do we know about school discipline reform? Assessing the alternatives to suspensions and expulsions. *Education Next, 17*(1), 44–53.

Steinbrenner, J. R. D., & Watson, L. R. (2015). Student engagement in the classroom: The impact of classroom, teacher, and student factors. *Journal of Autism and Developmental Disorders, 45*(8), 2392–2410.

Stephens, C. E., Widener, M. K., & Karge, B. D. (2019). *Thinking that matters for schools: School function areas from challenge to change* (2nd ed.). Vista, CA: The Discovery Source.

Stewart, C. (2014). Transforming professional development to professional learning. *Journal of Adult Education, 43*(1), 28–33. Accessed at https://files.eric.ed.gov/fulltext/EJ1047338.pdf on July 12, 2022.

Strogilos, V., & King-Sears, M. E. (2019). Co-teaching is extra help and fun: Perspectives on co-teaching from middle school students and co-teachers. *Journal of Research in Special Educational Needs, 19*(2), 92–102.

Tamakloe, D. (2020). Enhancing learning and development of young children with disabilities with assistive technology. In D. Chambers (Ed.), *Assistive technology to support inclusive education: International perspectives on inclusive education* (Vol. 14, pp. 141–161). Bingley, UK: Emerald.

Tefera, A. A., Hernández-Saca, D., & Lester, A. M. (2019). Troubling the master narrative of "grit": Counterstories of Black and Latinx students with dis/abilities during an era of "high-stakes" testing. *Education Policy Analysis Archives, 27*(1).

Theoharis, G., & Causton, J. (2014). Leading inclusive reform for students with disabilities: A school- and systemwide approach. *Theory Into Practice, 53*(2), 82–97.

Thornock v. Boise Independent School District No. 1, 115 Idaho 466, 767 P.2d 1241, 1250 (1988).

Thornton, B., Zunino, B., & Beattie, J. W. (2020). Moving the dial: Improving teacher efficacy to promote instructional change. *Education, 140*(4), 171–180.

Tomlinson, C. A. (2014). *The differentiated classroom: Responding to the needs of all learners* (2nd ed.). Alexandria, VA: ASCD.

Tomlinson, C. A., & Imbeau, M. B. (2010). *Leading and managing a differentiated classroom.* Alexandria, VA: ASCD.

Tracy-Bronson, C. P. (2020). District-level inclusive special education leaders demonstrate social justice strategies. *Journal of Special Education Leadership, 33*(2), 59–77.

Travis, T. A. (2021). *TrustED: The bridge to school improvement.* Denver, CO: Author.

Tremblay, P. (2013). Comparative outcomes of two instructional models for students with learning disabilities: Inclusion with co-teaching and solo-taught special education. *Journal of Research in Special Educational Needs, 13*(4), 251–258.

Twal, N. I. (2022). Leading and learning for equity is a collective journey. *The Learning Professional, 43*(1), 10–11.

Tyler, T. A., & Brunner, C. C. (2014). The case for increasing workplace decision-making: Proposing a model for special educator attrition research. *Teacher Education and Special Education, 37*(4), 283–308.

United Nations. (2019). *Empowering children with disabilities for the enjoyment of their human rights, including through inclusive education: Report of the United Nations high commissioner for human rights.* New York: Author. Accessed at https://digitallibrary.un.org/record/3791961?ln=en on April 4, 2022.

United Nations Educational, Scientific and Cultural Organization. (2009). *Policy guidelines on inclusion in education.* Paris: Author. Accessed at http://unesdoc.unesco.org/images/0017/001778/177849e.pdf on March 31, 2022.

United Nations Educational, Scientific and Cultural Organization. (2020). *Global education monitoring report 2020: Inclusion and education—All means all* (3rd ed.). Paris: Author.

United Nations Educational, Scientific, and Cultural Organization International Bureau of Education. (n.d.). *Resources.* Accessed at https://digitalcollections.ibe-unesco.org/resources on July 11, 2022.

U.S. Department of Education. (2002). *A new era: Revitalizing special education for children and their families.* Washington, DC: Author. Accessed at https://ectacenter.org/~pdfs/calls/2010/earlypartc/revitalizing_special_education.pdf on July 12, 2022.

U.S. Department of Education. (2007). *History: Twenty five years of progress in educating children with disabilities through IDEA.* Washington, DC: Author. Accessed at https://files.eric.ed.gov/fulltext/ED556111.pdf on March 31, 2022.

U.S. Department of Education. (2020). *41st annual report to Congress on the implementation of the Individuals With Disabilities Education Act, 2019.* Washington, DC: Author.

U.S. Department of Education. (2022). *IDEA section 618 data products: State level data files*. Accessed at https://www2.ed.gov/programs/osepidea/618-data/state-level-data-files/index.html#bcc on March 31, 2022.

VanDerHeyden, A. M. (2011). Technical adequacy of response to intervention decisions. *Exceptional Children, 77*(3), 335–350.

Vaughn, S., Bos, C. S., & Schumm, J. S. (2011). *Teaching students who are exceptional, diverse, and at risk in the general education classroom* (5th ed.). Upper Saddle River, NJ: Pearson Education.

Vignoles, A. (2016). What is the economic value of literacy and numeracy? *IZA World of Labor*, Article 229. Accessed at https://wol.iza.org/articles/what-is-economic-value-of-literacy-and-numeracy/long on July 12, 2022.

Villa, R. A., & Thousand, J. S. (2017). *Leading an inclusive school: Access and success for all students*. Alexandria, VA: ASCD.

von Ahlefeld Nisser, D. (2017). Can collaborative consultation, based on communicative theory, promote an inclusive school culture? *Issues in Educational Research, 27*(4), 874–892.

von der Embse, N., Rutherford, L., Mankin, A., & Jenkins, A. (2019). Demonstration of a trauma-informed assessment to intervention model in a large urban school district. *School Mental Health, 11*(2), 276–289.

Walker, H. M., Horner, R. H., Sugai, G., Bullis, M., Sprague, J. R., Bricker, D., et al. (1996). Integrated approaches to preventing antisocial behavior patterns among school-age children and youth. *Journal of Emotional and Behavioral Disorders, 4*(4), 194–209.

Walker, J. D., Johnson, K. M., & Randolph, K. M. (2021). Teacher self-advocacy for the shared responsibility of classroom and behavior management. *TEACHING Exceptional Children, 53*(3), 216–225.

Walsh, J. M. (2012). Co-teaching as a school system strategy for continuous improvement. *Preventing School Failure, 56*(1), 29–36.

Weatherly, J. J. (2021, October 28). *The leader's guide to coaching teachers in creating legally defensible IEPs* [Video file]. Accessed at https://vimeo.com/640146396 on March 31, 2022.

Werner, P. (Director). (2008). *Front of the class* [Film]. McGee Productions.

Wienen, A. W., Reijnders, I., van Aggelen, M. H., Bos, E. H., Batstra, L., & de Jonge, P. (2019). The relative impact of school-wide positive behavior support on teachers' perceptions of student behavior across schools, teachers, and students. *Psychology in the Schools*, *56*(2), 232–241.

World Health Organization. (2005). *Mental health atlas 2005* (Rev. ed.). Geneva, Switzerland: Author. Accessed at https://apps.who.int/iris/bitstream/handle/10665/43230/924156296X_eng.pdf?sequence=1&isAllowed=y on July 12, 2022.

World Health Organization. (2011). *World report on disability*. Geneva, Switzerland: Author. Accessed at www.who.int/teams/noncommunicable-diseases/sensory-functions-disability-and-rehabilitation/world-report-on-disability on July 12, 2022.

Wu, E. H. (2013). The path leading to differentiation: An interview with Carol Tomlinson. *Journal of Advanced Academics*, *24*(2), 125–133.

Wulandari, S. A. (2014). *Teaching speaking by using SLANT strategy on discussion text at senior high school* (Publication No. 2706) [Doctoral dissertation, Universitas Negeri Padang]. Universitas Negeri Padang Repository. Accessed at http://repository.unp.ac.id/2706 on July 12, 2022.

Zemeckis, R. (Director). (1994). *Forrest Gump* [Film]. The Tisch Company.

Index

C

D

E

F

G

H

I

J

L

M

N

O

P

R

S

U

V

W

Z

The General Education Teacher's Guide to Autism
Barbara Boroson
In this engaging title, you will find answers to all your questions about students on the autism spectrum in inclusive classrooms. Collect the information and strategies you need to create an effective, welcoming, and supportive environment for these neurodiverse students.
BKG055

Inclusion Strategies and Interventions, Second Edition
Toby J. Karten
In a world filled with diverse students, inclusive education is more important than ever. Rely on the second edition of this user-friendly guide to help you provide a strong learning path for all students, with a focus on special needs.
BKF963

Yes We Can!
Heather Friziellie, Julie A. Schmidt, and Jeanne Spiller
Utilizing PLC practices, general and special educators must develop collaborative partnerships in order to close the achievement gap and maximize learning for all. The authors encourage *all* educators to take collective responsibility in improving outcomes for students with special needs.
BKF653

When Actions Speak Louder Than Words
Kim Davis and Susan D. Dixon
Build your understanding of behavior as communication, and learn to interpret the messages behind the actions. This book provides information and tools to support all children whose primary way to communicate is through challenging behaviors.
BKF274